The Financial Times Guide to Pensions and Wealth in Retirement

FINANCIAL TIMES

In an increasingly competitive world, we believe it's quality of thinking that gives you the edge – an idea that opens new doors, a technique that solves a problem, or an insight that simply makes sense of it all. The more you know, the smarter and faster you can go.

That's why we work with the best minds in business and finance to bring cutting-edge thinking and best learning practice to a global market.

Under a range of leading imprints, including *Financial Times Prentice Hall*, we create world-class print publications and electronic products bringing our readers knowledge, skills and understanding, which can be applied whether studying or at work.

To find out more about Pearson Education publications, or tell us about the books you'd like to find, you can visit us at
www.pearsoned.co.uk

The Financial Times Guide to Pensions and Wealth in Retirement

John Greenwood

**Financial Times
Prentice Hall
is an imprint of**

Harlow, England • London • New York • Boston • San Francisco • Toronto • Sydney • Singapore • Hong Kong
Tokyo • Seoul • Taipei • New Delhi • Cape Town • Madrid • Mexico City • Amsterdam • Munich • Paris • Milan

PEARSON EDUCATION LIMITED

Edinburgh Gate
Harlow CM20 2JE
Tel: +44 (0)1279 623623
Fax: +44 (0)1279 431059
Website: www.pearsoned.co.uk

First published in Great Britain in 2010

© Pearson Education Limited 2010

The right of John Greenwood to be identified as author of this work has been asserted by him in accordance with the Copyright, Designs and Patents Act 1988.

ISBN: 978-0-273-72785-9

British Library Cataloguing-in-Publication Data
A catalogue record for this book is available from the British Library

Library of Congress Cataloging-in-Publication Data
Greenwood, John, 1964-
  The Financial Times guide to pensions and wealth in retirement / John Greenwood.
     p. cm.
  ISBN 978-0-273-72785-9 (pbk.)
  1. Retirement income--Planning. 2. Old age pensions. 3. Finance, Personal. I. Title.
  HG179.G729 2010
  332.024'014--dc22
                          2009038565

10 9 8 7 6 5 4 3 2 1
13 12 11 10 09

Typeset in 9pt Stone Serif by 30
Printed and bound in Great Britain by Ashford Colour Press, Gosport

The publisher's policy is to use paper manufactured from sustainable forests.

Contents

.

PART 4 WEALTH MANAGEMENT IN RETIREMENT / 191

Preface

This book is designed for anybody who wants to take control of their pension and retirement planning, whether they are avid readers of the financial pages or don't know the first thing about money matters.

The key to successful pension saving is knowledge. The pension landscape is full of traps that snare the unwary investor and avoiding them can make the difference between a comfortable retirement and one lived counting every penny. By following the recommendations set out in this book it is possible to end up with an income in retirement up to 50 per cent higher than you could get if you trust pension companies, your employer and the state to look after you.

Pension providers make most of their profits from uninformed customers. These profits come out of the money you invest, ultimately reducing your final return. Many dynamic providers also offer great value products but it is often only the smart investors who manage to track them down.

The complexity of the tax system can also be a barrier to efficient pension saving – the way you time payments and withdrawls can make a huge difference to how much tax you pay and the tax relief you receive, again having a big influence on your final retirement pot. And investment markets, which are likely to be the key driver of a large part of your pension savings, can rise or fall quickly and need to be handled with informed respect.

This book explains in simple language how to access the best deals, minimise your tax contributions, make the most of the state system and maximise your pension fund.

You can implement some of the solutions in this book yourself. Some more complex procedures will require the assistance of a financial adviser. Whichever way you proceed, this book aims to show you where you are losing money and what steps you need to take to get your pension planning back on track.

Acknowledgements

This book would not have been possible without the patience of the literally hundreds of financial advisers, tax specialists, provider representatives and other experts who have explained the intricacies of the UK pensions system to me over the years. Particular thanks go to John Lawson, head of pension policy at Standard Life, for his keen-eyed proofreading of this edition and his perceptive suggestions and criticisms.

Thanks are also due to Tom McPhail and Mark Dampier at Hargreaves Lansdown, Billy Burrows at William Burrows Annuities, Chris Curry at the Pensions Policy Institute, Billy Mackay at Skandia, Richard Jacobs at Richard Jacobs Pension & Trustee Services, Amanda Davidson at Baigrie Davies, the Department for Work and Pensions, Barclays Capital, Alexander Forbes Financial Services and Principle First Financial Services. Special thanks to Helen Adkins.

Publisher's acknowledgements

We are grateful to the following for permission to reproduce copyright material:

Figures and tables
Tables 9.3 and 9.4 from Barclays Capital. Barclays Bank PLC is authorised and regulated by the Financial Services Authority and a member of the London Stock Exchange. Barclays Capital is the investment banking division of Barclays Bank PLC and undertakes US securities business in the name of its wholly owned subsidiary Barclays Capital Inc., a FINRA and SIPC member. Neither Barclays Bank PLC nor any affiliate nor any officer or director of any of them accepts any liability or loss arising from any use of this publication or its content. This publication is for discussion purposes only and shall not constitute any offer to sell or any solicitation to buy any security nor is it intended to give rise to any legal relationship between Barclays Bank PLC or any of its affiliates and you or any other

person, nor is it recommended to buy any securities or enter into any transaction; Table 14.4 from William Burrows Annuities; Figure 15.1 from The Annuity Bureau.

Text

Text on page 217 from William Burrows Annuities.

In some instances we have been unable to trace the owners of copyright material, and we would appreciate any information that would enable us to do so.

Pensions: what they mean to you

1

Solving your own personal pensions crisis

What topics are covered in this chapter?

- How do I visualise my retirement?
- The 'pensions crisis'
- Planning for your retirement
- Pensions: an overview
- Are pensions the best way to save for retirement?

How do I visualise my retirement?

It is worth asking yourself what sort of retirement you visualise yourself having. Do you see yourself having the ability to spend freely on expensive hobbies, travel and other leisure activities? Or will you be happy to rein in your expenditure and spend your time doing things that cost less? Visualising your retirement is the first step towards making it financially secure.

You will need to work out what sort of retirement your current pension savings are on course to deliver and what extra income you will have to forgo today if you want to improve on that.

This can be an unpleasant process and there are many reasons why you might want to put off looking at your own pension arrangements. You might find pensions confusing and file them in the 'too complicated' box.

You may be daunted by the amount you need to save to achieve a decent income in retirement. Or perhaps the numerous scandals that have hit the industry over the last two decades have put you off pensions altogether. Yet burying your head in the sand is the worst thing you can do. The government has made it clear that it will only protect pensioners from the very harshest realities of poverty. Relying on the state is only a realistic option for those who are already used to living on benefits. As you read this book you will discover that responsibility for your retirement is increasingly being placed on your shoulders.

> Confronting the pensions system involves making a series of important decisions that can cost you dear if you get them wrong

Bearing this responsibility is a challenge. Confronting the pensions system involves making a series of important decisions that can cost you dear if you get them wrong. This book is packed with advice and ideas on how to be a smart pension investor, how to avoid the pitfalls uninformed savers fall into, and how to build yourself a healthy retirement income.

Inside this book

How to:

■ save tens of thousands of pounds of pension charges

■ receive commission normally paid to financial advisers

■ make the most of your investment portfolio

■ receive money in a pension for no net outlay if you are a higher rate taxpayer (unbelievable but true)

■ buy added years of final salary pension for a fraction of the market rate

■ get a bigger tax-free cash lump sum

■ reduce your Inheritance Tax bill

■ buy your business premises with your pension

■ lend money to your company from your pension

■ buy extra state pension at knockdown prices

■ get up to 30 per cent more for your annuity

■ trace unclaimed pensions.

Discover why:

■ higher rate taxpayers in some schemes are missing out on a fifth of their pension

■ transferring out of a final salary scheme can cut your pension in half

■ taking a cash lump sum on leaving a job can cost you thousands

■ sticking with your pension provider when you buy an annuity can cost you up to a third of your income.

The 'pensions crisis'

Many people will be reading this book because, rightly, they are worried they will not have enough to live on when they retire. If you fall into this category, you are not alone. In his 2004 report on the state of the nation's pension saving, Lord Turner identified more than 12 million Britons over the age of 25 who are not saving enough for their retirement, two-thirds of whom are saving nothing.

The causes of the so-called 'pensions crisis' are many and varied: poor investment returns, closure or collapse of company schemes, plummeting confidence and a lack of interest in long-term saving. But the single biggest factor underlying the chronic shortfall in UK pension saving is the welcome fact that people are living longer. In 1950 a 65-year-old man could expect to live for a further 12 years. Today, he will live for another 21 years, and by 2050 it is expected that a further 25 years will be the norm. Women can expect to live between two and three years longer than that. (See Table 1.1.)

> The single biggest factor underlying the chronic shortfall in UK pension saving is the welcome fact that people are living longer

Table 1.1 Life expectancy of a 65-year-old male/female

1950	77/79
2008	86/88
2050	90/92

Three decades or more of retirement

It is worth remembering that these figures are averages – millions of people will live considerably longer than this. Non-smokers and those who keep fit have a fair chance of making it well into their nineties, and even beyond. Wealthier people are also likely to live longer – even something as seemingly commonplace as saving in a pension is an indicator of relative wealth and people who do so are expected to live four years longer than the general population. Lifespans are expanding so quickly that the

Department for Work and Pensions predicts that one in four babies born today will make it to the age of 100.

A retirement lasting 30 years or more on a pension built up over a working life of 40 years is clearly going to cost more than 10 per cent of income. Finding out how much you will have to put away each month to even achieve half your working income when you retire can come as a massive shock. But it is also the first step towards setting a coherent strategy for funding your retirement.

Today it is not just a question of when to retire, but how. The traditional pattern of working 40 years and suddenly giving up work is becoming less common. Retirement for many is now a process rather than a cliff-edge event – people are working later, graduating their retirement by working part time, downsizing their property or releasing cash from their home. Many are now even keeping their pension invested in the stock market through retirement.

Pensions: a chequered history

The last 30 years have seen pensions in the headlines for all the wrong reasons. The pensions misselling scandal took place between 1988 and 1994 when more than a million people were wrongly advised to transfer out of company pensions into private personal pensions with high charges. After a lengthy government review, financial advisers and pension companies were ordered to pay back £11.8bn in compensation.

Pensions were back in the limelight in 1991 when Robert Maxwell was found to have stolen more than £400m from the Mirror Group pension scheme, leaving 32,000 employees and former employees out of pocket. The 1995 Pensions Act put in place stricter controls on pensions trustees and prohibited pension funds from holding more than 5 per cent of the sponsoring company's shares. In addition, those holding funds are now under stricter regulatory monitoring.

Equitable Life, the life insurance company founded in 1762, almost collapsed in 2000, forcing it to cut payouts to more than a million policyholders. In 2008 an investigation by the Parliamentary Ombudsman found the government guilty of failing to regulate Equitable Life adequately and compensation is now in the pipeline for many who lost out. Since then a regulatory overhaul has forced life insurers to hold increased reserves, to reduce the risk of a similar collapse of another life insurer in the future.

The precarious nature of final salary pensions was revealed between 2002 and 2004 when a succession of companies collapsed, leaving around 125,000 scheme members with next to no pension. Realising that many final salary schemes were as safe as a house of cards, the government quickly introduced the Pension Protection Fund, which guarantees to pay around three-quarters of scheme benefits up to a fixed level.

The payment of compensation to the actual victims of these various scandals has varied hugely in terms of both amount and speed of delivery. And the government has also been accused of playing its own part in increasing these pension deficits by taking £5bn a year off pension funds since 1997 through the introduction of tax on share dividends.

A serious consequence of this barrage of bad news is that many people have little trust in either the companies that provide pensions or the people who advise on them. Some people have had their confidence in pensions undermined to such an extent that they have decided to give up on them altogether, opting for property or ISAs instead.

How secure are pensions?

The government has taken steps to address the root causes of the problems that have beset pensions in the past. One by one, most of the historical problems with pensions have been addressed and the regulatory framework is now significantly more robust than it was. However, the fundamental issue of investment risk will always remain for those in pensions linked to the stock market.

The investor protection offered to different sorts of pension varies depending on what sort of arrangement it is. The security of each form of pension is covered in more detail in the relevant chapter.

Nobody knows where tomorrow's pensions scandal will come from, but today's savers can at least comfort themselves with the knowledge that there are now more rigorous controls on the way that pension schemes are administered, charges on personal pension products are levied and the solvency of life insurers is guaranteed than there were 20 or even 10 years ago. What is less clear is what happens if there is a serious prolonged collapse in the economy that turns into a slump. Such an outcome could pose serious problems for some of the investor protection arrangements currently in place, although the same issues would arise with all investments and not just pensions.

Recent economic history shows us that nobody, not even the people held up as investment gurus, can really predict the future. No book can insulate you from an economic depression. But this book can help make your retirement savings work harder while helping you to avoid some of the common pitfalls that can cost investors dear.

Planning for your retirement

There is much more to pension planning than simply putting away a portion of your salary each month, although that of course is a crucial factor. Those in the know utilise a whole range of tricks of the trade, which can make a huge difference to the income you will get in retirement. Maximising your tax allowances, getting the most out of the investments behind your pensions, opting for products with lower charges, getting all you can from your employer and the state pension system, drawing your income in an efficient way – these will all make a real difference to your retirement income and, taken together, can make the difference between constant money worries in later life and a comfortable lifestyle.

Reading this book you may be surprised at the number of situations where responsibility for complex decisions on pensions is placed on you. You may think that your employer, the trustees of your scheme or the government are responsible for making sure your pension saving is on the right track. But the system expects you to make crucial decisions about your pension saving throughout your life. Many people get many of these decisions wrong, often with devastating effects on their ability to fund the retirement they had hoped for.

This book has been put together with the aim of showing you how to make the most of what you already have, and what to do with the new savings that you will need to make. It is also designed to clarify much of the confusing jargon and cut through the marketing hype that surrounds many of the products on the market. You will be able to take forward many of the suggestions in this book without the assistance of a financial adviser, although there are some strategies where professional advice and assistance will be essential.

Small steps can make a big difference

Most of us have some pension savings somewhere, whether through the state system, workplace or a personal pension plan. By making small changes in the way you deal with these savings today, you can make a big difference in their value decades down the line. For example, by moving to a pension provider with lower charges today, you will benefit from higher net returns every month of every year for the rest of your working life. That could add up to thousands or even tens of thousands of pounds more pension.

It is not just those with low pension savings who need to take control of their pensions. People with top-class pensions, whether final salary plans or well-funded money purchase arrangements, can make a significant difference to their retirement income by using the most efficient strategies.

For those yet to start pension savings, it is crucial not to give up just because the amount you need to save seems too big. It is far better to start with what you can afford today with a view to increasing it in the future when your circumstances change. Like any long journey, pension saving starts with a single step.

> Like any long journey, pension saving starts with a single step

Pensions: an overview

The UK pensions landscape is a complex patchwork of laws and regulations that can seem complicated to a lay audience. The first step towards getting your pension saving on track is to understand what you have got, and what options are open to you. Pensions generally fall into one of three categories: state, workplace or individual. Most people have at least some pension benefits in at least one of these three sorts of pension and many people have all three.

The UK has one of the least generous state pensions in the developed world alongside one of the most developed private sector pensions systems. On the continent it is quite common for state pensions to provide 70 per cent of earnings. In the UK the average earner will get a state pension, including both basic and state second pension, equal to around 37 per cent of earnings. This parsimonious state pension has traditionally been considered politically acceptable because of the huge amount of assets in private sector pensions in the UK. These assets, held in both workplace and individual pensions, are worth more than £1 trillion, depending on the level of the stock market on the day you do the calculation – more than the rest of the European Union's private sector pension savings put together.

> The number of people on course for serious financial difficulty in retirement is huge

But while the UK private sector system has provided and continues to provide generous pensions for many, there are millions who get little or nothing at all. The number of people on course for serious financial difficulty in retirement is huge. In 2003 around 11.8 million Britons were not saving anything in a pension and the figures have got worse since then. Millions more have seen their expected retirement incomes fall as employers have switched from gilt-edged final salary schemes to less generous money purchase arrangements.

State pension

State income in retirement has three principal elements: basic state pension, additional state pension (currently called state second pension and formerly known as SERPS) and Pension Credit. The first two are based on National Insurance contributions, while Pension Credit is a means-tested safety net to take those with no other income off the poverty line. A pensioner solely in receipt of full basic state pension of £95.25 in 2009/10 would have that topped up to £130.00 by Pension Credit. This figure is the minimum that the government says people over 60 need to live on.

Personal pensions

Personal pensions are long-term savings plans that anyone under the age of 75 can save into. They are offered by life insurance companies, banks and investment houses. Contributions paid into personal pensions benefit from relief from income tax. The fund in the pension grows tax-free and at least 75 per cent of it must be used to buy an income, normally an annuity. Up to 25 per cent can be taken tax-free from age 55 (age 50 until April 2010).

Personal pensions can be risky as the investments contained within them are traditionally invested in the stock market, which can go down as well as up. As well as share price volatility, personal pensions also carry the risk that annuity rates will change by the time you come to buy a pension income. In recent years this has meant that investors have received less pension income than they would have done 20 years ago.

Stakeholder pensions

Stakeholder pensions are a form of personal pension with low charges and no exit penalties.

Workplace pensions

Pensions offered by employers range from the gold-plated final salary arrangements offered by blue-chip companies and public sector bodies, to risky money purchase plans with low contribution rates.

Workplace pensions can be divided into two distinct categories: final salary schemes, which are also known as defined benefit schemes, and money purchase schemes, also known as defined contribution schemes. The key difference between the two is who bears the risks inherent in the schemes. Employers offering final salary schemes promise to pay employees a proportion of their salary for life when they retire. These pensions benefit from index-linking to protect them from inflation and they also pay out an income to surviving spouses as well. Some defined benefit schemes are based on the average salary earned over your career rather than your final salary when you leave the company. However, the term 'final salary scheme' has become shorthand for all defined benefit schemes, whether the income paid is based on the final salary of the employee or their average salary over their career.

With final salary pensions it is the employer who takes responsibility for making sure that the assets it invests in the scheme generate a big enough return to meet the pension payments promised to employees. The employer also takes on board the longevity risk – the risk that the life expectancy of the members of the scheme grows, which means that pensions have to be paid for longer.

By contrast, it is the employee who bears all of these risks in a money purchase scheme. This shift of risk from the employer to the employee is the reason why these schemes have largely replaced final salary schemes in the private sector over the last decade. Employers have often taken the opportunity to reduce the contributions they pay into plans when switching from final salary to money purchase schemes. In a money purchase scheme the employer contributes a proportion of salary into a pension plan, usually on the understanding that the employee contributes too. Both the employer's and the employee's contributions benefit from tax relief. With time a pension pot is built up which the employee uses to buy an annuity or other income-generating product at retirement.

This presents the employee with two significant risks, both of which can have a serious impact on their income in retirement. First, if stock markets do not perform as well as hoped, the fund will not be big enough to buy the income that had been anticipated. Second, if annuity rates go down, whether because the insurers who offer them think life expectancy has increased or because long-term interest rates have gone down, then income will also be hit.

Money purchase schemes also come in different forms. Occupational money purchase schemes have boards of trustees, which monitor the assets in which members' contributions are invested and the annuity rates that are offered. Not all workplace money purchase schemes have trustees. Those that do not are either group personal pensions (GPPs) or group stakeholder pensions.

A GPP is effectively a group of individual personal pensions administered by an employer. Because it does not have a board of trustees, employees are responsible for choosing the investment funds held inside the pension. Members of a GPP who do not have a financial adviser acting on their behalf normally end up investing in a default investment fund that the pension provider allocates to the GPP. This default fund typically offers medium- to high-risk investments across either a range of asset classes or a blend of equity sector holdings.

Group stakeholder pensions are similar to GPPs, but are required to have fixed low charges and are not allowed to have exit penalties. GPPs and group stakeholder pensions are cheaper for employers to run than occupational money purchase schemes, which is why they are becoming increasingly common. These sorts of schemes place most risk on the individual. They also put the obligation on the individual to claim back higher rate tax relief on contributions made, which is not the case with occupational money purchase schemes.

SIPPs

Self-invested personal pensions (SIPPs) are a form of personal pension and are bound by the same tax rules. But unlike personal pensions, which only offer access to a limited range of investment funds, SIPPs allow pension savers to invest in a wide range of assets, such as commercial property, directly held shares, exchange traded funds and other instruments. They also offer access to a broad choice of unit trusts, investment trusts and other mutual funds.

Personal Accounts

You may have heard mention in the press of a new form of pension called Personal Accounts which is being launched as part of a government drive to boost pension saving. Personal Accounts are a new state-sponsored savings vehicle designed to offer an ultra-low-cost savings option for employees. Personal Accounts are being launched in 2012 in conjunction with a new requirement on employers to enroll all staff into a company pension scheme. Employers will be required to pay 3 per cent of earnings into this pension scheme, between a set band of earnings, with employees seeing a further 4 per cent deducted from payroll. The government will add another 1 per cent as tax relief. Those employers that do not already offer a pension scheme that meets these criteria are likely to enrol their staff into Personal Accounts.

Employees will have the right to opt out of Personal Accounts and other company schemes. The government is hoping that a combination of apathy and appreciating the value of having their own pension savings will mean that a majority of workers will not do so.

Are pensions the best way to save for retirement?

Many people have made a conscious decision to avoid pensions altogether, opting for residential property or ISAs instead. Each have their advantages and disadvantages, depending on your circumstances. And while buy-to-let investment is only for experts, for most people saving in both a pension and an ISA can make sense.

Tax relief on pensions is more generous than ISAs, particularly so if you pay tax at a lower rate, and buy-to-let investing does not attract tax relief on contributions although interest payments can be set off as a business expense. But money held in a pension is tied up until age 55 (50 until April 2010) and three-quarters of it must be drawn as an income. ISAs and property investments can be passed on more easily on death. However, for many people, the fact that they cannot access their cash until they retire is seen as an advantage.

Pensions have higher contribution limits than ISAs and money held in them is protected if you become bankrupt. Pension savings do not erode your entitlement for means-tested benefits if you lose your job.

By saving through pensions and ISAs you can spread your money across a range of asset classes, reducing your overall investment risk. Residential property investment can give you fantastic returns in rising markets, particularly if you have geared your investment by funding the purchase with a mortgage. But the property market could be in trouble when you come to retire and you might find that you cannot sell your property to give yourself an income. You should also bear in mind the hidden costs and expenses of running a buy-to-let property, such as void periods, wear and tear and fluctuating interest rates.

2

Drawing up your retirement saving plan

What topics are covered in this chapter?

- How much will I need?
- How much am I currently saving?
- Your pension shortfall
- How much will it cost to plug my shortfall?
- Other ways to reduce your pension shortfall
- Women and pensions
- The self-employed

If you are one of the 12 million Britons not saving enough for their retirement, you need a coherent plan to get your pension back on track. The bad news is that this is likely to involve having less money today. The good news is that the sooner you start, the less it will cost you.

There are three key areas you need to quantify before you can work out your retirement saving plan:

- how much you will need
- how much your current savings will give
- how big your retirement saving shortfall is.

Only once you have worked out where you currently stand and how much of a shortfall you have will you be able to consider what sacrifices you are prepared to make today for a higher income when you retire. You may decide that you are prepared to make do in retirement and will try to get by on the absolute minimum. Or you may have a fixed idea of the comfortable retirement that you want and be prepared to save hard now to pay for it.

This book contains many strategies for making your existing pension savings work harder for you. This will help you meet your target more quickly and may be enough to give you an income in retirement you will be satisfied with. For many people with low levels of current saving, however, ensuring a comfortable retirement will involve paying more today.

How much will I need?

The amount of pension income you will need will depend on the sort of retirement that you want. You need to ask yourself what sort of retirement you visualise yourself having. You may see work as an unpleasant but necessary prelude to a happy and comfortable retirement, enjoying hobbies and other leisure pastimes that you do not have time to do now. Alternatively you may be planning to take each day as it comes and accept that your standard of living will fall when you stop receiving your monthly pay cheque.

> You need to ask yourself what sort of retirement you visualise yourself having

Many people have a vague idea of retiring on half or two-thirds of current income. But even people starting saving in their late 20s and 30s will have to put away considerable sums to get anywhere near that figure unless they are in final salary schemes throughout their working lives. For anyone over 35 who has not started saving yet, retiring at age 60 on even 50 per cent of earnings, let alone two-thirds, is likely to be virtually impossible unless they have income from outside their pension as well. A 35-year-old would have to start saving 30 per cent of income to net 50 per cent of earnings from age 60 and would have to forgo any tax-free cash to get to that figure. For a 45-year-old the figure rises to a staggering 57 per cent, which is perhaps not surprising given that he or she may be expecting to live 30 years or more on a pension pot built up over only 15 years.

These figures show that it is also important to have a realistic expectation of your own retirement age. While we have seen our parents typically retire between the ages of 60 and 65, increasing life expectancy means that in the future, 65 to 70 is more likely to be the norm.

Rather than aim for a proportion of your income in retirement, it may be more suitable to work out how much pension you will actually need to enjoy the retirement you want, and then calculate how to get to that income. Remember, many of the expenses that you have when you are working will disappear by the time you reach retirement age, although some costs will go up. And the amount you need to save will be reduced by your state pension and any other pensions you have accrued. That said, the longer you have left it to start saving, the more expensive even a seemingly modest income can become. To secure a private income of £20,000 a year by age 65, a 25-year-old would have to save around £430 a month out of gross income. Start saving at 35 and you will have to fork out closer to £700 a month. Leave it until age 45 and you are looking at £1,260 a month to reach that target. (See Table 2.1.)

Table 2.1: Monthly pension contribution needed to secure a private income of £20,000 by age 65

Age starts saving	Monthly contribution
25	£430
35	£700
45	£1,260

Set a realistic target

If you have left it late and are staring at what seems an almost impossible savings challenge, the last thing you should do is give up hope and bury your head in the sand. Accept that a target of two-thirds or half of final salary is likely to be unachievable for you as it is for most people who are not in final salary schemes. By setting yourself such a target you are setting yourself up to fail.

A far better starting point is to calculate what you will actually need in retirement, and then seeing how far you are currently falling short. Your outgoings in retirement are likely to be lower than they are earlier in your life. What's more, most people already have some pension savings somewhere and factoring in your state pension will also help you meet your target.

Calculating your pension shortfall

The formula for calculating your pension shortfall is simple:

Calculate	Your projected annual expenses	A
Minus	Your current projected retirement income	$-$ B
Equals	Your pension shortfall	C

The following pages will show you how to calculate relatively accurate figures for A, B and C.

How much will you need?

A – Your projected annual expenses

Work out your projected monthly expenses using the list below and then multiply the figure by 12 to give yourself an annual figure:

- food/drink/cigarettes
- clothes
- dry cleaning
- utility bills
- home/car insurance
- car repairs
- car tax
- petrol
- other transport costs
- health costs – dental/private medical insurance
- entertainment/eating out
- holidays
- hobbies/club memberships
- housing costs – mortgage/rent/servicecharge/maintenance/repairs/decoration
- council tax and water rates
- replacing broken appliances (work out a nominal cost).

Remember – some costs will be lower in retirement . . .

- You may be able to benefit from pensioner rates for pub meals, theatre and concert tickets, free or reduced charge travel on buses and trains, prescription charges.
- You will be able to go on holiday off-peak when it is cheaper.
- You are likely to have paid off your mortgage by the time you retire, although people in rental properties will still have to meet these charges.

■ Downsizing to a smaller property is likely to cut your council tax, water rates, decoration and repair costs, service charges and home insurance.

■ The TV licence is free from age 75.

■ Children are likely to have left home, so food, clothing and entertainment costs will be lower. You may no longer be paying for their education or living costs, although those who had children later in life may still be doing so.

■ You will not be travelling to work or buying lunch away from home every day. You will not need to buy work clothes.

■ You will not be making pension contributions or paying for life insurance.

. . . but some will be higher:

■ You are likely to spend more time at home so your electricity and gas bills may be higher.

■ You will have more spare time on your hands so may want to spend more on entertainment, holidays and hobbies.

■ Private medical insurance and car insurance can get more expensive the older you are.

■ You may need to pay for home help.

■ You may need to spend money getting your home adapted for disability.

Couples

If you are living with a spouse or partner, add up all these expenses and then divide them by two. This will give you each an individual figure for your projected annual expenses.

Tax

Unless your projected annual expenses are below the threshold for income tax, you will have to make an allowance for the tax you will have to pay on the income you receive.

For people aged 65 to 75, income tax is paid as followed (thresholds for 2009/2010):

Up to £9,490	No tax
£9,490–£46,890	20%
£46,890 and higher	40%
£150,000 and higher	50% (from April 2010)

Calculate your pre-tax income requirement

To calculate how much gross income you need to give you enough net income to meet your projected annual expenses, multiply income at the 20 per cent tax bracket by 1.2 and income above the 40 per cent tax bracket by 1.4. Income in the 0 per cent tax bracket is unaffected.

For example, if you have projected annual expenses of £10,490, then when calculating the gross income you need to meet this amount, remember that £1,000 of your income falls in the 20 per cent tax bracket. So, £1,000 × 1.2 = £1,200 plus the £9,490 at the 0 per cent rate, giving you a figure for your total gross projected annual income requirement of £10,690.

A – Gross projected income requirement _____

How much am I currently saving?

Most people have some pension savings somewhere, and virtually everybody in the workforce is accruing state pension. You will not know exactly how much pension income you will have until you actually retire, but you can get projections on what your existing pension saving is likely to give you.

Company pensions

If you are in company pensions or have a personal pension of your own, the scheme or pension provider will send you an annual statement giving your accrued pension to date and a projection of what you will get when you retire if you carry on contributing at the same rate. People in final salary schemes will get pension projections based on salary in today's money. With final salary schemes the employer bears the risk of making sure that income is met. People in money purchase schemes, also known as defined contribution plans, get pension projections based on assumptions made about future investment returns and annuity rates. These may prove to be inaccurate. Getting a money purchase pension projection can be something of a shock, particularly after a fall in the stock market. You may find that your current projected pension is lower than it was one or two years ago, even though you have paid more in since then.

Even if your pension performs well, you may be surprised at how little you are on course to receive. Just because you are in a company pension scheme, and have been all your working life, it does not follow that you are necessarily in line for a comfortable retirement. Research carried out by Fidelity International in 2007, before the collapse in financial markets, concluded that half of employers offering staff a money purchase pension scheme do so knowing they are unlikely to provide their staff with an adequate income. Money purchase schemes are now the most common form of pension scheme in the private sector.

> Even if your pension performs well, you may be surprised at how little you are on course to receive

Personal and stakeholder pensions

As with workplace money purchase pensions, these can go down in value – projections for these plans are based on assumptions. Again, contact the provider for an update of what your projected pension is.

State pension

You can find out how much state pension you are likely to receive by requesting a state pension forecast from the Pension Service. Anyone who has paid enough National Insurance contributions or received credits for caring for others will have built up entitlement to a basic state pension. Full basic state pension stands at £95.25 a week for a single person for the year 2009/2010.

People earning a salary on a PAYE basis are also likely to have accrued additional pension, which is currently called state second pension and was formerly known as SERPS, unless they have contracted out into a personal pension or are in a final salary scheme. As a guide, someone aged 40 now who has been a higher rate taxpayer for 20 years could get around £4,600 a year when they reach state pension age. (For more on state pensions see Chapter 10.)

Non-pension income

You may also have other forms of savings and investments that you intend to use to support you in your retirement. These might include cash on deposit in bank and building society accounts, PEPs and ISAs, shares and premium bonds. You may also be planning to move to a smaller property and release some cash from your home, or you may have other properties from which you receive rent or that you intend to sell to generate capital when you retire.

Long-term savings and property can be a valuable extra source of revenue in retirement. But it is important to bear in mind that the income you receive can vary. Savings rates can fall drastically as well as rise. The value of shares can go down as well as up, and companies are likely to cut dividend payments when economic conditions are hard.

Many people have invested in rental property for their retirement. While for some it will have been a good investment, property prices can go down as well as up, and you may not make as much money as you thought. You also need to bear in mind that you will be liable for Capital Gains Tax at 18 per cent on all gains above £10,000 (for the 2009/2010 tax year) if you decide to sell up.

Because of these factors you should work out a cautious estimate of the income you are likely to derive from your non-pension assets when calculating your total projected retirement income.

How much are you currently saving?

B – Work out your current gross projected retirement income

Add up your total current projected gross retirement income from the list below:

■ state pension – includes basic state pension, additional pension (currently called state second pension, but formerly known as SERPS)

■ workplace pensions, whether final salary or money purchase

■ personal pensions, including those set up by contracting out of state second pension/Serps

■ income from investments, savings, property and other assets.

B – Current projected gross retirement income   _____

State pension

Find out how much basic and state second pension you can expect on retirement by contacting the Pension Service, online at www.thepensionservice.gov.uk/state-pension/forecast/home.asp or by calling 0845 300 0168, although it takes around 12 days from your telephone enquiry before the forecast is sent out to you. Online applications take around two days to process. To get a rough idea of how much you get straight away, turn to Chapter 10.

Workplace and personal pensions

The scheme's trustees or the pension provider that runs the plan will send you an annual statement of your current and projected retirement income. If you have lost it, ring up and ask for another one – they may be able to give you figures over the telephone.

Lost pensions and other investments

You may be entitled to pension from former employers. You should be receiving an annual pension statement from them, but if you are not you can track down lost pensions through the Pension Service's pension tracing service. See Chapter 17 for more details on tracing lost pensions as well as lost savings, investment and insurance products.

Calculate your shortfall

	A – Gross projected annual expenses	_____
Minus	B – Current projected retirement income	_____
Equals	C – Pension shortfall	_____

Your pension shortfall

If you are fortunate to have a generous pension already, or substantial income from other assets and investments, you may not have a pension shortfall at all. But the majority of people will find that their projected retirement income is less than their projected annual expenses. In many cases this shortfall will be considerable. Once you have calculated the annual amount of extra retirement income you are going to need, you must then work out how much extra you will have to save to get it.

If you are a member of a final salary scheme and are not currently on course to retire with a full pension, you may be able to wipe out or reduce your pension shortfall by buying extra years of pension or extra pension income, provided the scheme allows it. However, most final salary schemes only allow you to top up savings using money purchase additional voluntary contributions (AVCs).

For most people who are not in final salary schemes, tackling a pension shortfall involves building up a fund that will buy an annuity from a life insurance company that will pay out an income equal to that shortfall. When you come to retire you may not actually buy a conventional annuity straight away. For example, you may take income from your fund through income drawdown or live off your tax-free lump sum. But for the purposes of calculating how much extra saving you need to make, it is simplest to assume you will buy a conventional annuity.

How much will it cost to plug my shortfall?

Finding out how much you need to put away to achieve your target income can come as something of a shock. A 65-year-old single male today has to pay more than £23,000 to buy an inflation-protected annuity paying £1,000 a year. With no inflation protection it still costs over £14,800 for each £1,000 of annual income. For a woman of the same age the costs are £25,250 and £16,300 respectively. (Annuities are more expensive for women because they are expected to live longer than men.)

Seeing figures like these can leave you feeling downhearted, but if you have several decades to save, you will benefit from the effect of compound growth on your savings. You are also benefiting from tax relief on your contributions, and if you are in a company scheme you are likely to be getting at least some contribution from your employer. By increasing your monthly contributions and choosing a later retirement age you can make it easier to build up the amount you need to plug your pension shortfall.

Online pension calculators

The simplest, quickest and most efficient way of working out how much more you will need to put away to meet your target income is by using an online pension calculator. There are several available on the internet that you can use free of charge. Pension calculators ask you for a number of details about your circumstances. These include your age, projected retirement date, salary, percentage of salary pension contribution from both you and your employer, existing pension savings and contributions.

The better pension calculators then take these data and calculate how much your fund is likely to grow, how big a tax-free cash lump sum you will be entitled to and how much pension income you are likely to get, based on real-time annuity rates. Some, such as the one offered by Hargreaves Lansdown (an independent financial adviser), at www.h-l.co.uk/pension-calculator, also allow you to change details such as contributions, retirement age and tax-free cash onscreen with your mouse to see what even small changes to your saving strategy will make to your eventual income.

Strategies for plugging your pension shortfall

There are many ways of making your pension savings work harder for you, such as maximising what is on offer from your employer and the state, saving in a tax-efficient way, reducing charges and improving your investment strategy. These are covered elsewhere in the book and will help you to a greater or lesser degree depending on your particular circumstances. But for people with serious pension shortfalls there are effectively only two strategies that will make a real difference:

■ retire later

■ save more now.

Retirement age

It goes without saying that the earlier you want to retire, the more you will have to put away

How much extra you will need to save to make up your pension shortfall will be influenced to a great extent by the age at which you want to retire. It goes without saying that the earlier you want to retire, the more you will have to put away. Conversely, one way you can make your pension shortfall smaller is by opting for a later retirement date. For example, by opting for a retirement age of 68 rather than 65, your fund not only benefits from three more years' contributions and investment growth, but because your life expectancy is correspondingly shorter when you come to buy an annuity, you get a higher income. The downside is of course that you will have had to work for another three years and enjoy the income for three years less.

How delaying retirement and increasing contributions combine to give you a bigger pension

Contributing 10 per cent of a salary of £40,000, with a retirement age of 60:

Starting age	Total fund/tax-free lump sum	Income/percentage of salary
25	£280,161/£70,040	£9,736/24%
35	£151,399/£37,849	£5,090/13%
45	£76,136/£19,034	£2,468/6%

Contributing 15 per cent of a salary of £40,000, with a retirement age of 68:

Starting age	Total fund/tax-free lump sum	Income/percentage of salary
25	£597,222/£149,305	£26,167/65%
35	£382,673/£95,668	£16,456/41%
45	£227,101/£56,775	£9,528/24%

Note – All figures adjusted for inflation, assumes 50 per cent pension to spouse on death of policyholder

The age at which your other pensions start paying out

If you are making extra contributions into a private pension to plug your shortfall then you are free to start receiving it from any age between 55 (50 until April 2010) and 75. But not all pensions will start to pay out at the age you are planning to retire, so you will need to make arrangements to cover any shortfall in the intervening years.

Your state pension will normally start paying out at your state pension age – currently 65 for men and 60 for women, but rising to 65 by 2020, although you do have the opportunity to delay receiving it to either build up a cash lump sum or an increased income for life (see Chapter 10). Between 2024 and 2046 state pension age is increasing from 66 to 68 for both sexes. For many people this will mean they will not be receiving their state pension until several years after they plan to retire.

If your workplace scheme is an occupational scheme (i.e. it has a board of trustees), your pension statement will give a projected income from the scheme's normal retirement age. Occupational schemes will not normally let you change your retirement date, so if your scheme has a normal retirement age of 65 and you are planning to retire before then, you will suffer a shortfall.

If you have a workplace scheme without trustees, such as a group personal pension or a group stakeholder pension, or if you have your own personal or stakeholder pension or SIPP, the statement will reflect the retirement date you selected when you set up the plan. This retirement date is not binding and can be changed any time you like.

If you think that you need to change the retirement date you selected on a personal or stakeholder pension or SIPP, for example if you were overambitious in your expectation of how soon you might be able to retire, just contact your pension provider and they will make the change. This will give you a more realistic impression of what your projected retirement income is likely to be. If you make your retirement date later, it will make your pension shortfall smaller.

Increasing contributions

If you have a pension shortfall, the sooner you can start increasing your contributions, or even start making contributions for the very first time, the better. The cost of delaying doing so gets exponentially higher with every passing year. At 30 you have to contribute £27.32 a month to generate each £1,000 a year income. Leave it to 35 and the figure rises to £35.01. By 40 the cost will have gone up to £46.04.

But can I afford it?

Pensions are expensive and the idea of paying out the extra cash recommended by the online pension calculator you have consulted may seem unrealistic. Your other outgoings may be so high that to do so is simply not possible.

You may also have heard financial experts say that clearing existing debts should be your top priority. If you are struggling with chronic debt, unable to meet the minimum payments on your credit cards and other loans, then paying off these debts is a more efficient use of your resources than long-term saving, and you should arrange a debt repayment plan.

But waiting until you have cleared all of your debts, be they student loans, your mortgage, credit cards or other debts, could mean that you never start saving at all. Many people go through their lives without ever clearing all their credit cards or hire purchase contracts.

> If you think you can't afford to save, ask yourself whether you can afford not to

If you think you can't afford to save, ask yourself whether you can afford not to.

That said, you should not put every penny you have into your pension. Financial advisers always recommend putting some rainy day money aside as well. You could lose your job, have an accident or see your income cut for some other reason. Money paid into a pension is locked away for the long-term. It makes sense to save at least some money in a place where you can get at it if you really need to.

The psychology of saving

Behavioural psychologists say that one of the reasons why people shy away from saving is that they are put off by the size of the challenge and the length of time before they reap any reward. To be told that you need a pot of more than £60,000 just to secure an income of less than £360 a month can seem overwhelming.

But if you can't afford the contributions needed to meet your target today, start with what you can afford. That way, when you review the situation a year or so down the line, you will at least have made a start on addressing the problem.

It is also worth remembering that most people see their income grow considerably through their lives as they get promoted, and become more experienced and valued employees. While 5 per cent of today's salary may not be a huge pension contribution, it is a statistical probability that your salary will have increased considerably in 5, 10 or 20 years' time, and your pension contributions with it if you are in a company scheme.

A way of increasing contributions that taps into this factor is 'save more tomorrow', a concept developed by American academics Richard H. Thaler and Shlomo Benartzi. 'Save more tomorrow' is a method of encouraging people to increase their pension contributions with time. Under 'save more tomorrow', which is offered by AXA, among other pension providers, the individual agrees to increase their pension contributions in the future. Particularly popular in the workplace, employees often agree to increase their contributions by 1 per cent of salary a year, normally over three years. The increase is timed to coincide with their annual pay review, meaning they generally do not notice the extra money coming out of their pay packet.

The strategy is designed to address the problem that many people have in actually taking control of their finances, despite their best intentions. Research carried out for AXA found that 68 per cent of pension plan members think the amount they are saving is too low, yet due to apathy only 14 per cent of those planning to start saving actually do so.

Many pension providers, whether through the workplace or individual plans, will allow you to increase your contributions. This is known as automatic escalation. You can either tick a box saying you want your contributions to increase by a set amount, or if your pension plan is already in place and your provider does not offer this facility, you must write to them to let them know you want your contributions increased. It makes sense to make a date in your diary to review your pension recovery plan once a year. Increasing contributions by a small amount each year can be a good way to build up considerable savings in a relatively painless way. (See Tables 2.2 and 2.3.)

Other ways to reduce your pension shortfall

Aside from increasing your contributions and shifting your retirement date, other ways of addressing a pension shortfall include phasing your retirement, working part-time, downsizing to a smaller property and releasing cash from the value of your home. These strategies are considered in later chapters of this book.

Where to put your extra contributions

If you already have a money purchase company pension scheme, the chances are its annual management costs will be low, so paying extra contributions into that plan may be your best option. This will also give you the convenience of having all your pension savings in one place.

However, there are a number of different sorts of pension out there – personal pensions, stakeholder pensions, SIPPs and small self-administered schemes. The following chapters explain how you can put your retirement

Table 2.2: The cost of delay – how the return on a £100 monthly contribution shrinks the longer you put off saving

Age at which saving started	Monthly income for £100 monthly contribution*
20	£477
25	£384
30	£305
35	£238
40	£181
45	£132
50	£91
55	£55
60	£26

Table 2.3: Amount you need to save each month to generate £1,000 p.a. income as you get older

Age at which saving started	Monthly contribution required*
20	£18.96
25	£21.70
30	£27.32
35	£35.01
40	£46.04
45	£63.13
50	£91.57
55	£151.51
60	£320.51

* Assumes 20 per cent tax relief, charges of 1.5 per cent for first ten years and 1 per cent for remainder of term, average 7 per cent a year fund growth, before charges. On retirement the fund buys an annuity with a 50 per cent spouse's benefit and 2.5 per cent a year escalation.

planning on the right track and what sort of pension is best suited to helping you achieve your goal.

Women and pensions

There are a number of issues that are likely to affect women's retirement saving plans far more than men's:

■ *State pension age* For women, state pension age is rising to 65 from 60 between 2010 and 2020. The change affects women born between 6 April 1950 and 5 April 1955.

■ *State pension entitlement* Wives can claim basic state pension based on their husband's National Insurance contribution history.

■ *Divorce* If you are going through a divorce the court is required to take pension rights into account. When calculating a settlement, the court can order that pension assets be offset against other assets, earmark part of a pension to be paid to the other party at retirement or require that a pension be shared by giving the other party entitlement to a share of the other's pension or by paying a transfer value at the time of the divorce.

■ *Maternity leave* All paid maternity leave must be treated as pensionable service for the purpose of calculating entitlement to pension from occupational schemes. In final salary schemes, employee contributions are based on actual pay while employer contributions must continue at the pre-leave level. Similarly, employer contributions into group personal pension and group stakeholder arrangements must continue at the pre-leave level. The employee's contributions may be lower if her maternity pay is lower than her regular pay. Unpaid maternity leave does not count as pensionable service and there is no requirement for employers to make contributions.

■ *Part-time workers* If your employer excludes part-time workers from the company pension scheme and the majority of part-timers are women it may be possible to claim sex discrimination. This area of the law is complex and you should contact your local Citizens Advice Bureau or union.

The self-employed

People who run their own businesses face unique challenges in saving for their retirement. They do not have an employer contributing into a scheme on their behalf and do not accrue state second pension, formerly

SERPS, because they do not pay the National Insurance contributions necessary to do so. This means that the self-employed will have to make sure they put away enough to cover what they would have got through the state second pension as well as whatever extra they need.

Private pensions

3

How private pensions work

What topics are covered in this chapter?

- Tax relief
- Getting money into a pension for no net outlay
- Drawing an income
- Tax-free cash lump sum
- Pensions as medium-term savings vehicles
- Limits on pension saving
- Pensions for children and non-working family members

The government is desperate for people to save in private pensions so that they do not fall back on the state when they are retired. But why would anyone lock up their money until age 55 and then buy an annuity unless there was some incentive for doing so? The carrot for saving in a pension is tax relief, and for higher rate taxpayers in particular, that incentive can seem incredibly generous.

There are several different sorts of private sector pension: final salary and money purchase schemes in the workplace; personal pensions, SIPPs and stakeholder pensions for individuals. While all these pensions have their own features, they are all governed by a single tax structure.

This single structure was introduced in 2006 and replaced decades of laws, rules and regulations which had created a labyrinthine pensions system that few people fully understood. The 2009 Budget made things more complicated for people earning more than £150,000, but for everybody else, today's pensions system is based on three main principles:

1   Tax relief is given on your and your employer's contributions into pensions, limited to a maximum of £245,000 for the tax year 2009/2010. Within this limit you can make personal contributions of up to 100 per cent of your income.

2   A quarter of the fund may be taken as a tax-free lump sum from age 55, (age 50 until April 2010). The remaining 75 per cent of the fund must be used to buy an income.

3   Everybody is entitled to tax-advantaged pension saving worth up to £1.75m (for those retiring in tax year 2009/2010) in their lifetime.

The effect of tax relief may seem more relevant to those people saving in money purchase pensions than those in final salary schemes. But all types of pensions, including final salary schemes, are governed by the same rules when it comes to tax, tax-free cash and when benefits can be taken.

Understanding how pensions work will help you make pensions work for you. What follows is an overview of the way private sector pensions operate. All these issues are covered in greater detail further on in the book.

Tax relief

Tax relief for pensions comes in two parts: income tax on contributions, and the withdrawal of 25 per cent of the value of the fund as a tax-free lump sum from age 55. Investment growth is also largely tax-free, although pension income is taxable.

Basic rate tax is payable at 20 per cent on income above £6,475 for everyone under the age of 65, for the 2009/2010 tax year. That rises to a higher rate tax of 40 per cent on income above £43,875. From April 2010, income above £150,000 incurs tax at 50 per cent. However, for everybody except those with taxable income above £150,000, pension contributions are not subject to tax, so if the tax has already been levied at source, the person paying into a plan will get a rebate. Basic rate taxpayers therefore accrue £100 in their pension fund for each £80 of net income paid in. Higher rate taxpayers accrue £100 for each £60 of net income paid in.

From April 2011 people with taxable income over £150,000 will see their tax relief tapered down from 50 per cent to 20 per cent between £150,000 and £180,000. Contributions relating to income above £180,000 will only attract

20 per cent tax relief. Company and public sector pensions normally pay employers' pension contributions in gross, before tax is deducted.

From April 2011 those earning more than £150,000 a year will have their final salary pension benefits taxed as a benefit in kind. The government is consulting as to exactly how this tax levy will be calculated. But in the meantime, those with taxable income above £150,000 will only receive tax relief at their top rate on the first £20,000 of contributions each year, unless they were already paying in more on a regular basis on or before 22 April 2009.

How tax relief works

When individuals pay into personal or stakeholder pensions the pension provider claims their basic rate tax relief for them from the government. So if you pay £80 into a personal pension the pension provider will automatically credit you with a further £20 which it claims back from the taxman. (See Table 3.1.)

Table 3.1: Tax relief*

Marginal tax rate	Net contribution	Gross contribution
20%	£800	£1,000
40%	£600	£1,000

*For people earning less than £150,000.

Higher rate taxpayers making contributions into personal or stakeholder pensions have to complete a Self-Assessment tax return or make a claim by telephone or letter to HM Revenue & Customs to get their higher rate tax rebate back.

Whether higher rate taxpayers in company schemes get their tax relief automatically depends on the type of scheme they are in. The pension contributions of higher rate taxpayers in schemes that have trustees, such as final salary schemes and occupational money purchase schemes, are paid in gross, which means they do not have to claim back extra relief. GPs and dentists contributing into public service schemes are taxed as self-employed for some of their earnings so should claim tax relief through a Self-Assessment tax return.

Pension contributions of higher rate taxpayers in schemes without trustees, such as group personal pensions, group SIPPs and group stakeholder plans, do not get their higher rate tax relief automatically. To get the rebate they need to fill in a Self Assessment tax return or telephone or write to HM Revenue & Customs in the same way that individuals in personal pensions do.

Your pension fund grows free of tax on capital gains and investment income

Your pension fund grows free of tax on capital gains and investment income.

Getting money into a pension for no net outlay

For higher rate taxpayers in particular, tax relief on pensions is so generous that it is possible to effectively get money for nothing. Astounding as this may sound, higher rate taxpayers over the age of 55 (50 until April 2010), can get free money out of the pensions system. Make a contribution into a pension and within six years it is possible for a higher rate taxpayer to get out everything they put in and still have some cash left in their pension.

Money for nothing – how it works

June, a higher rate taxpayer, pays £8,000 into a personal pension. The pension provider automatically increases her pot to £10,000 to reflect the 20 per cent basic rate tax relief to which she is entitled. She also gets a £2,000 tax rebate on filing her tax return. This is paid back by HM Revenue & Customs as cash, outside the pension, making her net contribution into the pension £6,000.

Because she is 55 years old she is entitled to take retirement benefits immediately. She withdraws £2,500 from the fund as her 25 per cent tax-free cash lump sum.

Deducting this £2,500 from the £6,000 paid into the account makes her net contribution into the pension £3,500, yet she still has a pension pot worth £7,500. She then draws an annual income from that pot by taking what is called unsecured pension, also known as income drawdown. To recoup the original £3,500 outlay from a £7,500 pension pot will take around six years, without allowing for any growth in the pension pot at all.

After six years she has a pension pot of £4,000 for no net outlay whatsoever.

This 'money for nothing' strategy sounds too good to be true, but is entirely legal. There are limits on how much people can realistically use this mechanism, however.

First, you can only realise these returns on income on which you would normally be paying tax at a higher rate. So someone on £50,000 would only get 40 per cent tax relief on £6,125, as this is the amount of their salary that sits above the £43,875 higher rate tax threshold.

Second, there are annual limits on how much you can pay into pensions, although these will only present a problem to the super-rich or those who have already built up very big pensions. Total tax-relieved contributions, including both yours and your employers, into pensions are capped at £245,000 a year. You cannot pay in an amount greater than your annual salary as personal contributions.

Third, you have to be able to spare the money to do it. You will not get all the money back immediately, and the tax rebate in particular will take a year to come through.

Last, while the 25 per cent lump sum is always paid tax free, it is important to remember that with any pension you will pay income tax on the money you withdraw from the plan at your marginal rate.

Therefore, if your accumulated wealth means you are going to be a higher rate taxpayer when you retire, the income you receive from the pension will be taxed at 40 per cent, reducing much of the apparent gain shown in this example.

Tax relief on the way in, tax levied on the way out

This 'money for nothing' example underlines an important facet of pension saving. By saving in a pension you are not necessarily avoiding tax altogether, but shielding it from the taxman until a time when it is more efficient for you to receive your income.

If you were to take the 25 per cent tax-free lump sum out of the equation, pension saving would be of little or no benefit from a tax point of view for those who end up paying tax at the same rate both before and after retirement. Getting 40 per cent tax relief on contributions into a tax wrapper such as a pension is of little use if you are then going to be taxed at 40 per cent when you take the cash out again (although you would still avoid Capital Gains Tax on growth in your investments).

But the reality is that most people have a lower income in retirement than they do when they are working and a great many go from being higher rate to basic rate taxpayers. Some people also go from being basic rate taxpayers to not paying any tax at all.

Tax thresholds rise with age

Tax thresholds rise in big steps the further into retirement you get, meaning that more of your income will be taxed at a lower or zero rate. While the tax-free limit, known as the 'personal allowance', for anyone under 65 is £6,475 for the 2009/2010 tax year, this rises to £9,490 if you are age 65 to 74 and to £9,640 if you are over 75.

Tax thresholds (2009/2010)

Age	Tax-free personal allowance
Under 65	£6,475
65–74	£9,490
Over 75	£9,640

■ If your income is over £22,900, your higher age-related personal allowance reduces by £1 for every £2 of income over that limit. But your personal allowance will never fall below the under-65s' allowance of £6,475. For example, if you are 67 and your income is £23,900 – £1,000 above the income limit – your personal allowance of £9,490 falls by £500 to £8,990.

■ Registered blind people are entitled to a further allowance of £1,890.

■ Couples should make sure they maximise the use of both personal allowances (see Chapter 16).

These more generous personal allowances, combined with the fact that most people have less income in retirement than in their working lives, make pensions a useful tool for deciding when tax is paid.

Drawing an income

Annuities

While 25 per cent of the accumulated pension can be taken as a tax-free lump sum from age 55 (50 until April 2010), the remaining 75 per cent must be used to buy an income in retirement, usually through an annuity. For people with final salary pensions the process is simple – they receive the income they are entitled to under the terms of the scheme. Those in money purchase schemes usually buy an annuity, although it is possible to continue to keep your pension pot invested and take an income each year through a facility known as income drawdown or unsecured pension.

You can start drawing income from your pension at the same time as taking the tax-free lump sum, or you can leave the remaining three-quarters of your fund to carry on growing until you need the income. But you effectively have to start drawing income from your pot by age 75 because if you do not do so, you will still be taxed as if you are.

An annuity is a contract between an individual and an insurance company. You pay over your pension pot to the insurance company and in return they promise to pay you an income for the rest of your life. Buying an annuity is one of the most important decisions of your life – there are many different sorts of annuity and you could increase your income in retirement by up to a third if you choose the right one, yet two thirds of people do not shop around.

> Buying an annuity is one of the most important decisions of your life

Annuity purchase is also a once-in-a-lifetime decision – get it wrong and you will be stuck with that annuity for the rest of your life. There is an entire chapter devoted to the process in this book (Chapter 14), which you should read before buying an annuity.

Income drawdown/unsecured pension

Income drawdown, or, to give it its official title, unsecured pension, is a way to take income from your pension pot without buying an annuity. You can draw income from your pension from the age of 55 (50 until April 2010), up to your 75th birthday. There are rules that restrict how much you can draw from your fund each year which aim to make sure you do not leave yourself penniless, although it is possible to draw a large proportion of your pot out. As long as you are within the prescribed limits you can vary the amount you withdraw, and you can choose not to draw anything at all, even if you have taken your tax-free cash from your pension.

What happens at age 75?

At age 75 the ability to use income drawdown ceases and you must either buy an annuity or transfer your money into alternatively secured pension (ASP). This is a special form of income drawdown with very restrictive cash withdrawal limits, which is seen as extremely punitive by many financial advisers. Not only are withdrawal rates lower than those of income drawdown customers under the age of 75, but if you die while in ASP any funds left in your pension pot are taxed at a rate of up to 82 per cent. While a tax charge of 82 per cent may sound excessive, those who buy annuities lose the entirety of their pension pot when they die, unless they pay more for a guaranteed return to heirs.

ASP was introduced in 2006 following lobbying by the Plymouth Brethren, who were concerned at HM Revenue & Customs' original proposal that everybody should have to buy an annuity at age 75. Because annuities pool lives, those who live longer benefit from the pension pots of those who die younger. The Plymouth Brethren raised an objection to a product that relies on profiting from the death of others.

Tax-free cash lump sum

The ability to take a 25 per cent tax-free cash lump sum is one of the most attractive features of pension saving. Since the pension system was over-hauled in 2006, taking your tax-free cash is now much easier. As long as you are over the age for taking retirement benefits, age 55 (50 until April 2010), you can take your tax-free cash lump sum at any time before your 75th birthday, even if you are still working. You can take all of your tax-free cash in one go, or you can take it in tranches. And you do not have to take your pension income at the same time. What's more, you can pay more into your pension after you have withdrawn your tax-free cash and take tax-free cash from that too.

Example

> Thomas is 55 and has £40,000 in a pension fund. He withdraws a tax-free cash lump sum of £10,000 to spend today and leaves the remaining £30,000 to grow.
>
> He contributes another £15,000 into his pot and investment returns boost it to £60,000 by the time he is 60.
>
> Thomas can now take a tax-free lump sum equal to 25 per cent of the proportion of the fund he has not yet touched – in this case, a third. Thomas is therefore entitled to a further tax-free lump sum of £5,000.

People who are still working and contributing into a money purchase workplace pension can take their tax-free lump sum before they retire.

Pensions as medium-term savings vehicles

Because drawing tax-free cash lump sums is now so straightforward, many financial advisers are recommending that people use pensions as vehicles for saving for long-term spending commitments such as school or univer-sity fees or deposits on property for children. Many parents will not be called upon to fund these expenses until they are beyond the age at which pension benefits are taken. For higher rate taxpayers in particular, tax relief on contributions can make pensions a tax-efficient way of building up a lump sum and pension fund at the same time.

There are pitfalls to watch out for when drawing tax-free cash, which are covered in more detail in Chapter 15.

Limits on pension saving

Before the pensions system was overhauled in 2006, the amount you were allowed to contribute in any year was limited by a complex set of rules that related to your age and earnings. Today, contribution limits are both more generous and more straightforward.

Tax-advantaged pension saving is constrained by two limits: the annual allowance and the lifetime allowance.

■ *The annual allowance* In any tax year you can pay in a sum up to the same level as your earnings for that year up to an annual allowance, which has been fixed at £245,000 for 2009/2010. This is far more generous than the limit that was in place before 2006, and since then financial advisers have been quick to recommend that wealthy clients place large amounts in their pension to benefit from the generous tax relief on offer.

■ *The lifetime allowance* But there is also a limit on how much tax-relieved pension saving you are allowed to make through your entire lifetime, which has been set at £1.75m for 2009/2010. This has little effect on the majority of people but high earners need to make sure their total pension saving does not inadvertently break this limit.

Both these limits have been increased each year since the new rules were introduced in 2006. But in a move designed to reduce the amount of tax relief the Treasury is giving away, the government has said that there will be no further increases in the annual or lifetime allowances from their 2010/2011 level of £255,000 and £1.8m respectively until 2016/2017 at the earliest. This means in real terms the limits will come down.

If these limits are breached then punitive tax charges are levied. If the excess above the lifetime allowance is paid as a lump sum then a tax charge of 55 per cent is payable. If the excess is received as pension income then it is subject to a 25 per cent tax charge and the remainder taxed under the income tax rules.

Figuring out whether a money purchase pension breaks the lifetime allowance is straightforward – if the fund value is greater than £1.8m then the limit is broken. But things are more complicated if you are entitled to final salary benefits, which are expressed in terms of income, or if you are already receiving a pension, whether from an annuity, final salary scheme or through income drawdown.

Pensions already in payment are multiplied by a factor of 25 times the annual income received to calculate their value for the purpose of calculating the lifetime allowance. So somebody in receipt of a pension of £10,000 a year who is still working and accruing pension elsewhere will be deemed to have a pension asset worth £250,000. People in income drawdown are considered to have a pension asset worth 25 times the maximum they are allowed to withdraw each year under the drawdown arrangement.

Final salary benefits that are not yet being paid are multiplied by a factor of 20. Tax-free cash lump sum entitlement is not included where you have to relinquish some income to get it, but is included if it is given on top of the main benefit, as is common in some public sector schemes. In the latter case, tax-free cash lump sums are worth their face value and are added to the deemed pension value when measured against the lifetime allowance.

Another way to look at the limit is to divide the lifetime limit of £1.8m (for 2010/2011) by 20, giving you a maximum pension income of £90,000 a year before you hit the lifetime limit.

Example

A

Emma earns £50,000 a year and has ten years' service in a 1/60th final salary scheme. She has accrued a pension income of £8,333 so far.

Her pension is worth £8,333 × 20 = £166,666 for the purposes of the lifetime limit.

B

Joseph is receiving a pension of £20,000 a year from a final salary scheme but is also still working and contributing into a personal pension, which has a current fund value of £200,000.

His pension in payment is valued at £20,000 × 25 = £500,000. Adding this figure to his personal pension gives total pension assets of £700,000 for the purposes of the lifetime limit.

High earners and the lifetime limit

While probably 95 per cent of people will do well to come anywhere near the lifetime limit, for very high earners the risk of breaking it can present a real financial planning problem. Many high earners may find this is the case once they have projected forward their expected numbers of years' service and future salary increases.

Example

> Patrick earns £120,000 a year and is a member of a scheme offering one-sixtieth of final salary for each year of service. He is on course to build up a pension of £80,000 after 40 years' service. Multiplying this by 20 would give a pension value of £1.6m, within the lifetime limit.
>
> Then Patrick gets promoted and his salary rises to £180,000, putting his pension up to £120,000 a year. It is now worth £2.4m, breaking the lifetime limit.

Patrick's example relies on a number of assumptions, one of which is that the lifetime allowance will not keep pace with his wage increases. For many people, accepting the higher pension and taking the tax hit will be better than opting out of the pension scheme and getting nothing.

But if you think the lifetime allowance is going to present a problem it may be worth attempting to negotiate to receive more pay or bigger bonuses instead of pension contributions, particularly if you know you are close to or have already broken the limit. Private sector employees are far more likely to be able to negotiate such arrangements than those in the public sector.

Transitional protection against the lifetime limit

When the lifetime limit was introduced in 2006 special transitional provisions were put in place to protect people whose pensions were already over the lifetime limit or who were on course to break the limit by the time they retired. However, to benefit from these provisions, and to avoid a potential 55 per cent charge on pension benefits over the lifetime limit, you had to register your pension with HM Revenue & Customs by claiming either 'primary protection' or 'enhanced protection' before April 2009.

Most high earners in the private sector are likely to have registered for primary or enhanced protection because they are likely to have had a financial adviser looking after their affairs. But experts believe that many senior civil servants, doctors and surgeons, who have traditionally been less likely to take the assistance of financial advisers because of the security offered by their final salary pension schemes, will not have registered for primary or enhanced protection before the April 2009 deadline. They now face a tax rate of up to 55 per cent on pension income deemed to be above the lifetime allowance.

Primary protection

Primary protection was created to accommodate people whose total pension benefits already exceeded the lifetime allowance when the new rules were introduced in 2006. Primary protection allows an individual to have their own personal lifetime allowance, based on the factor by which their pension exceeded the actual lifetime limit at the date they registered for protection. For example, in 2006 the lifetime allowance was set at £1.5m. Somebody with a pension worth £3m in 2006 who registered for primary protection will in the future be deemed to have a personal lifetime allowance of twice the actual lifetime allowance. This individual is therefore entitled to a personal lifetime allowance of £3.6m in 2010/2011 when the actual lifetime allowance is £1.8m.

Enhanced protection

Enhanced protection was created to accommodate people who expect their pension to exceed the lifetime limit by the time they retire, either as a result of stock market growth or through increases in their final salary or the number of years of their service. To benefit from enhanced protection you had to claim by April 2006. Anyone who has claimed enhanced protection cannot make any further payments into their pension if it is a money purchase plan, but in return their lifetime allowance is unlimited. If they do make further payments, they will automatically lose enhanced protection, and could incur a tax charge of up to 55 per cent.

Pensions for children and non-working family members

You don't have to be working and paying income tax to benefit from the tax relief offered in pensions

You don't have to be working and paying income tax to benefit from the tax relief offered in pensions. Anyone under the age of 75 can pay into a personal or stakeholder pension and still get 20 per cent tax relief on their contributions. Even pension contributions paid on behalf of babies can receive 20 per cent tax relief.

The maximum you can pay into a pension if you are not earning is £3,600 gross. This equates to a net contribution of £2,880. Many people are now funding pensions for children or grandchildren, non-working partners or even friends.

If a parent or grandparent pays the maximum £2,880 into a pension for a child every year until they are 18, then with net growth of 7 per cent they will achieve a fund of nearly £1m by the time they are 55. This princely sum is achieved for a net outlay of only £50,544. Even assuming a real rate of return of just 3.5 per cent, the fund will still grow to £500,000, taking inflation into account.

Elderly relatives looking to pass on assets to their children should note that regular payments of this level fall below the £3,000 annual gift allowance for inheritance tax purposes.

People with non-working partners should consider paying £2,880 a year into a pension on their behalf so full use can be made of both parties' income tax personal allowances. If one partner is going to be paying income tax in retirement and the other is not, then further pension saving is most efficiently achieved in the name of the latter. He or she will not pay income tax at all up to the personal allowance of £9,490 for those aged 65 to 74, and £9,640 over 75, for the year 2009/2010. Furthermore, there may be the possibility of the non-working partner drawing a 'small pension' as a cash lump sum.

Small pensions

If the value of your pension is below a certain level you can take it as a cash lump sum rather than as an income. The limit for taking small pensions as cash is 1 per cent of the lifetime limit for pension saving, which stands at £1.75m for 2009/2010.

This means that anyone with total pension savings of less than £17,500 can take their pension as cash. Somebody with two pensions each worth £10,000 is therefore not allowed to take them as a cash lump sum and must buy an annuity. Combined pension savings below the 1 per cent of lifetime limit threshold are known as 'trivial pensions' and the process of taking them as cash is known as 'commutation'.

People with small amounts of pension in final salary schemes have the annual income multiplied by a factor of 20 for the purposes of the trivial pensions rules. So somebody with a final salary benefit of £500 a year is deemed to have a trivial pension worth £10,000 and can take it as a lump sum. However, that individual will find that they are offered a different sum by the scheme. This is because the '20 times' factor only relates to the value of the pension for the trivial pensions rules. The scheme actuaries will determine exactly how big a cash sum they offer based on how well the scheme is actually funded.

You can take 25 per cent of the trivial pension free of income tax, with the remaining 75 per cent taxed as income in the tax year it is received. For this reason it is worth drawing trivial pensions in a year when your income is low, if possible.

If you are in an occupational money purchase scheme, which is one that has a board of trustees, there may be special scheme rules governing how you can take small pensions as a lump sum.

Commutation of trivial pensions could be appropriate for people who get to retirement age without saving very much, or who only worked for an employer offering a pension for a short period of time.

You can only draw trivial pensions as cash between the ages of 60 and 75. If you want to cash in more than one small pension you have to do so within 12 months of cashing in the first one. After that no more small pensions can be cashed in. If your trivial benefits are cashed in without you asking for them to be, for example where an occupational scheme is wound up, they do not count towards your trivial commutation limit.

4

Personal and stakeholder pensions

What topics are covered in this chapter?

■ Personal pensions

■ Stakeholder pensions

■ SIPPs

■ How to beat the corrosive effect of charges

Personal pensions

Personal and stakeholder pensions are the most common plan for people who do not have access to company schemes. Personal pensions replaced the retirement annuity plans that preceded them and are governed by the tax and contribution rules set out in Chapter 3.

Created in 1988 to kick-start the idea of individual responsibility for pensions in the psyche of the nation, personal pensions did not get off to an auspicious start. Between 1988 and 1994 at least a million people were wrongly advised by financial advisers and pension providers to switch from company pension schemes to personal pensions with higher charges. An extensive review by the regulator found pension misselling had been widespread and providers and financial advisers were ordered to pay nearly £12bn in compensation to customers who lost out.

Since then the industry has largely cleaned up its act. Stakeholder pensions also arrived on the scene in 2001 as a government-designed plan structure with clean, simple and consumer-friendly features. These include a maximum annual management charge of 1 per cent and the right to transfer to another pension fund without exit penalties. The maximum annual charge had to be increased in 2005 to 1.5 per cent for the first ten years to allow life insurers to be able to afford to market the plans, because the profit margins were so tight at 1 per cent. Some experts say this demonstrates what good value stakeholder pensions have been for consumers.

Stakeholder pensions offer a more basic service and narrower range of investments than personal pensions. But although personal pensions are allowed to charge more than the stakeholder charge cap, in reality most providers have shied away from making them much more expensive. This is because, since stakeholder pensions were introduced, the FSA has required advisers to be able to demonstrate that if they recommend a pension product that is more expensive than a stakeholder plan, they must be able to justify why they did so.

Old products still have high charges

Millions of old pension contracts that are taking billions of pounds in charges out of the nation's pensions remain in place to this day

But despite the review and compensation that followed the pensions misselling scandal and the creation of stakeholder pensions, there are still bad personal pensions out there. Millions of old pension contracts that are taking billions of pounds in charges out of the nation's pensions remain in place to this day. Some may be in forgotten pensions that are no longer being contributed into. Others may be in pensions set up a long time ago, but which you are still paying into.

Either way, the amounts being deducted in charges can be eye-watering – a £50,000 forgotten pot with no new contributions going in at all will be still paying out £1,000 a year in charges under a pension contract with a 2 per cent annual management charge. By taking control of your pension and moving it to a cheaper plan you could save literally tens of thousands of pounds by the time you retire (see page 54).

How personal pensions work

Personal pensions offer individuals a tax-efficient way of saving over the long term, although most of the money you save in them has to be used to buy an income in retirement.

Contributions you make into a personal pension are boosted by tax relief at your marginal rate. Basic rate taxpayers paying £80 into a personal pension see it uplifted to £100 with tax relief. Higher rate taxpayers only have to pay £60 to see £100 credited in their pension plan. Over the years your fund will grow tax-free and when you come to retire you use the fund to buy a pension income, normally from an insurance company in the form of an annuity. As a way of incentivising you to tie up your money in this way, the government allows you to take a quarter of your fund as a tax-free lump sum.

Risk

Personal pensions are money purchase arrangements which means that, unlike final salary schemes offered by employers, there is no guarantee as to how much income you will receive in retirement. With personal pensions, the individual plan holder is responsible for dealing with a considerable amount of risk.

There are two key elements to this risk: how well the investments perform and what the annuity rate is when you come to retire.

Stock market volatility

Recent years have shown the devastating effect that stock market volatility can have on the retirement plans of people with personal pensions. But volatility can be positive as well as negative, depending on when you happen to come into and exit the market. Between October 2004 and October 2007 the balanced managed sector rose by 30 per cent and somebody retiring and buying an annuity at the peak in the market will have done well. Twelve months later an identical fund had fallen 30 per cent. A pension saver with a fund of £50,000 in October 2007 could have seen it fall to around £35,000 a year down the line.

This shows the extent to which the stock market behaves as something of a lottery. Two people retiring 12 months apart who have followed an identical retirement saving strategy would receive pensions differing in value by a third if they had failed to address the issue of risk in their portfolio.

There are ways to mitigate the risk that stock market volatility creates as you approach retirement. Most modern pensions have strategies that can do this built in to their systems. This is a process called lifestyling. Many people have pensions that were set up years ago that do not offer lifestyling solutions. These pension arrangements should be revisited. Lifestyling is explained in more detail later in this chapter

Annuity risk

Rollercoaster fund values are not the only risk borne by people with personal pensions. The annuity rates available when you come to cash in your pension for an income can vary significantly too.

At their peak in 1990, annuities for 65 year olds paid out at a rate of around 16 per cent. This means £100,000 could buy you an income for life of £16,000 a year. Since then increased life expectancy projections and lower long-term interest rates have pushed annuity rates steadily downwards. By 2006 they were below 7 per cent, meaning an income of less than £7,000, less than half of the 1990 figure, for the same £100,000 pension pot.

Stakeholder pensions

Stakeholder pensions are a low-cost form of personal pension which were created to protect consumers in the wake of the pensions misselling scandal of the late 1980s and early 1990s. The government created the concept of the 'stakeholder pension' as a kitemark-style product that adheres to a strict set of consumer-friendly features relating to charges, contributions and withdrawals. The intention behind the launch of stakeholder pensions was to encourage wider saving among those on low incomes. Very few stakeholder pensions have actually been sold to the target group, although large numbers have been and continue to be sold to wealthier people attracted by their low charges.

Requirements of a stakeholder pension

- ■ Total annual management charges, including fund management fees, capped at 1.5 per cent of fund value for the first ten years and 1 per cent a year after that.
- ■ Must allow penalty-free transfers to other pension providers.
- ■ Must accept contributions as low as £20, whether on a regular basis or as a one-off payment.

These low charges make stakeholder pensions a safe choice for anyone concerned that pension providers' fees will eat too big a hole in their savings.

But the downside of the cap on charges is that the range of funds available to invest in through stakeholder pensions is invariably less comprehensive than through personal pensions with higher charges. Star fund managers often have annual management charges that are already higher than 1 or 1.5 per cent a year, before the charges levied by the pension provider for administering the scheme are even taken into account.

When the two are added together, total charges can rise above 2 per cent. For this reason stakeholder pensions will never be able to offer pension savers access to the sort of investment funds that offer stellar outperformance over their peers. Whether or not star fund managers can deliver the outperformance needed to justify these fees over decades of pension saving is a separate matter, covered in more detail on page 144.

Investment choice

Personal pensions typically offer you a range of between 40 and 200 investment funds in which to invest. Stakeholder pensions usually offer less than 30 funds to choose from, and these are unlikely to include any star fund managers.

Charges on pensions are a combination of administration charges and fund management charges. Most personal pensions offer at least some funds that, when combined with the administration charge, fall below the 1.5 per cent a year stakeholder threshold. But because they also offer funds that cost more than that, they are not allowed to call themselves stakeholder pensions.

Service

You may get better service if you opt for a personal pension over a stakeholder pension. This could be in terms of the amount of information you are sent about your investment returns, access to online valuations and the speed with which your calls are answered at a call centre.

SIPPs

SIPPs, which stands for self-investment personal pensions, are, as the name suggests, a type of personal pension plan. SIPPs are allowed to offer access to a broader range of funds and a wider choice of asset classes than traditional personal pensions, which only allow savers to invest in a limited range of funds. SIPPs are covered in detail in Chapter 7.

Unless you are going to use the extra functionality that SIPPs permit, for example by putting directly held shares, commercial property or exchange traded funds in your pension, most financial advisers agree that a personal pension will do the job just as well. Some online supermarket SIPPs, which do not offer access to asset classes such as commercial property or directly held shares, do compete with stakeholder and personal pensions on price, however.

How to beat the corrosive effect of charges

Charges are one of the biggest drains on investment performance for pensions so it is important to buy a pension on the best terms available. Old pensions in particular, taken out in the 1980s and 1990s, can have charges way in excess of the current stakeholder limits, and will seriously damage your pension pot, in some cases reducing it by a third. Regulation may have made the pensions sold today cheap and consumer friendly but it has not required pensions taken out decades ago to reduce their charges.

Old-fashioned pensions with high charges

If you are still saving in a pension you took out more than a decade ago it is possible that your pension provider could skim up to a third of your investment returns from your pot through high charges.

Example

How one person saved £58,000 in pension charges by switching pension

This real-life example shows just how bad for your retirement an old-fashioned pension contract can be.

Mr X is currently saving in a high charging pension with NFU Mutual, one of the country's smaller life insurers. He still has another 20 years until his planned retirement date and is still paying £100 a month into a fund worth £70,216. Under the terms of the plan, which was taken out before stakeholder pensions had been created, he is charged 5 per cent up front on every monthly contribution as well as an annual management charge of 0.625 per cent a year on the entire value of the fund.

Assuming a return of 7 per cent a year on the investments held within the pension, the NFU Mutual plan is on course to grow to £177,250 by the time he retires. By moving to a stakeholder pension with Aegon charging 1 per cent a year, the same fund and contributions will grow to £236,000, saving over £58,000 in unnecessary charges.

Pension companies make vast amounts of money from these contracts, which is why they sit back and let you carry on paying the charges rather than publicise the effect it is having on your retirement. Many people think that the financial services industry had got rid of high charging products once and for all after it was forced to compensate customers with billions of pounds in compensation following the pensions misselling scandal. But while the arrival of low-cost stakeholder pensions has forced pension providers to clean up their act when it comes to selling new pensions, there are still plenty of costly old contracts out there eating into both funds that have already been built up and contributions that will be made for years to come.

When stakeholder pensions were introduced in 2001 only a few providers, including Aviva (formerly Norwich Union) and Standard Life, moved their existing customers' plans onto the same lower charges enjoyed by new customers. But companies such as Scottish Provident, Scottish Mutual, Abbey Life, Friends Provident, Scottish Life and Scottish Equitable (part of Aegon) between them have hundreds of thousands of existing customers who are being charged more than double the 1 per cent charge that is common in today's pension products. Scottish Widows moved all its personal pension customers onto 1 per cent charging contracts but its freestanding additional voluntary contribution (AVC) and executive pension customers are still paying considerably more.

Should I switch?

Moving your pension from a high charging contract can save you thousands of pounds, making a considerable difference to your retirement income. In many cases switching will save you money both on the pension you have already accrued and the contributions you make in the future.

For example, someone with an accrued fund of £50,000 who has another 25 years to retirement will save £49,180 in charges by switching from a pension with a level annual management charge of 2 per cent a year to one charging 1 per cent, assuming returns of 7 per cent a year before charges. This equates to an uplift in fund value of 28 per cent, bringing a projected pot of £174,068 up to £223,248. The effect that this has on retirement income is simple. A 28 per cent uplift in fund value translates through to a 28 per cent increase in pension income.

Regular contributions also grow more quickly if they are not held back by high charges. A contribution of £300 a month, or £3,600 a year for

25 years will grow to £209,362 in a plan with 1 per cent charges rather than £180,408 in a plan charging 2 per cent, an uplift of £28,954 or 16 per cent.

But it is not always a good idea to switch if you have already paid a lot of high charges. This is because some pension plans charge you more in the early years in return for lower charges later on in the life of the plan. Others levy high charges in the early years, but give you extra bonus units if you keep paying into the plan. These complex charging structures were created to allow the insurance companies to recoup money from you in the early years of the contract to allow them to pay commission to financial advisers. For this reason, it is always worth getting a detailed explanation of the effect of stopping payments into your pension plan from your provider before taking action.

For example, the NFU Mutual pension contract mentioned above eats away at pensions through a large upfront charge of 5 per cent on contributions, while its annual management charge is relatively modest, at 0.625 per cent. This charging structure makes it more worthwhile leaving the existing fund in the NFU Mutual pension but stopping future contributions into the plan and diverting them into a new low-cost arrangement.

Getting charges even lower: discount brokers

It is possible to cut your charges even lower than the stakeholder price threshold by using a discount broker. Pension companies do not publicise the fact, but you can get exactly the same product from them for almost half price by going through a discount broker rather than buying direct. Discount brokers are able to do this because they take part of the pension's annual management charge that normally goes to financial advisers and pay that back to you, the client.

You can also use discount brokers to get you better deals on ISAs, unit trusts and with-profits bonds as well

Discount brokers are, technically-speaking, IFAs that do not give advice. This means their running costs are a lot lower than regular IFAs. So by registering as your IFA with the pension provider they are able to receive the ongoing commission that providers pay, which is known as 'trail' commission, and give a proportion of it back to you. Some will rebate the entire amount of the IFA's commission back into your plan. You can also use discount brokers to get you better deals on ISAs, unit trusts and with-profits bonds as well.

Ongoing trail commission paid to financial advisers is normally around 0.5 per cent for pensions. It is paid every single year that the pension contract is live, whether you are paying money in or not and, crucially, whether you are receiving advice or not. It is supposed to pay for ongoing advice and service from the financial adviser that sold you the pension. If you do not have a financial adviser then the pension provider keeps the trail commission for itself.

It is reasonable for your financial adviser to get trail commission if they are giving you ongoing advice and assistance with your pension, but in many situations they do not. A large proportion of financial advisers continue to receive trail commission for many years after they have put the pension in place, effectively scooping big chunks of cash from your pension pot for no effort whatsoever. On a £100,000 pension pot a financial adviser could easily be receiving £500 trail commission a year for doing absolutely nothing. You can stop this happening by contacting a discount broker, which will rebate some or all of the trail commission into your pension pot.

Cavendish Online is one of the best value discount brokers. It rebates all trail commission back into your pension for the rest of the life of the product in return for a one-off administration fee of £35.

Example

Malcolm is paying £350 a month into a stakeholder pension with Aviva. The normal stakeholder pension charge is 1 per cent.

	Annual management charge	*Fund at 9% growth (after 40 years, assuming 2.5% inflation)*
Full commission	1%	£1,485,110 or £539,440 in today's money
Cavendish Online (discount broker)	0.55%	£1,674,745 or £608,321 in today's money

By switching to a discount broker Malcolm's pension pot is 12.7 per cent higher when he comes to retire, giving him an annuity income 12.7 per cent higher.

However, Malcolm is not getting the benefit of financial advice any more. If his IFA wasn't giving him regular advice anyway, he is better off switching. If he is getting regular advice, he needs to consider whether he thinks that advice is worth what he is paying for it.

Personal pension, stakeholder or SIPP – which is cheapest?

If you are going down the 'no advice' route, only want to invest in funds and are comfortable making your own decisions about investment strategy and tax issues, then finding the best pension for you is all about cost and range of funds.

It is impossible to say which form of pension is the cheapest (although a specific product is cheaper through a discount broker) because it all depends on what funds you invest in. This is in part because most pension providers like to be able to say their product has at least one or two cheap investment options. This confusion marketing, which makes it impossible to compare like with like, means that investing in some funds can be cheaper through personal pensions than stakeholder pensions, while others will not.

Online SIPPs can work out cheaper than both personal and stakeholder pensions for a wide variety of funds, and not for others. Arguably the cheapest private pension option on the market is investing in the HSBC FTSE All Share Tracker Index fund through Hargreaves Lansdown's Vantage SIPP. This will cost you an unbeatable 0.25 per cent a year, including charges for the pension wrapper and fund manager charges, even though it would cost you 1 per cent if you went to HSBC direct. If all you are bothered about is cost, then this deal is hard to beat.

But if you want to invest in star fund managers, you may wish to check how much the total cost of doing so will be with various providers before signing up. This exercise will be easier to achieve for online supermarket SIPPs than for life insurers' pensions because their charging structures are generally less complicated.

Investment strategy

As with all types of money purchase pension, responsibility for the selection of investments in your personal or stakeholder pension rests with either you or your financial adviser. For a more detailed explanation of which funds to invest in, turn to Chapter 9.

'Zombie' with-profits funds

Millions of pensions sold in the 1980s and 1990s had with-profits funds as the default option. Today there still remain millions of people paying monthly contributions into with-profits funds that have no chance of ever delivering good performance over the long term.

This is because most with-profits funds are unable to move between asset classes as market conditions demand. These funds have promised so many guarantees to some policyholders that they can only be sure of meeting them and remaining solvent by following a very cautious investment approach. Because these funds will never enjoy the good years of equity performance they can never expect to deliver above-average returns. Over a period of decades this sluggish performance could result in a seriously stunted fund. However, they have held up well during the market turmoil of 2008 and 2009, precisely because of that cautious investment approach.

Out of the 110 with-profits funds on the market, at least 66 are even closed to new business, with the providers running them down and maximising the profits on them. Closed funds represented £191bn of assets in 2004, a fifth of the entire long-term insurance investment market, according to the FSA. Closed with-profits funds include those from Abbey Life, Alba, Britannic, Cornhill, Royal & SunAlliance, Pearl, NPI and London Life.

Prudential, Aviva and LV= (formerly Liverpool Victoria) are some of the exceptions which do still have strong enough funds that can benefit from exposure to equities.

Leaving these 'zombie' funds, so called because of their aimless, lumbering investment progress, is generally considered a good idea provided you do not have to suffer a hefty exit penalty to get out. Some providers allow you a penalty-free opt-out on each fifth or tenth anniversary of the date you took out the plan. You should also stay put if you are entitled to a guaranteed annuity rate, large guaranteed bonus on maturity or a high guaranteed rate of return.

Security of personal and stakeholder pensions

Personal and stakeholder pensions are offered by providers that are authorised and regulated by the FSA. These are usually insurance companies, banks and investment managers.

If your pension provider went bust then the level of protection you would get would depend on the investments within it:

▪ *Unitised funds (except with-profits)* The investment funds in your pension are held in trust. So if the pension provider goes into liquidation, its creditors cannot touch your investments. However, the value of those investments can and does go up and down on a regular basis. If the companies your fund invests in go bust then the shares you hold in them are worthless so you lose your money.

▪ *With-profits funds* These count as insurance products and are covered by the Financial Services Compensation Scheme (FSCS), which would compensate you up to the level of 100 per cent of the first £2,000 and 90 per cent of the remainder of your loss. However, you are only covered if the insurer becomes insolvent and the fund is lost to creditors, and not just because the fund is performing badly.

▪ *Annuities* These are treated as insurance contracts and the FSCS would compensate you up to the level of 100 per cent of the first £2,000 and 90 per cent of the remainder of your loss, without a ceiling, in the event that the insurer could not pay what it had promised to. This would include inflation increases, spouse's benefits and other extras.

▪ *Share portfolios* These would only be held in SIPPs. As with unitised funds, the shares are held in trust for the plan-holder and so if the SIPP provider went bust its creditors would not be able to access the shares. The value of the shares themselves is not guaranteed. If the company whose shares you have invested in goes into liquidation, you will lose your money.

▪ *Cash on deposit* The situation about compensation cover for cash held on deposit is not straightforward and depends on the policy of the provider you are dealing with. If the money is held in the bank's account in the name of the plan-holder, which is often the case through a SIPP, then each individual will benefit from the full £50,000 FSCS bank compensation limit. However, with some insurance companies it is not clear whether each individual member is entitled to £50,000 cover if the cash is held within a provider's account with a bank, or whether the £50,000 limit applies to the entire sum deposited with the provider. This issue is particularly important in relation to offshore bank accounts offered through SIPPs. It is important to clarify what level of investor protection you get with any cash deposit arrangement set up through a pension. If you hold more than £50,000 cash in your personal pension or SIPP, you should spread it around a range of banks and building societies.

Retirement Annuity Contracts

Retirement Annuity Contracts (RACs) are a type of pension plan that individuals could take out before 1 July 1988, when personal pensions were introduced.

They used to allow more contributions to be paid in than were allowed through personal pensions. But since the pensions system was simplified in 2006 RACs have been put on the same basis as personal pensions and almost all of their special features no longer apply.

Charges can be higher than those available on modern pensions, which could make it worth switching. But check that you will not be giving up valuable guaranteed annuity rates before doing so.

5

Workplace schemes: money purchase

What topics are covered in this chapter?

- ▓ Will my workplace pension be enough?
- ▓ Occupational money purchase schemes
- ▓ Group personal pensions and group stakeholder pensions
- ▓ Recoup unclaimed higher rate tax relief
- ▓ Security of workplace money purchase schemes

Money purchase pensions are the fastest-growing type of retirement plan among UK employers. Companies that close down final salary pensions usually replace them with a money purchase scheme, usually with a lower level of contributions. Like personal pensions, they leave the individual exposed to the volatility of the stock market. How much pension you get depends on how much you and your employer contribute, how well your investments perform and how much it costs to buy an annuity at retirement. These schemes are also known as 'defined contribution' plans.

Workplace money purchase pensions have several advantages over individual pensions. Normally your employer makes a contribution into the plan, typically between 5 and 10 per cent of salary, provided you contribute a similar amount. This means you are saving up to twice as quickly as you would in a plan on your own. By not signing up, you are effectively turning down free money.

Because of their size, charges are usually lower than individual pensions, and in many cases the employer will bear all or some of the cost of running the scheme, allowing your pot to grow more quickly. Even though few money purchase schemes are as generous as final salary pension schemes, signing up to one is still a no-brainer for virtually everybody if the employer makes a contribution into it.

Every employer with five or more employees is legally bound to give you access to a stakeholder pension scheme through your payroll. However, not all employers make a contribution into it.

Will my workplace pension be enough?

Research from Fidelity International, the fund manager, shows that people contributing into the average money purchase pension are on course to retire on 38 per cent of salary, compared to up to 66 per cent for somebody in a final salary scheme. Those who put off joining their company scheme for just a few years will be on even less than that. If this applies to you, you need to work out a retirement saving plan (see page 15).

However, it should be mentioned that most of those in a money purchase pension scheme will receive a state second pension in addition to their private pension, whereas most of those in a final salary scheme will not.

Different types of workplace money purchase scheme

Workplace money purchase schemes fall into two distinct categories: those with a board of trustees and those without. Schemes with a board of trustees are called occupational schemes, while those without trustees are either group personal pensions or group stakeholder pensions. Both types of workplace pension place the burden of risk on individual members but they do differ in terms of oversight of investments and the way in which higher rate tax relief is received.

Occupational money purchase schemes

Occupational money purchase schemes, also known as occupational defined contribution schemes, are common among large and medium-sized employers. They are governed by a board of trustees, which is normally appointed from a combination of the workforce, management

Occupational money purchase schemes, are common among large and medium-sized employers

and professional pensions consultants. At least a third of the trustees must be nominated by members of the pension scheme.

Some occupational money purchase schemes require you to contract out of state second pension (formerly SERPS) as a condition of membership. The fact that you are likely to be getting an employer contribution as well means that it is still worth signing up to such a scheme.

Investment approach

Occupational money purchase schemes usually have a limited choice of one or more investment options which are selected by the trustees. The default fund option, chosen by more than 80 per cent of employees, is typically a passively managed fund and in some cases invests 100 per cent in equities, exposing scheme members to considerable volatility. These funds normally reduce exposure to equities as members approach their stated retirement age.

Schemes also accept additional voluntary contributions (AVCs). This can be a low-cost way of building up extra pension because the employer usually bears some or all of the management charges. However, investment choice may be limited and you could opt for a low-cost SIPP or personal pension for your extra savings.

Tax

One of the benefits of occupational money purchase schemes is that both your basic and higher rate tax relief is recovered for you by the scheme. This means that you do not need to fill in a tax return to get your higher rate tax relief, which is not always the case for people saving through group personal pensions or group stakeholder plans.

What are my options if I leave before retirement?

If you leave after two or more years:

- ■ a preserved pension, payable from the scheme's normal retirement date, or
- ■ a transfer to a new employer's pension scheme, or
- ■ a transfer to a personal or stakeholder pension.

A refund of contributions is not permitted.

If you leave before completing two years' service:

■ a refund of your own contributions or the value of your own contributions, if the scheme's rules allow it

■ the option to transfer to another pension scheme, if you have completed more than three months' service.

Watch out for cash offers if you leave early

Avoid taking a refund of contributions if you can – it is not a good idea unless you have an overwhelming need for cash in your hand at the time. This is because you will only receive your own contributions – those made by your employer will not be paid over, whereas if you transfer your fund to another pension scheme, your employer's contributions will be included. By accepting the cash in your hand you not only lose typically half of the contributions, but you also lose your tax relief and any investment growth as well.

Pension schemes are not required to spell out how much you will lose by taking a refund of contributions. Some will offer to pay it to you directly into an ISA. Do not be confused into thinking it is still in a pension just because it has been placed in an investment vehicle. You are still losing money by accepting.

Death benefits

Occupational money purchase schemes normally pay out death benefits to beneficiaries such as spouses, unmarried partners and civil partners. Where the member dies before taking pension benefits the payout is normally the fund value at the time of death, whether the member was still employed by the company sponsoring the scheme or had left. Some occupational money purchase schemes also pay out a lump sum of between one and four times salary.

If the member dies after starting to receive the pension then spouses, unmarried partners and civil partners will continue to receive an income at the level selected by the member if they took an annuity with a survivor's benefit.

It is also possible to opt for a five- or ten-year guarantee. If the pensioner dies within the guarantee period, a sum equivalent to the remainder of the guarantee payment will be paid to named beneficiaries, normally subject to 35 per cent tax.

Do not accept the annuity offered by your trustees until you have shopped around to see if you can get a better deal. You may be able to increase your retirement income considerably if you smoke or have health issues. See page 206 for more information on how to get the best annuity rate.

It is important to keep the names of beneficiaries you would like to receive death benefits up to date. For a more detailed explanation of what can go wrong if you do not, see page 238.

Charges

Charges on occupational money purchase schemes are often very low, with some schemes running on an annual charge of less than 0.5 per cent.

Ill health early retirement

While occupational money purchase arrangements do not pay out ill health pensions, some employers offer group income protection policies to cover staff whose poor health forces them to stop work.

Group personal pensions and group stakeholder pensions

If your employer offers a money purchase pension and it does not have a board of trustees then it is either a group personal pension (GPP) or a group stakeholder pension.

In the eyes of the regulator GPPs and group stakeholder plans are nothing more than a group of individual personal or stakeholder pensions that happen to be held together. Investment options, defaults, switching options, death benefits, annuities and tax-free cash arrangements are all exactly the same as for personal or stakeholder pensions, which are covered in detail in Chapter 4.

Many people think that their employer has some responsibility for the GPP or group stakeholder pension that they offer to their staff in the way that employers operating occupational money purchase schemes do through the board of trustees. This impression is wrong. GPPs and group stakeholders differ from occupational money purchase schemes in two key areas: tax and investment strategy.

Tax

Because a group personal pension is just another form of personal pension, the obligation is on the employee to make sure they receive their higher rate tax relief. To do this you must either fill in a tax return or contact HM Revenue & Customs and get them to change your tax code.

It is worth noting that it costs a higher rate taxpayer more up front to save through a GPP or group stakeholder plan than through an occupational money purchase scheme. This is because the person saving through an occupational money purchase scheme gets 40 per cent tax relief immediately whereas the person saving through a GPP or group stakeholder has to claim 20 per cent of it back, usually getting it a year later, and in many situations forgetting it or not getting round to claiming it at all.

So, somebody on £60,000 a year paying 10 per cent of salary into an occupational scheme sees £6,000 a year credited to their pension fund. The person who does so through an occupational money purchase scheme only sees a £3,600 reduction in take-home pay as a result. The cost to the person in the GPP or group stakeholder on the other hand is a reduction of take-home pay of £4,800. They have to then reclaim the remaining £1,200.

Recoup unclaimed higher rate tax relief

Many people make the mistake of thinking that their employer or the pension scheme does this for them (as is the case for occupational money purchase schemes). Around 250,000 people could be missing out on a fifth of their pension contributions in this way, according to figures from Standard Life. The numbers losing out in this way are likely to have risen in recent years since HM Revenue & Customs stopped requiring higher rate taxpayers to fill in a tax return as a matter of course.

By getting your tax code changed, you will notice an immediate increase in your take-home pay of 20 per cent of your monthly pension contribution. Reclaim it through your Self-Assessment tax return and you may have to wait a year to get your money. Even if you have filled in a Self-Assessment tax return in the past but are no longer required to do so, it is important to check that you are getting the rebate you are entitled to.

Reclaim for previous years

You can make a claim for higher rate tax relief that you have missed out on, going back up to five years and ten months after the end of the year to which the claim relates. However, there is a proposal to reduce this period for some backdated claims to four years. To make a claim simply write to your local tax office explaining why you believe you are entitled to a backdated rebate.

Example

> Peter and Paul both earn £60,000 a year and pay 10% of salary into their workplace pension.
>
> Peter is in an occupational scheme. His £6,000 annual contribution is deducted from his salary before tax is calculated so the net cost to him is only £3,600.
>
> Paul is in a GPP. He pays in a net contribution of £4,800, which is automatically grossed up to £6,000.
>
> Paul finds out that he has been missing out on his higher rate tax relief for eight years. He discovers he is entitled to a tax rebate of £1,200 each year, which is paid outside the pension. This makes his gross contribution each year £3,600.
>
> He makes a backdated claim to HM Revenue & Customs and is able to claim back for six previous tax years. He recoups a backdated rebate of 6 × £1,200 = £7,200.

Investments

Making your investments work as hard as possible is crucial to your retirement

Because GPPs and group stakeholders do not have a board of trustees, the individual member is entirely responsible for selecting the investments into which their contributions are placed. As with individual personal and stakeholder pensions and occupational money purchase schemes, the majority of members will end up selecting the default option. This is likely to be a one-size-fits-all fund picked by the life insurer offering the pension scheme or the IFA or pension consultancy that has arranged the scheme.

Making your investments work as hard as possible is crucial to your retirement. For a more detailed analysis of investment options see Chapter 9.

Charges

Charges on a GPP or group stakeholder are likely to be slightly higher than on an occupational money purchase plan, but are still usually cheaper than the stakeholder price cap (see page 50). Many schemes charge as little as 0.5 per cent for employees who opt for the cheaper funds on the range. This can make your GPP or group stakeholder scheme a good option for extra pension saving, although stakeholder plans will have limited investment options.

Penalties for staff who move on

Some GPPs or group stakeholders penalise staff who leave the sponsoring company by jacking up the charges once they move on. This practice is called 'active member discount' and is becoming increasingly common. Somebody who has been benefiting from a low annual management charge of 0.5 per cent on their GPP or group stakeholder could see it raised to 1 or 1.5 per cent after they leave. To get an idea of the corrosive effect that higher charges have on long-term returns, see page 54.

It is therefore important to check the charges on any plans you have with former employers and, if necessary, move to a cheaper plan.

Security of workplace money purchase schemes

Occupational money purchase schemes

The protection offered to occupational money purchase schemes exists in relation to the providers involved in running the investments, provided they are regulated and authorised by the FSA. As with personal pensions, levels of protection vary depending on the type of investment and provider involved in the scheme. For more details see page 59.

People saving in AVCs should be aware that cash deposit options offered by some trustees are only covered by the FSCS up to £50,000 of the value of the entire scheme's cash deposits. If the bank in which the trustees have invested the money goes bust, then the entire scheme's deposits may only be covered up to £50,000, meaning that you will only get a proportion of your money back.

GPPs and group stakeholder plans

The security offered to people investing in GPPs and group stakeholder arrangements is exactly the same as for those in individual personal pension or stakeholder pension plans, and is covered in detail at the end of Chapter 4.

6

Workplace schemes: final salary

What topics are covered in this chapter?

- Bad press for final salary schemes
- Security of final salary pensions
- Buying added years or additional pension
- Additional voluntary contributions
- Transfers out of final salary schemes
- Death benefits

Final salary pensions are by a long distance the most desirable pensions you can get, fully meriting the 'Rolls Royce of pensions' tag by which they are often described. Also known as defined benefit schemes, they pay a proportion of the salary you earned when you were working every year for the rest of your life. If you get offered one, you should accept it with open arms.

Like Rolls Royces, final salary schemes are incredibly expensive to run. Improvements in life expectancy and poor investment returns have sent the contributions that employers have to make into these schemes soaring.

This is why the last decade has seen most private sector employers offering the schemes doing everything they can to scale back the benefits they offer in a bid to save themselves cash. For the most part this has been limited to closing schemes to new employees, while leaving existing employees in the scheme. By the beginning of 2009, only 26 per cent of private sector final salary schemes were still open to new members, according to a survey by the National Association of Pension Funds.

But that survey also found that one in four employers is planning to close its scheme to existing members as well, in most cases offering them a riskier, cheaper and less generous money purchase pension instead. So far few big employers have taken this step, although Rentokil is one household name to have stopped its staff accruing final salary benefits. But experts predict it will not be long before more blue-chip companies start shifting their existing employees out of their final salary scheme.

That said, there are still around 2.4 million people in open final salary pensions in the private sector, according to the Office for National Statistics, with more than double that number of people entitled to final salary pension benefits from previous employers. But private sector scheme membership is dwarfed by the more than 5 million public sector workers still building up final salary benefits.

Bad press for final salary schemes

Final salary schemes have had more than their fair share of bad press over the last decade. Spiralling deficits totalling hundreds of billions of pounds have put the wind up investors, employees and pensioners alike. The danger of these deficits was highlighted in 2002 when several employers with underfunded schemes went bust, leaving more than 120,000 people with little or no pension, in some instances after a lifetime of contributions. Several years and a bitter pensioner campaign later, and the system has been more or less repaired as far as the vast majority of employees are concerned.

Bad headlines should not put you off final salary pensions – if your employer offers you one, you should not think twice about signing up.

Bad headlines should not put you off final salary pensions

What if I cannot afford it?

Many final salary schemes require an employer contribution, often between 5 and 8 per cent of salary. For some people, particularly younger employees struggling to pay off student loans and credit card debt, there can be a temptation to put off joining a company pension, even if it is a final salary scheme. A further disincentive for younger employees in particular is the remoteness of the benefit that will be received many decades down the line, when compared to the advantages of receiving cash in the hand today.

If you are in this situation it is worth doing everything you possibly can to remain in the final salary scheme. By not doing so, you are effectively turning your back on free money. To illustrate just how valuable final salary pensions can be, the financial advisers to the NHS estimate that the value of the benefits offered by that organisation's scheme are worth around 29 per cent of salary. Yet many NHS employees only have to contribute 6 per cent of salary to be in it.

Types of scheme

Final salary pensions are also known as defined benefit schemes or salary-related schemes. These pay a proportion of earnings at retirement, depending on the number of years that you work for the employer. Not all defined benefit schemes offer a proportion of final salary – some offer a proportion of the employee's average earnings over their entire career. But the term 'final salary scheme' has become shorthand in the media for defined benefit schemes of all types.

Final salary or career average?

The pension paid in a final salary scheme is calculated by reference to the employee's earnings when they leave the scheme. This makes staying with an employer particularly attractive as each time you rise up the pay scale, your entire pension accrued with that employer to date is increased too. Career average schemes are less generous, as they calculate benefits in relation to your average earnings throughout your working life, adjusted for inflation.

Benefits come in the form of a pension income and a tax-free lump sum, from a specified retirement age, normally 60 or 65. Final salary and career average schemes typically accrue income on a 1/60th or 1/80th basis. So somebody in a 1/60th final salary scheme who retires after 20 years service would be entitled to a pension of 20/60ths or one-third of final salary.

Early retirement

Early retirement is usually allowed, provided it is above the age of 55 (50 until April 2010), but because you will be receiving the pension for longer, the amount you get is reduced. This reduction usually works out to about 6 per cent off your normal pension for each year early that you take it.

Leaving service

If you leave service after two years the trustees of the scheme must give you a preserved pension. You can also request a transfer to a new occupational scheme or a transfer to a personal or stakeholder pension of your choice. You are not allowed a refund of contributions.

A preserved pension is one that is payable from your normal retirement date. It will be calculated in line with your salary when you left the scheme, updated in line with inflation. People with preserved pensions are called deferred members of the scheme.

If you left an employer before April 1975 you may have no preserved pension at all with that employer's scheme. This is because before this date there was no requirement for schemes to preserve pensions for departing staff. Instead contributions were normally returned at the time of leaving.

If you leave employment before completing two years' service you may be entitled to a refund of your contributions if the scheme's rules allow it, which most schemes do. If you have completed three months' service when you leave you are also entitled to have your benefits transferred to another pension scheme. This will almost always be a better option than a refund of contributions, as you will not only get your contributions paid into a pension, with tax relief, but you will also retain the employer's contributions, which could be half the entire fund, or even more in some situations.

Trustees and employers are supposed to tell you your options, but because they would rather not pay over the employer's contributions they will generally not explain that you will be worse off by doing so. Some trustees and employers will even suggest that they can pay your contributions into an ISA on your behalf. This can have the effect of leading departing scheme members to think that they are no worse off because the return of their contributions has been given legitimacy by having them wrapped into a financial services product.

Departing members may also want to get their hands on hard cash, without stopping to think about what they are giving up. But if you leave service between three months and two years of starting, you should always resist the temptation to take back your contributions as a cash lump sum and ask for your entire pension to be transferred to another pension when you leave or stay put. If you do not, you lose both the employer's contributions, your tax relief and any investment growth.

Contracting out and final salary schemes

Most final salary schemes are contracted out of the state second pension (formerly SERPS) so by joining such a scheme the decision whether to contract out or not has already been made for you. Membership of such a final salary scheme means you are not accruing any state second pension, but the scheme is required by law to be at least as good as the state second pension you would have got. In practice, final salary schemes are worth far more than the state second pension you will forgo.

Security of final salary pensions

It only takes a dip in the stock market to provoke headlines warning of multi-billion-pound holes in final salary pension funds. The truth is that the majority of people will be unaffected by these liabilities, which will be met over several decades. But if you are unlucky enough to have your employer go bust leaving behind a pension scheme that does not have enough assets to pay all its pensions, then you could get less than you had expected.

Final salary schemes: why pensioners got militant

Final salary pensions are far more secure today than they were before 2005 when the Pension Protection Fund was established. Before then, if an employer went bust leaving behind an underfunded pension scheme, some employees could end up with nothing. Government rules set a strict order of priority of who should be first to be paid out of the remaining assets in the fund. This priority order required that the pensions of those who had already retired be paid in full before anything at all could be paid to those yet to retire. In some cases paying retired pensioners' pensions swallowed up all the assets in the fund, leaving those yet to retire with nothing.

Tens of thousands of workers lost around 60 per cent of their pensions when a string of companies with in-deficit pension schemes collapsed. An illustration of how badly the members of the schemes were let down is the case of an employee of manufacturing company Dexion, who had been paying into the company's final salary scheme for 38 years. He had been told he would be retiring in three years' time on a pension of around £20,000 a year. Months later, the company went bust and he was left with a fraction of what he had been promised.

In response to plummeting confidence in final salary pensions, the Department for Work and Pensions (DWP) set up the Pension Protection

Fund (PPF), an industry-funded scheme to compensate employees whose pensions collapsed in the future. But the PPF did not cover around 140,000 people who lost out prior to its establishment in April 2005. A concerted campaign, led by former pensions adviser to 10 Downing Street Dr Ros Altmann, argued that they too should be compensated because leaflets from various government departments had told workers for years that their pensions were safe.

Only after the Parliamentary Ombudsman, Public Administration Select Committee, High Court and Court of Appeal all found in favour of the campaigners did the DWP relent and set up the Financial Assistance Scheme, which set aside £400m over 20 years to compensate those not covered by the PPF.

What will I get from the Pension Protection Fund?

If your employer goes bust you may end up being compensated by the Pension Protection Fund (PPF) if the pension scheme is unable to meet its liabilities.

Q *I am already receiving my pension. Will my income drop?*

A Provided you have reached the scheme's normal retirement age you will receive 100 per cent of what you were receiving before the scheme was wound up. You will also be paid in full if you have retired on ill health grounds and if you are receiving a pension as a surviving spouse.

Q *I have not yet retired. What will I get?*

A Compensation is limited to 90 per cent of benefits, up to a total annual pension income of £31,936.32 in 2009/2010. This works out at a maximum compensation of £28,742.69 a year.

Q *When will I start to receive my pension?*

A PPF benefits are only paid from age 65 if you have not yet started receiving your pension, regardless of your scheme's retirement age.

Q *I took early retirement and am still below my scheme's normal retirement age of 65. Am I covered?*

A You will get 90 per cent of benefits, subject to the above limit.

Q *What about inflation protection?*

A Both retired and non-retired scheme members will see their inflation protection reduced. The PPF gives no inflation protection for pension accrued before 1997 and gives retail price index inflation up to a maximum 2.5 per cent a year for benefits received after that.

Q *Taking all these factors together, how much worse off am I?*

A Bearing in mind these factors, most experts estimate the compensation you get from the Pension Protection Fund is worth around 70 per cent of your original benefits up to the limit.

How worried should I be about my employer going bust?

The thought of having to rely on your employer still being around to pay your pension in 30 or 40 years time may not inspire you with confidence. A comparison of the FTSE100 of today with that of 30 years ago (only a handful of companies are still in the index three decades on) shows the way that companies can rise and fall. And with global economic problems pouring more pressure on UK companies, the chance that some will go bust, leaving behind unpaid-for pension liabilities, is very real.

Some companies have pension scheme liabilities bigger than the value of the company itself. British Airways, for example, had a deficit of £1.74bn in September 2008, compared to a market capitalisation of £1.52bn. Pension deficits relate to liabilities that only have to be paid over several decades, but they still present a considerable drain on the parent company's profitability and therefore its solvency.

The establishment of the PPF means that this is a significant issue only for those people with large pensions above the cap, but even the thought of losing 30 per cent of overall benefits by having to take compensation from the PPF will be unappealing to many.

> Most experts believe that the vast majority of employers will be around to ensure that pensions are paid

Canadian telecom company Nortel's 43,000 UK pensioners have joined staff from Lehman Brothers and Woolworths who are already facing up to a retirement funded by the PPF. Many more companies are expected to enter the PPF in future.

But most experts believe that the vast majority of employers will be around to ensure that pensions are paid, while only a minority will not.

Bulk annuities – how safe is my pension?

Some final salary schemes have transferred their pension liabilities to insurance companies in a bid to get them off their books once and for all. The instruments used to do this are called bulk annuities. Instead of the pension scheme promising to pay the pension, the insurance company agrees to do so, in return for a fee.

Insurance companies operate under stricter regulation than final salary pension schemes and are regularly monitored by the FSA. Most experts agree that pension benefits transferred under bulk annuities are no less secure than those that are not.

In the event that the life insurance goes bust, the obligation to pay a pension would be treated as an insurance policy and would be covered by the Financial Services Compensation Scheme. This gives 100 per cent of the first £2,000 plus 90 per cent of the rest of the compensation, with no limit. This is set to change to change to 90 per cent of all benefits from February 2010. This is better protection for most people than that offered by the PPF because inflation increases are paid in full, and people with big pensions that go over the PPF limit see nine-tenths of their entire income protected.

Buying added years or additional pension

Some final salary schemes allow you to buy extra years' entitlement for cash payments. The sums involved can seem high, but compared to the cost of buying an equivalent income through an annuity, they usually work out as very good deal indeed. And, unlike annuities you can buy from insurance companies, they offer valuable ill health benefits.

This makes buying added years a good way of topping up your pension income if you think you will not have enough to live on when you retire.

Because it is such a good deal for the employee, many employers, including those in the public sector, are making changes to scheme rules to stop employees being allowed to buy extra years. Instead, they are replacing the extra years option with the right to buy a more limited level of additional pension. In 2007 and 2008 the NHS, civil service and teachers pension schemes all replaced their old schemes with new arrangements where employees are limited to buying back a maximum of £5,000 additional income.

Buying more pension – public sector schemes

The NHS scheme, for example, which is the biggest defined benefit scheme in Europe and has 1.2 million working members, allows employees under the age of 65 to buy additional pension in lumps of £250 a year income, up to a maximum of £5,000. The amount you pay depends on your age when you start buying it, your gender, your planned retirement date and whether or not you want an income that will cover your spouse, partner and dependent children after your death.

As with all pensions, the younger you start paying in, the cheaper it is to buy

You can buy additional pension either by paying a lump sum each year or by making regular monthly payments out of payroll. As with all pensions, the younger you start paying in, the cheaper it is to buy.

Additional voluntary contributions

If you want to build up more pension than you are accruing through your final salary scheme, you can also pay into an additional voluntary contribution (AVC) arrangement. This can be a great idea because it often means you can take out a bigger tax-free lump sum, without depleting your retirement income to the extent you would do if you took your lump sum directly from your final salary scheme.

AVCs are money purchase arrangements that are run by an insurance company. Because your employer usually pays for the cost of offering an AVC, it can be a cheaper way to save for retirement than paying into a personal pension of your own, although the choice of investment funds may be limited. As with personal pensions, AVC pots invest in a range of assets, which can go down as well as up.

The amount you can pay into your AVC arrangement is governed by the overarching pension contribution limits, which means your AVCs and other pension contributions cannot exceed a sum equal to your salary or the annual limit, which is £245,000 for the tax year 2009/2010, whichever is the lower.

You get tax relief on AVCs in the same way as you do for other occupational pensions, which means higher rate taxpayers do not have to worry about claiming back the top 20 per cent of their tax relief from HM Revenue & Customs by filing a tax return.

How AVCs can boost your tax-free cash lump sum

Until 2006, you could not even get any tax-free cash lump sums out of AVCs. But you can now not only take 25 per cent of your AVC fund as a lump sum, but you can also use the money in them to take tax-free cash up to a quarter of the value of your final salary benefits too. Because final salary schemes offer tax-free lump sums that are worth less than the pension income you have to give up to get them, this can make AVCs a very efficient way for employees to save and draw benefits.

Some companies will offer as little as £10 for every £1 of annual pension income given up, when the cost of buying the same income with an annuity from an insurance company could be more than double that figure. This 10:1 ratio is called the commutation rate – the rate at which the scheme calculates the value of the pension for the purposes of tax-free cash.

But when drawing tax-free cash you are allowed to value the final salary benefits at their full market value and then take a lump sum of 25 per cent of the combined value of your final salary pension scheme and money purchase AVC out of the AVC fund.

Not everyone will be able to take advantage of this efficient way of drawing tax-free cash because it is only permitted if the trustees have amended the scheme rules to allow it, but many have done so,

Example

James has a £20,000 a year pension and an AVC pot worth £125,000. He is offered £50,000 cash in return for surrendering £5,000 income, because the scheme is using a commutation rate of £10 for £1 income surrendered, even though the market value of the income is £20 per £1.

By taking the tax-free cash from the final salary scheme, James ends up with a tax-free cash lump sum of £50,000 plus £31,250 (a quarter of the AVC), making a total lump sum of £81,250, plus an annual income of £15,000 a year.

By taking the tax-free cash from the AVC, James ends up with a lump sum of £125,000, being £100,000 in relation to the final salary pension plus a further £25,000 in relation to his AVC pot.

For people yet to start paying into AVCs who are on the verge of taking their tax-free cash, it is worth paying as much as possible into an AVC now to maximise the lump sum and preserve pension income. If you are in this situation it is even worth getting a loan to maximise the AVC contribution and pay it off straight away as soon as the lump sum is received. People in schemes that do not allow this strategy and who are retiring before 2011 should consider whether they can afford to delay their retirement and live off other income and wait for the rules to change.

Free-standing additional voluntary contributions

Free-standing AVC (FSAVC) arrangements are vehicles that allow people in final salary schemes a broader choice of ways to invest their extra contributions. These became largely redundant when the pension system was overhauled in 2006, allowing for the first time those in occupational schemes to contribute into a personal or stakeholder pension as well as their employer-sponsored scheme. FSAVCs were more expensive than AVCs because the employer did not subsidise the plan's annual management charges.

Today, anyone can pay into as many pension schemes as they want, provided they do not break the contribution cap of a sum equal to their salary or the annual allowance, which is £245,000 for the tax year 2009/2010, whichever is the lower. People who want up to top up their pension saving can therefore opt for a personal or stakeholder pension, or a low-cost online SIPP, if they do not want to save in their AVC.

AVCs versus Personal Pensions or SIPPs

AVCs

- Usually cheaper as the employer meets some or all of the annual management charges.
- Can substantially boost your tax-free lump sum.
- Higher rate taxpayers get their full tax relief automatically, without having to claim it back from HM Revenue & Customs.
- Trustees of scheme monitor investments (but may be in a basic default fund).

But:

- Limited range of investment choice.
- Cannot take benefits before retirement date specified in scheme rules, which could be 60 or 65, unless scheme permits.

Personal pensions or SIPPs

- Broader range of investment choice.
- Can take benefits, including tax-free cash, from age 55 (50 until April 2010).
- No way your employer can find out how much extra cash you are putting into your pension.

But:

- No opportunity to boost tax-free cash from final salary pot.
- Responsible for own investment strategy.
- Charges likely to be higher.
- Higher rate taxpayers will have to fill in a tax return to get their higher rate tax relief of 20 per cent.

Transfers out of final salary schemes

Almost all members of final salary pensions have the right to transfer their benefits to a money purchase plan. For most people, this will not be a good idea, and such a drastic move should never be made without the advice of an independent financial adviser. By transferring to a money purchase plan you expose yourself to stock market risk and also the risk that annuity rates will be worse by the time it comes for you to retire. Final salary schemes, on the other hand, bear both of these risks on your behalf.

Furthermore, if you transfer out of an underfunded scheme, the transfer sum you receive is reduced below what is predicted to duplicate the benefits you would have got by staying in the scheme, in order that you do not get more than your fair share of what is in the pot. This in turn will lead to a reduction in the pension you ultimately receive.

But due to growing mistrust in final salary pensions, coupled with increased incentives being offered by pension schemes to get former employees off their books, we are seeing a renewed interest in transfers. If you do decide to go ahead with a transfer, your fund can be switched to your new company scheme or to a personal or stakeholder pension or a SIPP.

You are entitled to transfer out any time up to a year before you are due to retire. People who accrued benefits during employment in the public sector who left that job before January 1986 are barred from transferring out.

The mechanics of transfers

If you make a written 'statement of entitlement', the scheme is obliged to furnish you with a statement confirming the transfer value that you are entitled to receive. The scheme guarantees to pay this to you if you confirm your intention to proceed within the next three months. It then has six months to pay the sum over to the pension plan of your choice.

The size of the transfer figure is crucial to whether it is in your interests to proceed. If you have left the employer, and so have deferred benefits, it is meant to represent the cost to the scheme of funding today the benefits you are entitled to receive from your normal retirement age. This figure uses actuarial projections of returns on equities and gilts.

If the scheme has a deficit, the sum you receive is reduced by the percentage of it. The deficit could reduce in the future, either as a result of improvements in asset values or because the employer has paid more in. This would give you a bigger transfer value if you asked for a statement of entitlement at a future date. On the other hand, if the company offering the pension scheme is in trouble, its ability to fund the scheme may get worse, making the deficit increase and pushing down the transfer sum you will be offered.

How do I know whether it is worth transferring?

It is essential to get advice from an independent financial adviser (IFA) before committing to transferring, because once you have made your decision you will not be able to change your mind.

Your IFA will consider your age, health, prospective retirement date and other financial circumstances, as well as your attitude to risk. Your IFA will also calculate a 'critical yield'. This is expressed as a percentage and is the investment return your fund will need to achieve year in year out, net of pension plan charges, to replicate the income you would have got had you not transferred out. You then have to consider whether the flexibility you will get by transferring out outweigh the risks of transferring out.

It cannot be overstressed that the risk borne by the individual in a money purchase scheme for several decades is considerable. This risk is not just in terms of rollercoaster stock markets. In the 12 months between February 2008 and February 2009, the cost of annuities rose 10 per cent, meaning 10 per cent less income for people using an identical fund to buy a pension one year later. Annuity rates have more than halved since the early 1990s as a result of increased life expectancy and lower long-term interest rates.

But there are some situations where transferring out of a final salary pension can be beneficial.

Incentives to leave final salary schemes

Some employers have been so desperate to get final salary scheme liabilities off their books that they have offered cash incentives to pension scheme members. In many situations these have been disastrously bad value for the employees or, more typically, former employees who have accepted them. This is because the amounts offered are a fraction of the value of the benefits surrendered.

In recent years employers have preyed upon hard-up pension scheme members' desire to get their hands on cash, a practice that some financial advisers have dubbed the 'flat-screen TV effect' – a reference to the way the lump sum is often spent.

In some cases transfer sums have been worth only a tenth of the benefits surrendered. These poor value transfer offers are normally done without the offer of financial advice, often on a 'limited period only' offer basis to hurry members into what will turn out to be a bad decision.

The Pensions Regulator, the body that oversees final salary schemes, is so concerned about some of the poor transfer offers being made that in 2007 it issued a reminder to trustees that they should whistleblow if they see any situations where below-value transfers are being offered.

But there are also some final salary schemes targeting employees and former employees with enhanced transfer values, where the extra incentive to transfer out is contained as an enhancement to the pension fund, and not as a cash-in-hand payment. These scrupulous transfer exercises are being conducted in a legitimate attempt to find situations where it is in the interests of both the scheme and the individual for a transfer to take place. Scheme members offered transfers in these programmes are offered face-to-face financial advice from an IFA acting on their behalf. In this situation it could be worth considering a transfer, although in many situations it will not be.

Reasons why you may want to transfer out of a final salary scheme

For most people, switching out of a final salary scheme will expose them to more risk and is likely to make their pension income smaller. But there are some factors that can make it worthwhile switching out:

■ You will be able to access your 25 per cent tax-free cash at the age of 55 (50 until April 2010). Most final salary schemes only allow lump sums at the scheme's retirement age, which is usually 60 or 65. If you do switch out, the lump sum you will get may be smaller, however.

■ If you are very successful in the way you manage the investments in your personal pension or SIPP you may be able to build a higher income. However, in most situations experts say there is no certainty this will happen, particularly as people taking transfers from schemes with deficits see their fund reduced by the percentage by which the scheme is underfunded.

■ Some people who are sure that they will never get married could receive more cash by switching because transfer sums reflect the sum needed to buy a pension with a 50 per cent spouse's benefit.

■ People with particularly severe medical conditions that mean they have very short life expectancies may be able to get a bigger income through an impaired life annuity than they would have got through the final salary pension scheme.

■ The employer who is sponsoring the scheme could be in financial trouble, and the scheme itself may have a substantial deficit. If there is a risk of the employer becoming insolvent, people with benefits above the compensation level of the Pension Protection Fund (90 per cent of benefits up to a limit of £31,936.32 in 2009/2010) risk losing everything above that level.

Should fear of the sponsoring employer becoming insolvent make me transfer out?

People with large final salary pensions could see their income decimated and even pensions under £30,000 a year will be cut by as much as a third if the employer behind the scheme goes bust.

The bigger the final salary pension you have, the bigger the dilemma you face about whether to transfer on account of concern that the company sponsoring the scheme could go bust. This dilemma is particularly challenging for those who have built up a big pension with their current employer. This is because you can only transfer your benefits out of the scheme if you leave it altogether, thereby forgoing future accrual of benefits.

Normally, virtually everybody in a final salary scheme would do well to stay put. But in circumstances where business insolvencies are high and funding levels in pension schemes are low, increasing numbers of people with big pensions may want to transfer their benefits to a money purchase plan such as a personal pension or a SIPP.

Transferring to a money purchase scheme also carries its risks, as both the fund's investments and annuity rates can go down as well as up. Furthermore, if the scheme has a shortfall, the transfer value will be reduced by the proportion of that shortfall, giving the scheme member a smaller fund.

Low pension

For example, a member of a final salary pension scheme with a deferred pension of £10,000 per annum has five years to retirement age, and is concerned that the sponsoring employer may become insolvent and leave a substantial deficit in the pension scheme. Transferring to a money purchase scheme is projected to generate a pension of around £10,000 a year, but with no guarantee that even that figure will be reached. But even if the company does become insolvent, the PPF will pay 90 per cent of the pension, totalling £9,000 a year. The risk of investments underperforming is arguably greater than that of the scheme going into the PPF, so the member should probably stay put.

High pension

Consider a member of the same scheme with a deferred pension of £100,000 a year who also has five years to retirement age. Transferring to a money purchase scheme is projected to generate a pension of around £100,000 a year. But if the company becomes insolvent, then compensation from the PPF will be limited to around £28,700 a year, a loss of about two-thirds of the original defined benefit pension. Even if the transferred fund only achieves half of its projected target value, the member will be better off. However, bear in mind that the percentage of schemes expected to go bust is in low single figures.

Death benefits
Who is entitled to death benefits?

Many pension schemes pay death benefits, also known as survivor benefits, to unmarried partners, as well as spouses and civil partners. Dependent children can also receive death benefits from final salary schemes.

> Dependent children can also receive death benefits from final salary schemes

But unmarried partners will generally only receive survivor benefits provided they have been living with the pension scheme member for two years or more at the time of death, are legally entitled to get married and the relationship is one where both partners are financially interdependent.

Keep details of beneficiaries up to date

Many people forget to notify their pension scheme of changes in their personal circumstances that result in them wanting a different beneficiary. This is particularly the case where people divorce or split up from their long-term partners. Pension trustees and administrators regularly find themselves having to deal with distraught bereaved family members who find that a former spouse or partner from several decades ago is the person nominated to receive their loved one's pension because the deceased scheme member failed to notify the pension scheme of the termination of the relationship. If you have ended a relationship with someone you have nominated as a beneficiary to your pension benefits you should write to the pension scheme to cancel your nomination and name a new beneficiary.

If you neglect to nominate an unmarried partner as your beneficiary, he or she may still be able to receive death benefits but this will be down to the discretion of the trustees. By registering them as a beneficiary it will make it more straightforward for them to receive benefits in the event that you die. However, not all schemes pay survivor benefits to unmarried partners, so if you are in a long-term relationship but are not married it is worth asking the scheme what its policy is.

What do you get?

The death benefits you receive from a final salary scheme depend on whether you are still working for the employer and a member of the scheme, a former employee who has not yet retired, or have retired and are receiving income when you die. All schemes have their own rules, but death benefits generally differ depending on which of these three categories you are in when you die.

Active members

If you are still employed and contributing to the scheme, death benefits come in three different ways: a death-in-service payment, a refund of contributions and a survivor's income in retirement. Not all members get all three, however.

> Most schemes offer a death-in-service payment of a multiple of your salary

Most schemes offer a death-in-service payment of a multiple of your salary. This sum can be tax free if it falls below your available pensions lifetime allowance. The lump sum is normally payable to a beneficiary you will have already nominated when you filled in the forms to join the scheme. But the trustees retain a discretion to pay the sum to whoever they want, such as dependants, in the event that they do not agree with the person you have selected to be your beneficiary.

Some schemes will also pay a survivor's benefit of up to two-thirds of the pension the deceased member would have received, either to surviving spouses or civil partners.

Deferred members

On the death of a deferred member, who is no longer an employee of the company offering the scheme but who has not yet retired, their spouse may receive a pension regardless of whether the scheme is contracted in or contracted out of the state second pension. Where schemes are ones that have contracted out of the state system, which means members' National Insurance contributions go into the fund rather than towards accruing state second pension, the surviving spouse or civil partner will receive at least a guaranteed minimum pension from the scheme on benefits earned up to April 1997 and a 50 per cent spouse or partner's benefit on pension accrued after April 1997. This is broadly equal to what they would have got from the state system.

Unmarried partners, regardless of whether or not they have lived together for decades and have children together, do not get death benefits where a deferred member dies before pension payments have started as of right.

A small proportion of schemes will, however, pay a pension of up to two-thirds what the deferred member would have received to surviving spouses and civil partners.

Retired members

On the death of a member of a final salary scheme who is past the normal retirement age and receiving their pension, surviving spouses, civil partners and qualifying unmarried partners normally receive benefit in two different ways: through a guarantee and through a survivor's pension.

Some final salary pensions, such as the NHS scheme, include a guarantee that either five or ten years' pension income will be paid in full, although this practice is far less common in the private sector. For example, if the pension offers a five-year guarantee, and the income is £10,000 a year, the beneficiary will receive a one-off guarantee payment of £30,000 if the scheme member dies two years after starting to receive the pension.

The surviving spouse, civil partner or qualifying unmarried partner will also receive a survivor benefit of up to two-thirds, but normally half of the member's pension income for the rest of their life.

If the beneficiary is more than ten years younger than the deceased scheme member then the trustees have the right to decrease the amount of the pension income paid to reflect this.

Death benefits and tax

Lump sum benefits based on multiples of salary are expressed as being paid at the discretion of the trustees so they fall outside the estate of the deceased for the purposes of Inheritance Tax.

Lumps sums paid under guarantee periods generally incur tax at 35 per cent. The one exception to this rule is in relation to payments for guarantees that started before April 2006. In this situation, no tax is payable, even if the payment is received after April 2006. Income received from survivor pensions is subject to income tax in the usual way.

7

Self-invested personal pensions (SIPPs)

What topics are covered in this chapter?

- What is a SIPP?
- Different types of SIPP
- SIPP charges
- Transfers into SIPPs
- Investing in commercial property
- Borrowing
- Shares
- Drawing benefits
- Family/own-trust SIPPs

SIPPs have captured the imagination of the public to such an extent in recent years that they are now one of the most talked-about types of financial product. Self-invested personal pensions, to give them their full name, have been around since 1990. But they only really started to reaching a wider audience in 2006 when a new simplified pension regime ushered in an era of unprecedented flexibility in retirement saving. Since then hundreds of thousands of investors have taken out SIPPs, and billions of pounds have been invested in the plans, attracted by a seemingly limitless array of investment choices and flexible features.

The two words that best sum up SIPPs are flexibility and choice. You have complete control over how much you pay into and withdraw from a SIPP, subject to the usual legal limits. And the range of investments on offer is huge – some providers offer literally thousands of investment funds, as well as the option of putting your money in gilts, corporate property, land, investment trusts and other asset classes. You can also use them to hold and trade shares, benefiting from tax relief on contributions and exemption from Capital Gains Tax on your profits. Many SIPPs allow you to check how your portfolio is doing over the internet and switch investments at any time of day or night.

The government had even proposed allowing you to invest your pension in residential property through a SIPP, as well as esoteric investments such as wine, fine art and classic cars. But it dropped the idea when it realised how many people might try to use SIPPs in this way, and how much tax relief it might have to fund as a result.

The range of pension assets you can hold in SIPPs has widened in recent years, however. Since 2008, protected rights, the funds built up through contracting out of the state second pension (formerly SERPS) can now be moved into SIPPs. More than 6 million people have contracted out of the second tier of state pension at one time or another, so there is a fair chance you could benefit from this new freedom.

Restrictions on who can take out a SIPP have been removed as well. Before 2006, people in occupational pension schemes were only allowed to save in AVCs if they wanted to make extra pension savings on top of their employer-sponsored plan. Today these people are allowed to have as many private pensions as they want, provided the amount they pay in does not breach the overall contribution limits. Many of these people have opted for SIPPs as a low-cost, transparent way to top up their occupational plan.

Simply opting for a SIPP is not going to solve your pension problems. Your money is not going to grow any quicker just because you have moved it to a SIPP. But if you do take out a SIPP and invest wisely, keeping a close eye on asset allocation and product charges, it will offer you a range of product features and investment choice that other pension products do not. That is why SIPPs are here to stay and remain popular with investors who appreciate their simplicity, flexibility and investment potential.

What is a SIPP?

A SIPP is a type of personal pension and is governed by exactly the same rules on contributions and withdrawals as any other private pension such as a personal or stakeholder pension. But unlike a personal or stakeholder pension, which invests your contributions in a limited range of insurance funds offered by the life insurance company offering the plan, SIPPs allow a far wider choice of investments.

You can control the investments in the SIPP yourself or you can get an IFA, stockbroker or fund manager to run them for you. If you do decide to go down the do-it-yourself route it is important to be aware that managing your own SIPP is not for novices – you will need a certain level of investment expertise to run a SIPP by yourself and you will have nobody to complain to if you get things wrong. So if you are planning to go it alone, make sure you do as much research as possible and make sure you monitor your portfolio regularly.

> It is important to be aware that managing your own **SIPP** is not for novices

Group SIPPs

SIPPs can be held individually or on a group basis – an arrangement that is known as a group SIPP. A group SIPP is, technically speaking, a group of individual SIPPs that are held together. Each individual's pot belongs to them, and they are responsible for the selection of investments in it.

Group SIPPs can be offered by a big employer or by a small group of business professionals who want to invest together. Some employers, such as BT, have started offering group SIPPs as their company pension scheme. Other employers are offering a group SIPP alongside their existing final salary or occupational pension scheme as a replacement for an AVC arrangement or to allow employees to roll shares from maturing company share schemes directly into their pension, thus getting the benefit of tax relief. The tax advantages of doing so for people with an income of more than £150,000 a year are less significant, however.

Solicitors, accountants, company directors and other professionals also use small group SIPPs to club together to buy commercial premises, either to rent back to their own business or as a standalone investment.

SIPPs – permitted investments

■ Stocks and shares traded on a recognised UK or overseas stock exchange, including shares listed on AIM; also includes fixed interest securities, debenture stock, warrants, permanent interest-bearing shares, convertible securities and exchange traded funds (ETFs).

■ Unlisted shares (only offered by a few SIPP providers).

■ Investment trusts.

■ UK Real Estate Investment Trusts (REITs).

■ Venture capital trusts.

■ Futures and options – these must be traded on an HM Revenue & Customs or FSA recognised futures exchange.

■ Contracts for Differences (CFDs).

■ Depositary interests.

■ Unit trusts and Open-Ended Investment Companies (OEICS).

■ Insurance company funds.

■ Traded endowment policies.

■ Structured products.

■ National Savings & Investments products.

■ Commercial property.

■ Deposit accounts.

■ Hedge funds.

Different types of SIPP

There are different grades of SIPP on the market depending on the range of the permitted asset classes that they permit you to invest in. These SIPP providers range across a spectrum from specialist SIPP providers who allow you to invest in absolutely anything permitted by HM Revenue & Customs rules, to online providers only offering access to funds and quoted shares. But they can be broadly classified into two categories: full SIPPs and low-cost online supermarket SIPPs.

Full SIPPs are offered by specialist SIPP providers and by life insurance companies. Supermarket SIPPs are offered by some SIPP providers, IFAs and stockbrokers. They effectively consist of a fund supermarket and a share dealing service held in a pensions tax wrapper. A key difference between full SIPPs and supermarket SIPPs is that one is accessed through a financial adviser while the other is not.

Setting up a full SIPP will require the assistance of an IFA, even if you only intend to use it to invest in funds and shares. This is because the providers who offer full SIPPs will generally not deal directly with members of the public. Virtually all the SIPPs offered by life insurance companies can only be accessed with the assistance of a financial adviser.

You can set up a supermarket SIPP on your own. If you set up a SIPP without the assistance of an adviser you do so on what is described as an 'execution-only basis'. This means that you are responsible for all the investment choices you make and agree that you have no comeback against the SIPP provider if things go wrong.

Supermarket SIPPs set up on an execution-only basis generally work out cheaper than those set up through IFAs. This is because you are not paying for or benefitting from professional financial advice. However, because full SIPPs have fixed charges, they can work out cheaper if you have a very big fund that gives you economies of scale.

For both full and supermarket SIPPs, charges vary according to the range of asset classes that are permitted and utilised.

Full SIPPs

Full SIPPs, as the name might suggest, can give you access to all or the majority of the permitted investment classes. They are available through specialist SIPP providers and some life insurers. Full SIPPs are usually used by investors who want to invest in more complex assets, such as commercial property or in a broader range of financial instruments than is available through personal pensions. You will also need a full SIPP if you want to borrow money to invest through your pension.

Some providers who offer full SIPPs also offer specialist own-trust SIPPs that allow family members and small business partnerships to hold commercial property in an efficient and flexible way. These own-trust SIPPs can also be of use to families who want efficient estate planning strategies. Own-trust SIPPs are described in greater depth at the end of this chapter.

As well as niche specialist SIPP providers, most big life insurer pension providers now offer SIPPs as an alternative to their personal and stakeholder pensions. Some life insurers offer hybrid products that start off as personal pensions but allow you to use SIPP functionality in the future if and when the need arises, for example on the maturity of a company sharesave scheme to allow the individual to roll the shares over into the pension. Hybrid SIPPs only charge you for SIPP features when you actually use them.

Supermarket SIPPs

Supermarket SIPPs are designed to be low-cost, efficient ways for people to invest in a wide range of investment funds and shares. Their name comes from the fact that they are run by providers who offer online fund supermarkets.

Unlike full SIPPs, supermarket SIPPs are accessed without the assistance of a financial adviser. Dealing with a financial services provider without advice on an execution-only basis means you have no comeback to anybody if the investment choices you make or the way you arrange your tax affairs turn out to be wrong.

Anyone proceeding on an execution-only basis must be aware of the responsibility they are taking on, and should do as much research into pensions and investments before they start. If you are not confident of what you are doing, it is recommended that you see an IFA.

However, those who do understand financial markets and tax can cut a substantial amount of the cost out of their pension savings by running a SIPP themselves. If you take advice from an IFA who is remunerated through commission you will end up paying for it through the annual charges in the pension product. Similarly, money you pay in IFA fees cannot go into your pension.

By removing these charges from the equation, your fund will grow more quickly, provided you manage to achieve similar investment performance. However, an IFA will be able to help you with fund selection, asset allocation and tax mitigation, all of which could more than outweigh the extra cost, depending on your circumstances and the size of your fund.

If you do proceed alone, it is important to remember that high earners have to reclaim their higher rate tax relief themselves. This is not automatically credited to their pension. Money paid into SIPPs is grossed up by 20 per cent to reflect basic rate tax relief. Somebody investing £80 will therefore get their fund immediately boosted to £100 in the SIPP (as with any form of personal pension arrangement). Higher rate taxpayers, however have to claim back their higher rate tax relief.

SIPP charges

Charges vary so it is important to do some research before you pick one. Charges can be divided into three broad categories: set-up and administration, share dealing and fund switching costs, and charges for drawing benefits. Charges can quickly erode your pension if you are not careful so work out how you intend to use the SIPP and you can then figure out which charging structure will work best for you.

Some financial experts argue that SIPPs are a bandwagon that has got out of control. They claim that many people who have been advised to move into SIPPs would have done just as well to stick with their existing personal or stakeholder pension plan, which in many cases will have lower charges. In 2007 the FSA issued a warning to financial advisers that they should not recommend personal pensions or SIPPs when cheaper stakeholder pensions would be more suitable. It is concerned that people who are only ever likely to invest in a limited range of investment funds who are advised to move into SIPPs or personal pensions will end up paying for services they will never use.

Comparing charges between SIPPs and personal pensions and between different SIPP providers is difficult. Some will be cheaper on one arrangement and more expensive on another. For a more detailed analysis of charges on different sorts of pension turn to page 50.

Charges – full SIPP

Charges on full SIPPs depend on what you are using the product for. The basic principle is that you pay for every single thing you do with your SIPP.

> The basic principle is that you pay for every single thing you do with your SIPP

If you are investing in a range of complex assets such as unlisted shares or commercial property, perhaps with a loan to finance it, then charges will be higher. Set-up costs are typically between £300 and £500 with an annual management charge of between £400 and £600. Some providers will also charge you extra for holding protected rights from your contracted-out saving in the SIPP. These higher charges reflect the complexity of the transactions you will be making and the technically qualified staff needed to administer them. Purchases of property or unlisted shares will cost around £800 a time, while sale of these assets will cost around £400 to £500. Setting up third-party loans can cost around £500. You will also be charged for drawing benefits, with the price depending on how you choose to do so.

People using life insurer SIPPs for their fund range and for share dealing will pay less than this. Life insurers tend to charge the same or slightly more for their SIPPs than they do for their personal pensions. Some life insurers require SIPP investors to invest only in in-house funds until their total fund value rises above a certain threshold.

If you are using a full SIPP then your IFA is likely to guide you towards the product they think is most suitable for your purposes. If you are only going to be using your SIPP to hold investment funds you should ask your financial adviser whether you will be paying more by opting for a SIPP than you would through a personal or stakeholder pension. If charges are higher, ask your adviser to justify why this is the case and why it is worth proceeding on this basis.

Charges – supermarket SIPP

To choose the most cost-effective supermarket SIPP for your circumstances it is important to understand what sort of investor you are and how you intend to use it. Some SIPPs are more suitable for people who are only investing in funds, while others work out cheaper for those using their plan to buy and sell shares on a regular basis.

Account charges

Some supermarket SIPPs on the market, such as the Vantage SIPP offered by Hargreaves Lansdown and the product offered by Sippdeal, allow you to set up and run a SIPP for free provided you are only investing in cash or investment funds. The only charge these SIPPs levy before you draw benefits is the annual management charges on the funds themselves, a slice of which the SIPP provider receives back from the fund manager. However, as soon as you start holding and dealing shares or other assets through the SIPP, you will be charged a quarterly or annual management fee. For example, the Vantage SIPP charges 0.5 per cent of fund value plus VAT for other forms of investment, such as shares, up to a maximum of £200 a year.

Other supermarket SIPPs carry either an annual or quarterly charge and/or a set-up charge, even if you are only investing in funds. Alliance Trust's SIPP has no set-up charge but has an annual administrative charge of £75.

Dealing charges

Dealing charges vary, so if you intend to buy and sell a lot of shares in your SIPP, look out for one with charges that will match your usage. Some also charge you each time you buy into a unit trust. Charges normally vary between £10 and £30 depending on the size of the transaction, although Alliance Trust's comes in at £12.50 a time, regardless of transaction size, making it attractive for somebody trading regularly, despite its annual £75 administrative charge. While good value for investment funds, the Vantage SIPP is more expensive for people using their SIPP for share dealing, with costs rising from £9.95 to £29.95 depending on the size of the trade.

Fund charges

You will pay the annual management charge of the funds held on your SIPP whatever product you go for. SIPP providers derive a substantial proportion of their revenue from taking a share of the fund manager's annual management charge.

For quality funds these charges generally range between 1.5 per cent and 2 per cent a year, putting them at roughly the same cost as personal pensions. Passive funds that track indices can cost as little as 0.25 per cent a year.

Watch out for upfront charges on investment funds through some SIPP providers. Supermarket SIPPs such as Vantage and Sippdeal negotiate deals with fund managers that mean you usually pay no initial charge when you first invest, although Sippdeal charges you £20 each time you invest in a fund.

Some do not offer a discount on initial charges, however, or only do so on a limited list of funds. For example, if you invest in the immensely popular Invesco Perpetual High Income fund through some SIPP providers, you can end up paying an initial charge of 5 per cent of the sum you are contributing, as well as a 1.5 per cent annual management charge.

If you invest through Vantage or Sippdeal, you will pay the same annual management charge but you will pay no initial charge, meaning for every £1,000 you pay in gross, £1,000 will be credited to the fund, rather than £950 through costlier SIPP providers. Some SIPP providers only offer initial charge discounts on a select few of the funds on their range.

Other charges

All SIPPs charge for drawing benefits such as setting up unsecured pensions and alternatively secured pensions, both typically charged at £150, and some (but not all) charge £10 a time for paying you pension benefits, whether on a monthly or annual basis.

Transfers into SIPPs

SIPPs have been a buzzword in pensions for several years now and hundreds of thousands of people have transferred billions of pounds' worth of assets into the plans.

Advantages of transferring your pensions into a SIPP

■ Consolidating all your pension pots in one place makes life easier and can help you to make more informed decisions about asset allocation strategy.

■ You may have assets stuck in poorly performing with-profits or other default pension funds or in funds with high charges (see page 50 for more details on pension charges).

■ The bigger your fund is, the lower the charges you may able to negotiate with your pension provider.

■ You will get access to a wider range of investments.

■ You may want to borrow money to fund commercial property purchase.

When it is not a good idea to switch to a SIPP

■ *Guarantees* You may lose access to guaranteed rates of return or guaranteed annuity rates available on some old pension arrangements. By inadvertently doing so, you could accidentally cut your retirement income in half.

■ *Tax-free cash* Some pensions allow you to take more than 25 per cent of the fund as a tax-free lump sum. By switching such a pension to a SIPP you would restrict yourself to a 25 per cent tax-free lump sum, increasing the amount of tax you pay and reducing your flexibility.

■ *High penalties* Some old pension products reward you with extra units if you carry on paying into the scheme. By pulling out of the contract you may forgo valuable added units. For pension contracts like this it may still be worth leaving in some cases, but in others it may not. Each case needs to be judged on its merits and you need to ask your pension provider exactly where you stand.

■ *Higher charges* You may have already paid the bulk of the charges on your pension in the early years. Many old-fashioned personal pensions had exorbitant charges in the early years (some took large portions of the first and second years' contributions as upfront charges). While these pensions may be bad news over the life of the plan, if you have already suffered the pain of the charges, the cost of these plans going forward may be lower than even ultra-low charging online SIPPs.

■ *Exit penalties* Pension savings in with-profits funds may be subject to exit penalties known as market value adjustments (MVAs). Whether it is worth suffering the MVA and moving to a SIPP will depend on the circumstances of the plan, the provider and the length of time you have to go until it matures. In some cases it will be, in others it will not. Most with-profits allow you windows where you can get out of the plan with no penalty. For more information about pulling money out of with-profits plans, see page 59.

■ *Special with-profits windfalls* A small minority of life insurers have been looking at ways to distribute the so-called 'orphan assets' in their with-profits funds. These are assets that have been held back in years of good investment performance and have not been allocated to any with-profits investors. Under a reattribution of these assets, bonuses could be paid to with-profits policyholders. Cashing in such a policy would exclude you from any bonuses that were paid.

Transferring your old pension to a SIPP

The following types of pension can be transferred into a SIPP without the assistance of an IFA:

■ personal pension

■ stakeholder pension

■ another SIPP

■ Free Standing Additional Voluntary Contribution (FSAVC)

■ protected rights (built up through contracting out of state second pension or SERPS)*.

* Most SIPP providers will not accept transfers from final salary pension schemes on an execution-only basis. If you wish to do this, you will need to do so with the advice and assistance of an IFA. In many cases taking such a step will not be in your interests. Read the warnings on page 82 before you proceed.

How to transfer your old pension plan into a SIPP – step by step (for non-advised transactions)

1 Contact your SIPP provider and notify them of the name, address and reference number of the pension you wish to transfer.

2 Your SIPP provider will contact your existing provider, asking them to transfer the pension to them.

3 Your existing pension provider will contact you asking for your authority to effect the transfer. Complete this confirmation letter and return it to them.

4 Your existing pension provider will transfer your pension fund to your SIPP provider.

■ There is normally a minimum transfer value of £5,000. SIPP providers accept combinations of smaller plans provided the total value is £5,000 or more.

■ Some (but not all) SIPP providers charge an administrative fee of £50 for receiving transfers.

Investing in commercial property

One of the key attractions of SIPPs over personal and stakeholder pensions for some investors is the ability to hold commercial property directly within your plan and even borrow up to 50 per cent of your fund value to do so.

If you run a business you can even buy your own commercial premises and rent it back off your pension fund. Groups of solicitors, accountants and other professionals often use group SIPPs to purchase properties together. Pension contributions from a company used to purchase premises will benefit from corporation tax.

Once the SIPP has bought the premises it has to charge the company a market rent. Rent paid by the company is kept in the SIPP in the same way that income from shares and investments is, and growth in the value of the property is not subject to Capital Gains Tax on sale.

There are some downsides to small business owners buying their own premises with their pension. The company can no longer use it as an asset for raising capital. It will also be precluded from claiming capital allowances for commercial buildings. And the individual will bear more risk through having a large proportion of their pension invested in a single asset.

Furthermore, if the business goes bust then not only has the individual lost their day-to-day income, but their pension fund has also lost its tenant. And it is important to remember that the premises will be owned by the trustees of the SIPP and not by the company itself, although some SIPP providers will let the SIPP holder also hold a role as trustee.

Business partners or others buying commercial property together through a group SIPP or through several of their own SIPPs should be aware that they will incur conveyancing costs if one of them wants to sell up and leave. An agreement will also need to be reached on how this process will be conducted, before the property is purchased.

Borrowing

SIPPs holders can borrow up to 50 per cent of the value of their pot to fund a commercial property purchase.

The amount you can borrow through a SIPP was reduced in 2006. Before that date you could borrow up to 75 per cent of the value of the property. This meant that somebody with a £50,000 pension pot could borrow a further £150,000 to purchase a property worth £200,000. Today somebody with a £50,000 pension can only borrow half that figure, making a maximum loan of £25,000 and a maximum property purchase of £75,000.

Where people still have loans taken out under the old rules they are permitted to rebroker mortgage deals even if they are for more than 50 per cent of fund value.

Example

Peter has a pension fund worth £300,000. He arranges a mortgage of a further £150,000 to enable his SIPP to purchase the premises occupied by his own business for £450,000. His business pays his SIPP a market rent of £31,500 a year, reflecting a yield on the property of 7 per cent.

After ten years the mortgage on the premises is paid off in full. The SIPP now owns 100 per cent of the equity in a commercial property, the value of which may have gone up or down in the ten years since it was purchased. The SIPP continues to receive the rent, which may have increased or decreased, tax-free into the pension.

More freedom to invest protected rights through SIPPs

■ Since 2008 it is now possible to hold protected rights (built up through contracting out of the state second pension or Serps).

■ Protected rights funds within SIPPs can be included when calculating total fund value for borrowing limits, and can be used to pay off SIPPs borrowing.

■ You may be able to get access to better fund managers and lower charges by switching your protected rights fund to a SIPP.

But:

■ Protected rights must be ring-fenced from the rest of your SIPP assets until at least 2012 when contracting out is set to be abolished.

■ The survivor benefit rule, which currently requires people with a spouse or civil partner to use their contracted-out fund to purchase a joint life annuity, will also be abolished, but not until 2012.

Shares

Aside from using a SIPP to play the stock market, you may wish to transfer your maturing holdings in company share schemes into your plan. Shares from Sharesave or share incentive plans can be transferred into SIPPs within 90 days of maturity. You can move these plans over without cashing them in by making what is called an in-specie transfer. In-specie transfers into pensions attract tax relief in the same way that cash contributions do, at the value of the shares on the day of the transfer in.

Somebody earning £80,000 making an in-specie transfer of £8,000 of shares into their SIPP would see a further £2,000 added to their fund through basic rate tax relief. They would also be entitled to higher rate relief of a further £2,000 through their tax return.

Making an in-specie transfer counts as a disposal for Capital Gains Tax purposes, so if your shares have grown in value by more than your annual CGT allowance (£10,100 in 2009/2010), then a tax liability will arise. Such a transfer would also raise a stamp duty liability of 0.5 per cent, adding up to £40 on £8,000 of shares.

Turn shares to cash with a SIPP

Directors with substantial company shares that they cannot access until some time the future can unlock 40 per cent of their value now by making an in-specie transfer into a SIPP. This manoeuvre could be useful for those with large holdings that they must hold until retirement or some other specified later date.

Example

A director has shares worth £50,000 which cannot be sold for ten years. The director, who pays tax at a top rate of 40 per cent, makes an in-specie contribution of £40,000 of shares into a SIPP. After around six weeks £10,000 tax relief is paid into the SIPP. The remaining £10,000 worth of shares are transferred into the SIPP in exchange for £10,000 cash from the SIPP.

A further £10,000 tax relief is received when the director's tax return is filed. The director still has the £50,000 in shares but also £20,000 in cash now. However, when the restriction on sale of the shares is lifted, the director is not in a position to access the cash other than through drawing tax-free cash and income from the pension in the usual way.

People with taxable income of more than £150,000 will be restricted in using this strategy because their pension tax relief is reduced.

Drawing benefits

SIPPs allow benefits to be withdrawn in exactly the same way as personal pensions. Pension and tax-free cash can be drawn from age 55 (50 until April 2010). The remaining 75 per cent of the fund must be used to provide a pension income, either through buying an annuity from a life insurance company or through an unsecured pension before age 75 or an alternatively secured pension (ASP) after age 75, also known as income drawdown.

Most people will need all the pension income they can get in retirement. But there are some people who resent the idea of buying an annuity or going into income drawdown because both avenues involve losing a potentially large amount of their pension savings either to a life insurer or the taxman. As a result, many wealthy savers with income from other sources try to get as much of their money out of their pension as they can as quickly as possible.

Why would I want to run my pension fund down to nothing?

Many wealthy investors with retirement income from other sources do not like the idea of having to buy an annuity at age 75 or stay in income drawdown and risk a hefty tax charge on death of up to 82 per cent of fund value. Both SIPP and Small Self-Administered Scheme (SSAS) arrangements allow pension investors to draw income at a rate that could ultimately exhaust the fund, although SSAS plans allow you to do so at a slightly faster rate.

Advisers usually recommend that people with this attitude to death benefits draw as much income as possible by drawing the maximum through either income drawdown for SIPPs or scheme pension for SSAS (see Chapter 8). Specialist own-trust SIPPs can also pay scheme pension (see below).

Income attracts Income Tax at the individual's marginal rate, and is a potentially exempt transfer for Inheritance Tax purposes. But annual allowances of £3,000, gifts to grandchildren of £250 a year each, and regular payments of excess income can all be made without incurring a potential Inheritance Tax liability.

Family/own-trust SIPPs

Specialist SIPPs can offer many of the advantages of SSASs for families wanting to minimise Inheritance Tax or small business professionals buying property together. Sometimes called family SIPPs, these arrangements differ from regular SIPPs because they are set up under their own trust deed, in the same way that SSAS plans are.

They can be used to pass wealth to children, grandchildren or in fact anybody you choose to include as a member of the arrangement. This is because the actuary running the scheme can apportion the investment growth on your assets to another scheme member without creating a liability for Inheritance Tax. Specialist family SIPPs and SSASs are allowed to do this because they are effectively mini final salary schemes. The same rules that allow actuaries to shift money from one scheme member to another in a final salary scheme permit a similar reapportionment of assets in these specialist arrangements.

Family SIPPs can also take cost out of the process of buying and selling partners in and out of shares of commercial property held through group pensions. This is because, as with an SSAS, property held by a specialist family SIPP is owned in its entirety by the scheme, and not owned in parts by each member of the scheme as is the case with traditional group SIPPs.

Family or own-trust SIPPs have been a niche product until recently. For years there have only been a handful of small players actively marketing their full potential. This had led many financial advisers to be cautious as to whether HM Revenue & Customs is entirely happy with the way the product can be used to mitigate tax. But in 2009 AXA, one of the largest insurers in the world, launched a new product in the sector, which many experts say demonstrates that family SIPPs can now be considered more mainstream.

Estate planning – passing on pension investment growth

A family SIPP or SSAS allows individuals with large pension pots and potential Inheritance Tax liabilities to pass on the investment growth on their pension fund to the pensions of their relatives or friends in a tax-efficient way, provided they are also members of the arrangement.

Example

Anne is a member of a family SIPP or SSAS, together with her son David, his wife Maureen and their daughter Elizabeth.

Anne is aged 60 and has a pot worth £500,000 held within this plan. This generates growth of £15,000 a year. Anne has her own home and substantial other assets, and is concerned at her growing potential Inheritance Tax liability.

She can pass the annual £15,000 investment growth to her granddaughter's family SIPP pot without creating a tax liability.

Estate planning – scheme pension

Another advantage of the family SIPP and the SSAS over regular SIPPs is both plans' ability to pay a scheme pension. This allows greater flexibility in drawing cash from their fund than is possible from other types of SIPP, making it easier to pass on assets to heirs.

However, the benefit of this facility may be marginal in many cases, and opting for a SSAS on the grounds of estate planning alone should not be done without a thorough scrutiny of the additional costs that come with it. Furthermore, somebody doing so should be fully aware that if they live longer than the actuary predicted, the scheme pension runs out and their other assets are dissipated, they will have nothing left to live on.

Advantages of family SIPP and SSAS over traditional SIPP for estate planning

Family SIPPs and SSASs allow you to draw more money out of your pension fund than is permitted through a traditional SIPP, both while you are alive and after your death.

While many people will need all their pension assets to fund their own retirement, for wealthy people who are looking to reduce their income and assets and want to pass on as much of their cash to their family and friends, a family SIPP can be a useful tool for mitigating death duties. However, using a family SIPP in this way involves making your pension as small as possible, which will only be an option for those people who have sufficient assets elsewhere to fund their retirement.

You can draw more out of the fund while you are alive through a family SIPP or SSAS. The scheme pension pays an income agreed by an actuary, who has the flexibility to decide how much income the individual can receive without risking depleting the pension pot before they die. While the actuary can only recommend a scheme pension that is sustainable, based on industry practice standard calculations and assumptions, this will be higher than the fixed Government Actuary's Department rates that are used to govern traditional SIPP drawdown payouts after age 75.

If your physical condition is such that your life expectancy is below average, that payment could be considerably higher. By drawing this higher income, it is possible to run down the pension fund more quickly through a family SIPP or a SSAS. Supporters of traditional SIPPs argue that most people who start draining as much as possible from their SIPP pot in their early sixties will in any event be able to get the majority of their money out of the fund by the time they reach 75, at which point they can probably get the remainder out through a ten-year guarantee.

Family SIPPs allow you to withdraw more of your fund by your 85th birthday, whether you live to see it or not, by guaranteeing income. Family SIPPs have the ability to drain virtually all the remaining money in the fund by fixing a ten-year guaranteed income at age 75, thus avoiding a potential 82 per cent tax charge. Actuaries can approve income levels of between 10 and 11 per cent of the value of the fund when they calculate a ten-year guarantee for a 75 year old. Scheme pensions of this level mean that 100 per cent of the plan-holder's pot can be withdrawn from the scheme. If they die before the age of 85, their nominated beneficiaries will continue to receive the income for the remainder of the ten-year guarantee period.

However, if their other assets become depleted, they may not have enough to live on if they survive after the fund has been run down.

The commercial rates offered by insurance companies are lower than those allowed for scheme pensions

People with traditional SIPPs have the right to buy a guaranteed ten-year income at age 75 too, but they have to do so by buying an annuity with a ten-year guarantee option. The commercial rates offered by insurance companies are lower than those allowed for scheme pensions.

Commercial annuity rates for 74 year olds are closer to 8.5 per cent, which would mean that for people with traditional SIPPs only 85 per cent of the fund at age 75 is paid out through the guarantee. Any remaining funds in the traditional SIPP on death are then subject to a tax charge of up to 82 per cent.

But specialist arrangements such as family SIPPs and SSASs cost more than regular SIPPs and for many people the benefits will be unlikely to outweigh the extra costs involved in running one.

8

Small self-administered schemes (SSASs)

What topics are covered in this chapter?

- How a SSAS works
- Investing in the sponsoring company
- Lending your pension to your company
- Commercial property
- Drawing income from a SSAS
- Estate planning: scheme pension

A SSAS, which stands for small self-administered scheme, is a type of occupational pension scheme that has unique features offering small businesses attractive and efficient ways to grow wealth and own property.

SSAS plans allow directors to use their existing pension assets to make loans to their business and buy shares in it. They also offer a convenient way of holding commercial property that allows joining and departing partners to transfer ownership of their share of the property with a minimum of administrative hassle and expense. SSAS plans can also borrow money to fund property purchase.

For wealthy investors with small businesses who are facing Inheritance Tax liabilities, they also offer a way to pass pension assets to family or friends so that death duties can be minimised. A SSAS is an occupational pension scheme with less than 12 members, usually used by director-controlled businesses. The majority of SSAS plans have only two or three members, often husbands and wives.

The majority of SSAS plans have only two or three members, often husbands and wives

The freedom to invest in a wide range of asset classes, including shares, mutual funds, gilts, exchange traded funds and commercial property, and to borrow to fund property purchase, is not unique to SSAS plans. Self-invested personal pensions (SIPPs) also permit these activities.

But unlike SIPPs, SSAS plans can also lend money to the sponsoring company, provided they do so at a commercial rate. They are also allowed to hold shares in the company running the SSAS. SSAS plans also offer greater flexibility in the amount of pension that can be drawn from the scheme than is offered by most personal pensions and SIPPs. This is possible because, unlike personal pensions and SIPPs, which pay out income either through an annuity bought from a life insurer or through income drawdown limits fixed by the Government Actuary's Department, SSAS plans are able to pay out a 'scheme pension'. This is an income determined at the discretion of the scheme's own actuary. Specialist family SIPPs can also do this, often at a lower cost than a SSAS.

However, SSASs are not for everybody. This extensive range of functions comes at a cost and many of the features that the plans offer require intensive financial and actuarial advice. For most people the extra cost of a SSAS will outweigh the financial planning advantages they offer. But for small businesses or for family groups with complex finances, a SSAS can offer a flexible and tax-efficient way to save for retirement. Since 2006 SSAS plans have achieved a new relevance to small business owners, not least because of their ability to offer finance to enterprises at times when credit from banks has been squeezed almost out of existence.

How a SSAS works

A SSAS is a small occupational pension scheme set up under a trust deed with its own set of rules. Its members are all trustees, and the SSAS provider also acts as the requisite independent trustee. SSAS plans themselves are not regulated by the FSA, although the investments held within them may be. Like any other pension scheme, they have to be registered with HM Revenue & Customs. Because SSAS plans are occupational schemes there must be an employer/employee relationship but not all the members have to be employees of the company. This means that where there are partnerships, such as solicitors or accountants, the SSAS can be set up if there is a single employee, such as a secretary or assistant. All partners can then also join the scheme. The SSAS can only have 11 members or less.

Contributions from the employer attract Corporation Tax relief, while member contributions receive tax relief at the member's marginal rate. Limits on contributions into and the withdrawal of benefits from SSAS plans are governed by the same rules as all other pensions.

SSAS plans are technically small occupational schemes but because of their size they are not required to have all of the regulatory protection mechanisms that big occupational schemes have. This lighter regulatory regime means the SSAS's trustees do not have to meet the same requirements of knowledge and understanding of pensions law that bigger schemes do.

SSAS plans are also exempt from having internal dispute resolution mechanisms provided everyone who is in the scheme is also a trustee. They do, however, have to prepare an independent actuarial report on the scheme every three years. In practice these issues are dealt with by the SSAS provider, but this does mean that these are services that will have to be paid for by the company offering the scheme. You will need the assistance of an IFA to advise you on whether setting up a SSAS is the best option for you and your business.

Investment options

Like SIPPs, SSAS plans allow access to a broad range of asset classes. Many SSAS providers offer SIPPs as well, so you will often get access to an identical broad range of mutual funds whichever pension structure you opt for.

Permitted investments in SSAS plans

- Land and commercial property.
- UK quoted shares, stocks and gilts.
- Stocks and shares quoted on recognised overseas stock exchanges.
- Futures and options quoted on recognised stock exchanges.
- OEICs and unit trusts.
- Investment trusts.
- Hedge funds.

- Insurance company funds.
- Bank and building society deposits.
- Gold.
- Unquoted shares in sponsoring companies – up to a maximum of 5% of fund value.
- Other unquoted shares.
- Loans to sponsoring companies.

Investing in the sponsoring company

SSAS plans are able to invest directly in the company sponsoring the scheme. Investment in sponsoring companies is limited to 5 per cent of the value of the SSAS fund. If the fund is big enough it can own 100 per cent of the company's shares, provided it does not exceed 5 per cent of the value of the SSAS fund.

If there are several companies sponsoring the SSAS, it can invest 5 per cent in each one, provided that the total investment in sponsoring companies does not exceed 20 per cent of the value of the SSAS fund.

Lending your pension to your company

SSAS plans are generally the only pension arrangements in the UK that allow pension funds to lend money to the company offering them. This has proved a key attraction to profitable small businesses that have been starved of capital as credit has dried up in the wake of the collapse in confidence in the banking sector.

Loans to related businesses are governed by strict rules:

- The loan cannot exceed 50 per cent of the scheme's assets. So a SSAS with assets worth £1m can lend up to £500,000 to the sponsoring company.
- The loan must be secured on assets of the company by a first charge.
- The loan must be repaid within five years.
- The company taking the loan must pay interest at a commercial rate, which must be at least 1 per cent above the average base lending rate of six UK high street banks.

While the minimum interest charged is 1 per cent above bank base rate, it is common for SSAS plans to charge 2 or 3 per cent above bank base rate. In the current economic climate, for many businesses this may be cheaper than the commercial rates on offer from banks, if indeed they are offering the company any loans at all. The SSAS meanwhile is getting a guaranteed return from a trusted source, the company itself.

Pension advisers who deal with SSAS plans stress that small business owners must be aware of the risks involved when it comes to borrowing money from their pension pots. The loans must be repaid, and if they are not, the trustees of the SSAS have a duty to take action against the company to recover any money outstanding. This could involve the enforcement of legal charges over company property.

Furthermore, owner-directors who use SSAS plans to keep failing businesses going risk losing not only their company but also half their pension assets. It is possible to transfer money from other pensions into your SSAS to increase the amount of borrowing available to your company, although it is advisable to be wary of throwing money at lost-cause enterprises.

Commercial property

One of the primary uses of SSAS plans is for holding commercial property

One of the primary uses of SSAS plans is for holding commercial property. By doing so, small businesses can buy their own premises with the help of tax relief. You can also invest in commercial premises, whether of your own business or as a standalone investment, through a SIPP.

Because the SSAS is set up under its own trust, commercial property can be held by the trust in an efficient and convenient way. By holding the commercial property through a SSAS in the name of all the directors, rather than each director owning a portion of the property through their own SIPP, lengthy and costly conveyancing procedures can be avoided when business partners leave and join. This is because the trust is the legal owner of the property in the eyes of HM Land Registry. SSAS members own an entitlement to a portion of the SSAS's funds, but not a direct share in the property itself.

Owning assets in trust in this way offers greater flexibility for managing payments to members at differing stages of their lives, without having to sell them. Assets can therefore be apportioned to different members of the

SSAS without having to buy and sell them. This is particularly beneficial for family businesses where there are two or more generations participating in the enterprise. When an older SSAS member comes to draw their pension income they can do so out of liquid assets such as cash and quoted shares that are held in the SSAS fund, leaving the younger members owning a greater share of the commercial property. No conveyancing transactions are required to effect this transfer of assets.

When commercial property is held by a small business through a group of SIPPs, on the other hand, someone wanting to realise their investment in the business's premises held in it will have to formally sell it to the other members of the business.

Buying a company's premises through a SSAS is cheaper than doing so out of the company's own coffers because the contributions paid into the SSAS benefit from Corporation Tax relief. The company, on the other hand would have to buy the property out of net profits.

The SSAS must charge the company a fair market rent, which is paid into the SSAS. The rent paid is an allowable expense for the company's Corporation Tax liability. Once in the SSAS there is no further liability for Capital Gains Tax on sale of the property.

There are some downsides to SSAS ownership of commercial property. First, the company can no longer use it as security for its own capital-raising exercises. The company will also be precluded from claiming capital allowances for commercial buildings. Furthermore, if the property represents a large proportion of the SSAS's assets, the SSAS will by definition have an undiversified portfolio. If the value of the commercial property is low when the directors come to retire then their pension will be negatively affected.

Borrowing

The SSAS can borrow from banks and building societies to fund commercial purchases such as property. The maximum amount of borrowing permitted is 50 per cent of the value of the scheme's assets.

One disadvantage of SSAS plans over SIPPs is that they are not allowed to accept pension assets that you have accrued by contracting out of the state second pension. These assets are called 'protected rights'. SIPPs, on the other hand, are allowed to hold protected rights. If you have a large protected rights fund this means the amount of money you can access to fund a commercial property purchase through your pension can be greater through a SIPP than a SSAS.

For example, somebody with a protected rights pot of £100,000 and a non-protected rights pot of £200,000 would be able to borrow up to £100,000 through a SSAS compared up to £150,000 through a SIPP. This would mean the SSAS investor could only put a maximum of £300,000 towards funding the purchase of a commercial property. Transferring the protected rights pot into the SIPP would boost its size to £300,000, and with 50 per cent borrowing on the combined pot, the investor would be able to use up to £450,000 to fund a commercial property.

Protected rights as a concept, and the restrictions on assets held in protected-rights funds, are set to disappear in 2012 when contracting out of the state second pension is due to be abolished. After 2012 SSAS plans will be able to facilitate an identical level of funding of commercial property purchase as SIPPs because former protected rights will be allowed to be transferred into SSAS plans.

Drawing income from a SSAS

SSAS arrangements allow the member to withdraw greater amounts of income from their pot than most SIPPs do. As with other pensions, income and tax-free cash can be taken from age 55 (50 until April 2010). The maximum income that can be paid out is determined by an actuary that has been appointed by the scheme. The actuary determines how much the member's portion of the scheme's assets can justifiably be paid out while still leaving enough to pay an income for the rest of the member's life. This amount will vary depending on a number of factors that the actuary must take into account, such as the member's age and life expectancy and the actuary's prediction of the likely investment returns on the fund.

Because the actuary has this discretion to set the income level it is normally possible to achieve a higher withdrawal than is possible through most SIPPs, particularly where the member's medical history suggests they may have a shorter life expectancy. Unsecured income withdrawal limits apply to everybody at the same rate, and are set by the Government Actuary's Department. These rates are linked to gilt yields, and have fallen considerably during the period of the global banking crisis, restricting the amounts of income withdrawals allowable from SIPPs. However, actuarial valuations come at a cost to the SSAS.

What happens after age 75?

SSAS plans continue to pay income out of the fund after age 75, subject to the same actuarial valuations of the member's age and the ability of the fund to provide them with a lifetime income. But SSAS arrangements are also allowed to fix a ten-year guaranteed income, a facility akin to the ten-year guarantee allowed on annuities.

To reduce the risk of the member dying and leaving a large amount of assets in the SSAS, it is therefore normal practice to arrange a ten-year guaranteed income at age 75. The income fixed under the ten-year guarantee will then continue to be paid to beneficiaries even if the individual dies before they are 85.

The residual fund will normally be invested in secure assets but will continue to accrue investment growth. At the end of the ten-year guarantee period there may therefore be some investment growth remaining in the fund.

If the SSAS member is still alive, this is used to continue paying the scheme pension after the guarantee expires at age 85, at rates the scheme's actuary will determine. Assets left in the SSAS fund on death after the age of 75, excluding funds required to pay the ten-year guarantee, are distributed under the death benefit rules set out below.

Reducing the pot before death

Because the income level of the ten-year guaranteed payment is fixed by an actuary, it is possible to receive an income of 10 or 11 per cent of fund value. Such an income level will mean the full value of the fund at age 75 will be paid out over the ten-year guarantee period.

SSAS death benefits

Member dies before taking pension benefits

Where a member dies before taking benefits from their fund, the total value of their fund can be paid to beneficiaries as a tax-free lump sum, provided it is below the lifetime allowance (£1.8m for 2010/2011). Alternatively it can be paid out to dependants as a pension income. Income taken in this way will be liable for income tax at the marginal rate of the person receiving it.

Member dies after starting to take benefits, before age 75

Where a member has died after starting to take benefits but before he or she has reached the age of 75, the remaining fund in the SSAS can be paid to beneficiaries nominated by the member, subject to a 35 per cent tax charge. Alternatively, it can be paid out to dependants as a pension income, without a 35 per cent tax charge being made.

Member dies after age 75

Where a member is over the age of 75 when they die, leaving a residual fund in the SSAS, that fund cannot be paid out as a lump sum. Beneficiaries are not entitled to receive any of it. The residual fund can be used to pay an income to dependants, either through a scheme pension, annuity or income drawdown. Alternatively, if there are no dependants, the residual fund can be given to a charity named by the deceased, free of tax.

Estate planning: scheme pension

The ability to pay a scheme pension is one of the advantages of SSAS plans when it comes to passing on wealth to the next generation. Scheme pension allows members of the SSAS greater flexibility in drawing cash from their fund than is possible from most other types of pension, making it easier to pass it on to heirs. Estate planning can be facilitated by using cash extracted from the pension to use up Inheritance Tax (IHT) annual gift allowances, set up regular gifts from income (which are also exempt from IHT) or make potentially exempt transfers and hope to survive the seven years from the date of the gift required to avoid an IHT liability.

If passing on your pension assets to beneficiaries is your main objective then an own-trust SIPP is likely to be a more suitable option

However, the benefit of this facility may be marginal in many cases, and opting for a SSAS on the grounds of estate planning alone should not be done without a thorough scrutiny of the additional costs that come with it. If passing on your pension assets to beneficiaries is your main objective then a special kind of SIPP called an own-trust SIPP is likely to be a more suitable option.

For a more detailed analysis of the way a SSAS can be used to mitigate death duties through payment of a scheme pension, turn to page 104 in Chapter 7. A SSAS has the same ability to pay a scheme pension as a trust-based SIPP, and therefore can use that facility to manage Inheritance Tax in the same way.

Family pension arrangements – trust-based SIPPs

To make use of a SSAS you need to have an employer/employee relationship. But there are situations where some of the flexibility of the SSAS would be useful to those who are not employers. This could be the case where there are several members of the same family who part-own a commercial property related to the family business. Another example is where accountants and solicitors are self-employed but hold premises in partnership. For these groups, holding a property in a trust can be more straightforward than everybody's individual pension holding a share of it discretely.

Wealthy families looking to mitigate Inheritance Tax liabilities and pass assets down the generations would also benefit from many of the benefits of SSAS arrangements.

Fortunately for people in these situations, there are special forms of SIPP that allow those who are not in an employer/employee situation to get many of the benefits of a SSAS. These special SIPPs are able to do this because they are set up with their own trust deed. These own-trust SIPPs are sometimes called family trust SIPPs.

Own-trust SIPPs cannot lend money to connected parties in the way that a SSAS can, but they can hold property in trust for members. They can also pay a scheme pension, and have an advantage over SSAS arrangements in that they can pass investment growth of one member's assets to another, such as from a grandparent to a grandchild, without creating an Inheritance Tax liability. For a more detailed explanation of how own-trust SIPPs work, turn to page 103 in Chapter 7.

9

Investment strategy: constructing your portfolio

What topics are covered in this chapter?

- The relationship between risk and return
- What can I invest in?
- Asset allocation
- Asset classes and their risks
- Your attitude to risk
- How much risk can you afford?
- Building your portfolio
- Ethical investing

The performance of your pension investment portfolio has a massive impact on how much income you get when you retire. Deciding which funds you include in your portfolio is one of the most important stages of your retirement saving plan. Regular reviews of those decisions are equally important.

The choice of investment options available to you through modern pensions can appear bewildering. Deciding which fund or funds to pick can seem like an impossible task if you are left to do it all on your own. This is why around 90 per cent of people investing in money purchase pensions without the help of an IFA end up ticking the box that says 'default option'.

Default investment options on pension plans are by definition middle-of-the-road funds, designed to be fairly appealing to most people, and are often with-profits or insurance company balanced managed funds. Most experts argue you can achieve better returns by opting for alternatives, provided you do your homework.

Pensions can invest in a wide range of assets, from volatile emerging market equity funds and shares in single companies to cash on deposit and gilts. Picking the right asset classes, and the right fund managers, investment houses and other providers offering those asset classes will have a huge influence on how much pension you ultimately receive. Picking winners without the benefit of hindsight is very difficult, and some people argue it is not possible to pick fund managers that beat the market year after year. But there are things you can do that can make your investment strategy fit more closely to your requirements, giving you a better chance of reaching your retirement saving target.

You may be happy to get a financial adviser to deal with constructing your investment portfolio. If you are paying a fee for an adviser, or your adviser is receiving commission for advising you, it makes sense to get the benefit of that professional advice.

If you wish to deal with your affairs yourself, this chapter will show you how to do so, showing you the key steps to building a portfolio and pointing you towards sources of further up-to-date information to help you on your way.

The relationship between risk and return

Portfolio construction is about understanding risk and return. When putting together your portfolio you need to consider how much of a return you want or need to make on your investments and how much risk you are prepared to take to get that return.

Investments tend to pay you for taking risks. Sometimes a risk will pay off and you get the reward for taking it. But on other occasions risks can blow up in your face, so a level of informed caution is needed. But risk should not be treated as evil – without taking some risk you will not be able to build the pension you need in retirement.

Risk works both ways – it is not as simple as saying 'I'm risk-averse therefore I am going to invest all my pension savings in cash on deposit.' Taking this attitude will expose you to the very real risk of missing out on the outperformance that equities are likely to generate over the years.

The key is to make sure you construct your portfolio so that you have the right level of risk in your portfolio for the different stages of your life.

Changing risk profiles

In the early years of pension saving you will want to go for higher risk assets that offer a higher potential return such as shares. As you approach retirement you will probably want more security and less volatility and so will restructure your portfolio so you are invested in less risky assets that have more certain, lower returns. Some of today's pensioners remain invested in the stock market long after they have retired and even well into their seventies through income drawdown arrangements. The same core principles of portfolio construction apply to these investors as they do to those just starting pension saving. Their investment horizons are different, however.

The importance of getting your investment portfolio right cannot be overstressed. Some fund managers are better than others and some asset classes, industry sectors and geographical regions will perform better than others at different times in the cycle.

Choose well and your money could grow into a healthy sized pot by the time you come to retire. Get it wrong and your retirement saving plan can fall seriously short.

How 1 per cent of investment outperformance can turn into 32 per cent more pension

Because pension saving is such a long-term game, even small improvements in performance make a big difference in the end. Somebody contributing £3,000 a year for 40 years will see their fund grow to £497,000 if it achieves an average return of 6 per cent a year net of charges. If they can manage to construct a portfolio of good funds that generates an extra 1 per cent performance a year, it will grow to £656,000. Compounded over 40 years that extra 1 per cent return on your investments will mean an extra 32 per cent pension income.

Should I trust 'star' fund managers?

Some star managers have delivered fabulous returns through bull markets. Just a handful of these have managed it through the bad years as well. The most celebrated fund manager this country has seen in recent decades is Anthony Bolton, formerly of Fidelity International. An investor who had put £1,000 in his Fidelity Special Situations fund when it was set up in 1979 would have seen it grow to around £148,200 by the time he stepped down in 2007. That adds up to an annualised return of 19.5 per cent a year.

But for every Anthony Bolton there are hundreds of fund managers failing to deliver. Many people argue it's not even worth trying to second-guess which fund managers or market sectors will do best, and that you are better off putting your money into a fund with low annual management charges that tracks an index. But all financial experts agree that allocating your funds to the right asset classes at the different stages in your pension saving is crucial. Some academic studies have concluded that asset allocation has a greater influence on the outcome of a portfolio than the ability to choose the best managers within an asset class.

Equities, bonds, gilts, cash on deposit, commercial property, single company shares, with-profits funds and traded endowment policies are all permitted investments for pensions. All carry different levels of risk and all offer different levels of potential upside. The process of deciding how much of your money should go into each of these different asset classes is called 'asset allocation' and forms an essential part of your retirement saving plan.

What can I invest in?

You may have a personal or stakeholder pension plan, either individual or through the workplace, or you could be topping up an occupational scheme with an AVC. Alternatively you may have chosen to invest through a SIPP or SSAS. All these forms of pension offer a range of investment choices. It is up to the individual to choose which ones they put their money in, either with or without the assistance of an adviser.

People saving in occupational money purchase schemes and some in-house AVCs, on the other hand, have no or only a very limited amount of investment choice, because these decisions are taken by the trustees of the scheme.

Investment options in different types of pension

Personal pension (individual or workplace)

Offers access to a range of investment funds across different asset classes, geographical regions and industry sectors. Typically offers between 20 and 200 different funds that are available through the insurance company running the pension scheme.

Stakeholder pension (individual or workplace)

Like personal pensions, offers access to a range of investment funds, but typically limited in number to between 15 and 30 different options. Funds run by star fund managers or offering access to niche areas of investment are unlikely to be available as their charges would raise overall costs beyond what is permitted by the stakeholder charge cap.

SIPP and SSAS

Offer a wide range of investment funds, normally in excess of 1,000, as well as access to a range of other asset classes. Funds available are not just limited to insurance company offerings but include unit trusts and investment trusts. Shares, commercial property, gilts, UK Real Estate Investment Trusts (REITS), futures, options, traded endowment policies and cash on deposit are also permitted investments through SIPPs and SSASs. Not all SIPPs offer all these investment choices. Some SIPPs offered through the workplace only allow investment funds and shares, while some low-cost online SIPPs, also known as supermarket SIPPs, only offer access to investment funds available through a fund supermarket.

Occupational money purchase pension scheme

Many occupational schemes offer you no choice at all. In this situation the scheme's trustees set the investment strategy, normally with the assistance of professional investment advisers. Some occupational schemes allow you a limited range of funds to choose from.

AVCs

Some in-house AVCs and all free-standing AVCs offer you a choice of life insurance company investment funds similar to that offered through a personal pension. Some in-house AVCs require you to invest in a pre-determined fund that has been selected by the scheme's trustees.

Asset allocation

Put simply, asset allocation is how you balance the various asset types in your pension portfolio, or any other investment portfolio for that matter. Different asset classes tend to perform well or badly at different parts of the economic cycle. So by spreading your money across different types of asset class you can take some of the risk out of your portfolio. The idea is that, in the same way that street vendors sell sunglasses and umbrellas so they can make money whatever the weather, you can benefit from investment growth whatever the market conditions. Many investment experts say that deciding what proportion of your fund you should put in each asset class is more important than being able to pick the best fund within an asset class.

Depending on the sort of pension you have, you may hold equity investment funds, bonds, gilts, cash on deposit, commercial property, single company shares, exchange traded funds and traded endowment policies. You may also be invested in with-profits or balanced managed funds, which contain a range of different asset classes, but can usefully be looked at together with these asset classes because they are common pension investments and have a risk/reward profile of their own.

Diversification

Diversification is in essence the fundamental principle of not putting all your eggs in one basket. This means you should spread your money across a range of investments so that you reduce the risk in your portfolio. Diversification should take place at two levels – between asset classes and within asset classes.

Your pension asset allocation strategy may require that you do not diversify between asset classes at all. This may be the case if you are in your twenties or thirties and opt for an aggressive portfolio investing entirely in equities. People in their fifies and sixties, on the other hand, who are drawing income from their fund through unsecured pension are less able to deal with stock market volatility. By allocating their portfolio to different asset classes they can reduce much of the volatility in their fund.

Asset classes and their risks

Cash deposits – low risk

SIPP and SSAS investors will often have a portion of their fund invested in cash at times when they are restructuring their portfolios or waiting to buy a particular asset. Some investors have moved into cash at times when they have been worried about the prospects for other asset classes such as

Cash deposits are generally safe as long as the bank or building society does not go bust equities and bonds. Cash deposits are generally safe as long as the bank or building society does not go bust. In the event that it does, individual investors are usually protected up to the value of £50,000 by the Financial Services Compensation Scheme for each banking institution they have invested in. However, not all overseas banks do, so check with the bank how much protection is offered in that jurisdiction.

Cash deposits do have a risk for pension investors: the risk that they will miss out on the potential higher growth that other assets can offer. This risk is sometimes dubbed 'reckless caution'.

Cash on deposit should not be confused with cash funds, which are also known as money market funds. Many pension providers offer access to these funds, which aim to get returns slightly higher than cash on deposit, for slightly more risk. These funds invest in the same money market instruments that banks and building societies do, and can in normal economic circumstances beat cash on deposit, making them attractive to people just about to retire and buy an annuity. But during the global banking crisis of 2008/2009 some of these funds surprised investors by generating a negative return.

Gilts – low risk

Gilts are generally considered one of the lowest risk forms of investment because they are backed by the UK government, which has so far never reneged on a debt. The government issues gilts to fund its borrowing – when you buy gilts you are effectively lending money to the government. Gilts promise to pay a fixed income over a fixed term. Investors are repaid the capital value when the gilt matures.

Gilts come in a variety of lengths, ranging from just a few years to up to 50 years. Conventional gilts pay a fixed sum each year but less common index-linked gilts pay income and capital payments that are adjusted to take inflation into account. Others are 'strippable', which means that the individual interest and capital redemption payments may be bought and sold separately. The most common category is the conventional gilt.

Because they are secure, their returns are consequently low. Older investors who need to be able to guarantee that their income is maintained and capital returned may want to use them as part of their portfolio. They can be bought directly from the Debt Management Office, or through a stockbroker. Alternatively, you can get access to gilts through an investment fund that invests in a range of the instruments.

Corporate bonds – from low risk upwards

Considered riskier than gilts but less risky than equities, corporate bonds have become increasingly popular in recent years among both private and institutional investors. Corporate bonds are similar to gilts, promising a fixed annual return for the investor effectively lending the company cash. The difference is that the security of getting the income and principal sum back is given by the company issuing the corporate bond and not the government. Investors also get their initial capital investment back at the end of the bond's term. The capital return is known as the 'coupon'.

Corporate bonds are higher up the risk scale than gilts because of the possibility that the company will go bust and be unable to pay back the investor. To reward the investor for this higher risk, companies have to pay a higher return than the government does on gilts. The less secure the company is, the higher return it has to offer investors to fund its bonds.

Corporate bonds are split into two types: investment grade and non-investment grade. Investment-grade bonds deliver a lower yield, reflecting their lower risk. Non-investment-grade bonds, often known as 'junk' bonds, pay higher income levels. Companies issuing bonds are rated by agencies such as Standard & Poor's and Moody's – with the most secure being rated AAA, down to precarious companies rated DDD and E. Non-investment-grade bonds are arguably higher risk than some equities.

A stockbroker will be able to buy corporate bonds for you and recommend which ones are considered good value. Most retail investors, however, access this asset class through a corporate bond unit trust or OEIC. These invest in a diversified range of corporate bonds that are chosen and managed by a professional fund manager.

Corporate bonds can be bought off and sold to investors, and their value can rise and fall depending on returns on gilts and bank interest rates. The return an investor gets from a corporate bond is called the 'yield'.

> The return an investor gets from a corporate bond is called the 'yield'

When the price of a corporate bond goes up, the yield falls. High demand for corporate bonds causes yields to fall and therefore the difference between returns on corporate bonds and gilts, known as the 'spread', narrows. The narrower the spread, the less scope there may be for corporate bond prices to rise.

Investment-grade corporate bond performance tends to be driven by interest rate movements. Interest in corporate bonds has risen as interest rates have fallen in the wake of the international banking crisis, as bond returns have looked relatively more attractive. Conversely, rising interest rates and inflation are bad news for investment-grade bonds.

While the performance of investment-grade bonds relies heavily on interest-rate and gilt movements, non-investment-grade bonds are more closely linked to the general economy and the likelihood of companies going bust. Higher yield bonds are riskier in times of recession, although some experts argue that, provided you buy a fund investing in a broad range of corporate bonds, the chance of all of them defaulting is slim. However, even a low level of corporate bond defaults will erode your capital investment.

When the economic climate is positive, on the other hand, concerns that companies will not be able to repay bond debt are eased. Investment-grade corporate bonds may be at the lower end of the risk scale but it is essential to remember that your capital is still at risk.

Structured products – low to high risk, depending on guarantees

Structured products are also known as guaranteed products and are offered by banks, insurance companies and investment houses. They are usually share-based products that allow you some investment growth provided that an index, fund or basket of shares achieves a certain return, while guaranteeing the return of some or all of your initial investment at the end of a fixed period, normally five or six years. Those that do not guarantee a full return of capital are known as 'capital at risk products'.

High income versions of the product offer an income above that available from cash on deposit. However, some or all of the initial investment is not returned if the stock market falls below a certain point. Stock market growth structured products pay out no income during the term of the plan, but may pay out the growth in the index. However, you normally miss out on the dividends that would have been paid during the term of the plan.

Variable annuities, also known as 'third way annuities', are a type of structured product designed for those approaching or past retirement who want to remain exposed to the stock market through their retirement but do not want to risk their capital. These are low-risk products, with no risk of forfeiture of income and typically have added features such as death benefits or options to take out annuities at the end of the term.

With-profits funds – low to medium risk

With-profits funds are designed to give investors the benefit of growth in the stock market while mitigating much of the volatility of direct equity investment. They were a common option for mainstream pension investors in the 1980s and 1990s. All investors pool their cash in a single fund, which is then invested in different types of assets, such as shares, commercial property, gilts, corporate bonds and cash deposits.

Policies pay out a guaranteed sum at the end of the term and older policies from the early 1980s and earlier may offer guaranteed annuity rates, which can be a lot higher than those available on the open market today. Policies also allocate bonuses to your fund each year to reflect investment growth. You may also get a final bonus at the end of the term to make sure you get your fair share of the investment fund. These bonuses are not an exact proportion of the investment returns. Instead, a process called 'smoothing' is used to hold back some of the profits in good years so it can pay out at least something in the bad years.

Different insurance companies invest different amounts in each type of asset; some have mainly gilts and corporate bonds, others have more shares or property. Some with-profits funds that have closed to new business have had to shift to more cautious investment strategies because they cannot afford to risk not being able to pay the guarantees they have already promised policyholders when their policies mature. Many of these funds have less than 35 per cent of their portfolio invested in shares, with the remainder in more secure asset classes such as bonds, gilts and cash. This means they are lower risk, but have less potential to deliver returns over a long period. These funds have been dubbed 'zombie' funds by the press, because of their slow, directionless investment performance. While they are technically lower risk, for pension investors with many years to go to retirement they carry a risk of underperformance.

A handful of insurers, such as Prudential, Aviva (formerly Norwich Union) and LV= (formerly Liverpool Victoria) have stronger with-profits funds and remain committed to them as a vehicle for long-term equity growth. At the end of 2008, Prudential's with-profits fund had 70 per cent of its assets in equities or property. This makes it riskier than closed with-profit funds but also means it has greater potential to deliver high returns.

Commercial property – medium risk

Commercial property is a useful component of a diversified portfolio because it tends to perform in different cycles to equities, thereby reducing overall risk.

The commercial property market is different to the residential property market. Commercial properties are let out to companies and tend to be on long leases, often 25 years. So the value of the investment is generally reflected by the financial strength of the company paying the rent and the number of years left on their lease.

You can get access to the commercial property market through investment funds investing in a range of properties. Commercial properties are long-term investments and cannot be bought and sold overnight in the way equities can, which means that getting your money out of a commercial property fund immediately is not always possible. Fund managers keep a small level of cash to allow some investors to redeem their investments, but if the asset class falls out of favour and investors stampede for the exit, they reserve the right to make you wait six months or a year before you get your money back. This is so that the fund is not forced to dispose of properties in a fire sale to generate cash to pay redemptions.

SIPP and SSAS investors may invest in their own commercial premises, and may borrow up to 50 per cent of fund value to do so. While investing in a single property has its own risks, that risk is arguably reduced because the SIPP or SSAS owner has inside knowledge of the company's ability to pay the rent. On the other hand, the person investing in their own company's premises is increasing their overall risk by having their employment income and a proportion of their pension dependent on the success of their business. That risk is increased if they borrow money against the security of their other pension assets to fund the property purchase.

Life insurance managed pension funds – medium to medium/high risk

Managed pension funds are offered by all of the big life insurance pension companies. They attempt to address the issue of asset allocation for mass-market pension savers. Cautious managed and balanced managed funds all offer exposure to a range of assets such as different types of equities, commercial property, corporate bonds and cash. This blend of assets means they will be less volatile than funds invested 100 per cent in equities, making them more attractive to investors who do not have the stomach for dealing with high volatility.

These funds, together with with-profits funds, have often been used as the default option on personal, stakeholder and company pension schemes as a safe haven for those people who do not have a view on which investment funds they want to invest in. Critics of the funds argue that they claim to be actively managed but almost invariably aim to deliver performance as close to their benchmark as possible, meaning investors might as well be invested in a tracker fund with lower charges. This conservative investment philosophy arises from a fear of falling short of their benchmark. These funds are less likely to deliver outperformance, say their detractors. Supporters of the funds say that that is precisely what they are designed to do – offer a blend of exposure to equity markets with a conservative approach to risk.

Cautious managed funds have a maximum 60 per cent exposure to equities, both overseas and in the UK, while balanced managed funds are allowed to have up to 85 per cent in equities.

Equities – high risk

Equities, or company shares, are high-risk investments, a fact that is demonstrated by the daily fluctuations in the stock market. Some equities are higher risk than others – many investors lost every penny they put into certain internet start-up companies in the dot.com bubble at the end of the last millennium. Others, such as blue-chip companies, are less risky. But even these shares carry risks, as has been demonstrated by the collapse of household name banks and other financial institutions in 2008 and 2009.

While risks are high when you invest in equities, so are the potential returns. Equities are likely to be the main driver of your pension saving right up until a few years before you are ready to retire. The reason for this is simple: history has shown that equities generally outperform other asset classes over the longer term.

> While risks are high when you invest in equities, so are the potential returns

Barclays has been comparing the returns delivered by asset classes since 1899 in its Equity Gilt Study. The 2009 edition of the study showed that £100 invested in equities in 1899 would be worth £17,571 today, with dividends reinvested, once inflation has been taken into account. The same sum invested in gilts would be worth £365, while cash on deposit would have returned just £303.

Of course the potential to deliver high returns is coupled with potential to lose a large proportion, or even all of your investments. As the health warning goes, the value of equities can go down as well as up, and if the company becomes insolvent or is nationalised by the government, you may lose all your investment.

Most pension savers invest in equities through investment funds offered through their pension. Because these funds invest in lots of companies, risk is reduced as the chance of all the companies doing badly is lower. SIPP and SSAS investors are able to hold shares of individual companies in their plans.

There are many different sorts of company share, all of which have different characteristics. Many of the investment funds on the market are designed to invest in a particular type of company share. It is important to understand the types of shares you are investing in and the returns they are likely to deliver when constructing your investment portfolio.

Blue-chip shares are big, household-name companies and are generally supposed to be less volatile than smaller company shares. However, like any share they can fall drastically, as was borne out by the fate of many banking stocks in 2008.

Growth shares focus on sales growth and aim to grow their earnings faster than the average for the market. They don't tend to pay dividends because profits are ploughed back into the company to facilitate business growth. The theory is that if the company can grow quickly, then the value of the shares should go up more quickly. In the late 1990s prime examples of growth stocks were the internet and technology companies of the late 1990s – which were newer companies attempting to grow their businesses fast.

High yield stocks are typically old established businesses that have a history of paying stable dividends. Many high yield stocks perform relatively well in a downturn because they are the sorts of businesses that provide staple goods or services that people want irrespective of the stock market cycle, such as utility and tobacco companies. This counter-cyclical performance makes them a suitable component for most pension portfolios, unless you have an ethical objection to them. They can also be suitable for older pension investors looking for a regular income stream and some protection against inflation through remaining invested in the stock market.

Some investment funds will target medium-sized or small companies, called mid-cap and small-cap respectively. Others will track indices. Single sector funds, such as commodities, healthcare or banking are high risk as they can do well one year and badly the next. Overseas equities are a good way of diversifying your portfolio and thus reducing its risk – if the UK performs badly, you don't want your entire investment in that single economy.

Investing in the stock market is not for novices. A considerable amount of time and research is needed before it is possible to have an informed view of whether a company is going to perform well or badly. Unless you are an avid reader of the financial pages and spend time poring over company accounts, the best way to get exposure to the stock market is through a collective fund such as a unit trust, open-ended investment company (OEIC) or an investment trust, rather than buying individual shares. That way your risk is spread across a large number of companies and you get the benefit of the investment expertise of professional fund managers.

Many employers that offer SIPPs to staff promote the idea of rolling over shares from the company share scheme into their pension when the scheme matures. There are tax benefits in doing this in certain situations but it should also be remembered that having a substantial proportion of your pension invested in a single company's shares raises the risk profile of your portfolio.

Your attitude to risk

Your own personal attitude to risk will have an influence on how you construct your investment portfolio. You need to make sure that you not only understand the risks that the investments you have selected carry, but also that you are comfortable with living with the consequences of those risks becoming a reality.

Risk is a difficult thing to quantify. Most people, when asked where they see themselves on a spectrum of attitude to risk ranging from high to low, will put themselves somewhere in the middle. But unless the question of risk is put in some form of real-world context, such assessments have little meaning. Check out what your attitude to risk is by answering the questions on page 133.

You can also use online risk profilers to test your attitude to investment risk. Your pension provider or company pension scheme may offer such a service. One simple, straightforward service is offered online for free at www.principlefirst.co.uk/investment-risk-profiler.htm. This service, offered by Principle First, an IFA, also offers suggestions of portfolios of investment funds that match these various risk profiles.

Your attitude to risk can change the more you learn about financial matters, particularly when you discover that every investment you make carries risk. Some people who are initially cautious can become more comfortable with investment risk when they understand the risks inherent in *not* taking risks.

The prime example of this is the risk of being too conservative in your investment approach, a phenomenon known as 'reckless caution'. You may think that something as important as your retirement income demands an ultra-cautious investment strategy. If this was the case, we should all be investing for our pensions in savings accounts at the local building society. But even the FSA warns pension investors against taking this attitude because of the opposite risk that they will not have a big enough fund when they retire. This is why financial advisers and company pension schemes will attempt to educate savers about the situations where some level of risk in a portfolio is beneficial. That said, with equity investment there is always a risk that you will be unlucky and not get the returns you have projected, so if you are not prepared or cannot afford to take risk then you should adopt a more cautious investment strategy.

There are other factors to bear in mind when considering risk with pension saving. You cannot access your money until it is time to retire, so even if markets do fall drastically, for much of the time you are saving it will not matter because share prices may have decades more to recover. In the years coming up to retirement it is recommended that you shift gradually to more cautious assets to reduce risk when it matters most.

It should also be remembered that because regular pension contributions are paid on a monthly basis, you are buying shares every month. This means that when markets are low you are buying cheap but when they are high you are paying more for them. This effect, known as 'pound/cost averaging', takes out much of the volatility of equities for regular pension investors in comparison to lump sum investors.

But equity-based pension funds can still swing violently and if you are unable to deal with that prospect you need to go for a more cautious portfolio. Having a portfolio that does not match your risk profile can be disastrous: people who lose faith in equities and switch to 'safer' assets at the bottom of the market end up with the worst of both worlds – their fund size is reduced, they have less potential for future fund growth and they are not buying shares when they are cheap.

Risk profiler: what sort of investor are you?

Decide how you feel about each of the statements in Table 9.1. Do not look at the second part of the table on page 134 until you have gone through the process. Add up your score and see what your risk profile is.

Once you know what your risk profile is, match it with the suggested asset allocation splits in Table 9.2 to create your investment portfolio.

Table 9.1: Investment risk profiler

Risk profiler	Strongly agree	Somewhat agree	Somewhat disagree	Strongly disagree
1. I would feel comfortable if my investments could easily rise and fall by a quarter (25%) or more in a year	7	5	2	1
2. If my investments fell significantly in value I might see this as an opportunity to buy more at cheaper prices	7	5	2	1
3. I would not feel comfortable if my investments could fall in value at all	1	1	4	7
4. I prefer the security of bank accounts to stock market related investments.	1	1	4	7
5. I can sleep at night knowing that my investments might rise and fall quite rapidly in the short term.	7	4	2	1

▶

Table 9.1: Investment risk profiler *continued*

Score	Risk profile
0–5	Very defensive
6–9	Defensive
10–14	Cautious
15–19	Balanced
20–24	Moderately aggressive
25-35	Aggressive

Source: Principle First Financial Services

Table 9.2: Suggested asset allocation splits for investor more than 10 years from retirement

Definitions	Target asset allocations										
	UK Eq.	EU Eq.	N.Am	Jap.	Pac. X Jap	GEM	Prop.	UK Gilts	UK Corp.	Int. Bond	Cash
Very defensive	0%	0%	0%	0%	0%	0%	10%	10%	0%	0%	80%
Defensive	0%	0%	0%	0%	0%	0%	26%	15%	46%	8%	5%
Cautious	27%	1%	1%	1%	1%	1%	17%	4%	42%	0%	5%
Balanced	38%	7%	11%	3%	5%	0%	3%	0%	26%	0%	7%
Moderately aggressive	52%	11%	6%	0%	10%	6%	0%	0%	10%	0%	5%
Aggressive	22%	2%	4%	0%	5%	66%	0%	0%	0%	0%	1%

Source: Principle First Financial Services, data supplied by Distribution Technology

Certainty of outcomes

When you get a projection of how much pension you are likely to get from your pension provider or scheme, it has worked out a figure based on a range of assumptions. Typical assumptions are that your fund will generate an investment return of 6 per cent a year net of charges, that inflation will be 2.5 per cent throughout the period you save and that today's annuity rates will be around when you retire. But predicting what an investment will return in 20, 30 or 40 years time is not an exact science. Virtually nobody will retire on exactly the figure set out in their pension projection.

Pension providers are required by the FSA to give you predictions based on a projected 5, 7 and 9 per cent annual return, before charges. But a more accurate way of representing the way that risk affects your likely pension is through a process called 'stochastic modelling'. Stochastic modelling uses computers to run thousands of different possible scenarios and calculate a range of possible outcomes.

Returns are therefore given in terms of a range of possible outcomes and a statistical likelihood that the return will fall within that range. For example, a stochastic modelling tool could predict that your eventual pension has an 80 per cent likelihood of being between £15,000 and £20,000, and that £17,500 is the most likely outcome. This also means that there is a 20 per cent likelihood that it could be either below £15,000 or above £20,000.

You may think that this makes financial planning even more complicated. But stochastic modelling and portfolio planning tools can grade the risk profile of your selected investment portfolio by modelling the likely returns of each of the funds you have selected. Some systems will also send you prompts when your portfolio becomes unbalanced as a result of different sectors delivering different performance. For example, if you decided that your portfolio requirements are to have a 20 per cent exposure to emerging markets equities, and those funds do so well that they now represent 40 per cent of your whole fund, you need to cash in your gains and rebalance your portfolio.

Free access to stochastic modelling tools on the internet is limited. Most pension providers that have such sophisticated portfolio management tools limit access to clients and their IFAs. Some private and company pension schemes offer access to stochastic modelling tools.

Rebalancing your portfolio

Rebalancing is the process of readjusting your portfolio so that it reflects the original asset allocation strategy that you had decided upon. By doing this you can make sure you have the best chance of staying on target to reach your retirement goal. As a very simple example, you could have a situation where your asset allocation analysis process determined that you need a 70 per cent holding in equities and 30 per cent in bonds. A year later your equity holding has grown considerably more than your bonds holding, to the extent that equities make up 80 per cent of your portfolio.

To get back to your original asset allocation spread you need to either sell some of your equities or buy some more bonds, or do both.

To achieve this you can either cash in your equity holdings and use the money to buy bond holdings, or pay a higher proportion of your new contributions into bonds. Before cashing in any holdings you need to make sure there are no charges for doing so. The vast majority of pensions allow you at least one free fund switch a year, and many allow you considerably more, but you need to check first. There are unlikely to be any tax consequences of rebalancing your portfolio because all the assets you hold in it are not liable for Capital Gains Tax.

Selling discipline is immensely hard for investors to adopt

Getting out of an asset class that is rising may feel counter-intuitive, but it means that you actually bank your winnings. Selling discipline is immensely hard for investors to adopt. Psychologically, when we see a stock rising, we can tend to think it will carry on rising for ever. But by sticking to the rules for rebalancing your portfolio in this way you can ensure that you sell when stocks are high, leaving you to buy other assets when they are cheap.

Your age

How old you are and how long you have got to go until you reach your target retirement date will also have a key bearing on the structure of your portfolio and the types of assets in it.

Most experts agree that a large part, if not all of your portfolio should be in equities right up until at least 10 years before your projected retirement. At the very least, most experts agree that somebody with more than 10 years to go to retirement should at least have 60 per cent of their fund invested in equities. The proportion of equities that you ultimately go for will be influenced by your attitude to risk and the level of risk that you can afford to take.

De-risking your portfolio

As you approach retirement it makes sense to start gradually moving assets out of equities and into less risky asset classes, so that by the time you come to retire you have no equity exposure at all. This is a process called 'de-risking your portfolio'.

The risk of not de-risking your pension was highlighted to devastating effect following the stock market collapse of 2008. Tens of thousands of people within months of retirement who had saved in personal or stakeholder pensions saw their retirement pots cut by up to 30 per cent because they had not taken steps to de-risk their pensions. The combined effect of these asset falls and lower annuity rates resulting from falling interest rates, plus the government's policy of quantitative easing, resulted in some cases in pension incomes 40 per cent lower than those retiring two years earlier.

There are a number of theories around about how long before retirement you should start de-risking, with suitable periods ranging from five to ten years. Most modern pension arrangements will do this for you because they offer a process called 'lifestyling'. Your pension will also be de-risked for you if you are in an occupational money purchase scheme.

Lifestyling

Through lifestyling, your pension provider automatically de-risks your fund by switching a proportion of it into more stable assets such as cash on deposit and gilts in the years before you retire. A five-year lifestyling strategy will switch over 20 per cent of your fund each year up until your selected retirement date. This means you will not be hit so badly if markets fall off a cliff the day before you retire. The flip side of this is that your fund will not grow quite so much if equities soar in the months before you retire.

Some people argue that people who can afford to live off other income when they reach retirement age should avoid lifestyling, stay with equities and simply wait for the market to rebound if there is a steep fall just before they plan to retire. The risk they face is that equity markets do not rebound and fall further, making the problem even worse. As a general rule, the smaller your investment fund, the less likely you are to be able to afford to stay in equities and wait for the market to rebound because you cannot afford the risk of it falling even further.

As has already been described, the risk of leaving your pension entirely exposed to stock market volatility right up to the day before you retire is too great to ignore for all but those with considerable assets elsewhere that they can live off. But many personal or stakeholder pensions taken out before the millennium still have no lifestyling process assigned to them. You should check with your pension provider to find out whether your plan has a lifestyling strategy in place.

If it does not, you may be able to get one put on for nothing. Lifestyling funds are offered by almost all pension companies today, and many will allow you to switch to them for free. Some will allow you to do this online or over the telephone. You do not need to change your investment fund. Simply ask for a lifestyling option on the fund you are already investing in – for example, if you are currently invested in the Lifeco balanced managed fund, ask to be switched to the Lifeco balanced managed (lifestyling) fund.

Not all providers allow free switches to lifestyle options. If this applies to you then you should contact your provider and ask them what your options are. Most pension providers allow you to switch funds every year for free, so you could operate your own lifestyle strategy and move tranches of your fund into more stable funds such as cash and gilt funds in the years before you retire. However, this is best done with the help of a financial adviser.

Lifestyling and with-profits

With-profits investors are not exposed to the volatility of the stock market in the same way that those in balanced managed or other unit-linked funds are. Therefore they do not need to de-risk their investments in the years before retirement.

Is your stated retirement age correct?

It is common for savers to have selected a retirement age for their pension that no longer meets their circumstances. For example, you may be 58 now, and 20 years ago when you took out your pension plan expressed a wish to retire at 65. You may now be planning to retire at 60. If your plan has a lifestyling option that starts de-risking your fund five years before your retirement date you could inadvertently find yourself 100 per cent invested in equities right up to the date you plan to retire.

Conversely, if you selected a retirement age of 60 but now realise that you will have to work until you are 65, your lifestyling process will start pulling you out of equities five years earlier than you need, thus limiting your potential for achieving higher fund growth.

How much risk can you afford?

As well as your age and attitude to risk, the amount of risk you take with your pension saving will also be governed by how much you can afford to take. As a basic principle, the more money or other assets you have, the more risk you can afford to take. The issue of how much risk you can afford to take only really becomes relevant from the final years of your retirement saving onwards.

Before the lifestyling phase you risk missing out on growth so may not want to be too cautious. But once you have retired and are faced with having nothing to live on but your pension pot and state pension, the issue of risk becomes increasingly relevant. As already explained, you may decide to forgo the safety of lifestyling and remain exposed to equities right up to your planned retirement age and even beyond.

People retiring in their sixties face a number of choices ranging from buying a conventional annuity to remaining invested in the stock market through unsecured pension, also known as income drawdown. Between these extremes lies a number of options, such as unit-linked annuities, with-profits annuities and variable annuities, all of which offer some exposure to the stock market. These options are explained in greater detail in Chapter 14.

With retirement stretching well into three decades for most of today's retirees, the idea of benefiting from growth in the stock market for as long as possible is gaining ground among financial advisers and some clients.

Whether pensioners can afford to take such risks will be influenced by how big their pension pot is, what their living expenses are and what other assets they hold. Put simply, if your pension is only big enough to buy you an annuity that will barely cover your living expenses then you have no alternative but to take that annuity. If you can afford to lose some of your fund, you can afford some level of risk and hope to benefit from the potential upside that can bring.

Why should I put my faith in equities?

Financial advisers and pension providers talk about the outperformance of equities over other asset classes as though it is a sure thing. Even the FSA website says that equities are likely to be your best bet for long-term saving. Yet shares have delivered dreadful performance over the last decade. In the 10 years to December 2008, equities turned out to be the worst performing asset class of all, generating an inflation-adjusted average annual return of –1.5 per cent a year. Over that decade you would have been better off putting your money in cash on deposit or gilts, both of which would have given you a return of 2.4 per cent a year. The decade ending in 1978, covering the oil crisis of the early 1970s, was even worse than that ending in 2008, with an average annual return of –3.5 per cent. It should be added, however, that rampant inflation meant that even gilts and cash in the bank gave negative real returns over that decade.

But despite this poor performance, the majority of economists argue that equities are still the best bet for long-term saving. The Barclays Equity Gilt Study is published every year and has been tracking the relative performance of equities, gilts and cash since 1899. The 2009 study shows that in the 110 years since the turn of the twentieth century there have been 19 ten-year stretches where equities have underperformed gilts and 8 where equities have done worse than cash.

But those 19 years where equities have underperformed over a ten-year period must be seen in the context of the 81 occasions where they have outperformed. And, crucially for pension savers, for periods longer than ten years, the likelihood of equity outperformance increases considerably.

The Barclays study also looks at the relative performance of the three asset classes over the 92 discrete 18-year periods covered by the data. It shows that equities performed better than cash 91 times, with cash managing just a single 18-year period of outperformance. Barclays models these figures to give a 99 per cent probability of equities outperforming cash over an 18-year period.

Gilts fared better than cash over an 18-year period, managing to beat equities on 9 occasions out of 92. The other 83 18-year periods saw equities outperform, which Barclays models to a 90 per cent probability that equities will outperform gilts.

The long-term power of equities to not only keep up with inflation but deliver returns above it is also revealed in the Barclays study: £100 invested in equities in 1899 would be worth £1.15m by 2009 before inflation is taken into account, and £17,571 in real terms. The same sum invested in gilts would be worth £23,916, or £365 adjusted for inflation. Cash on deposit would have returned £17,571, a real return of just £303. (See Tables 9.3 and 9.4.)

Critics of the cult of equities point to the experience of Japan, where the stock market remains at a fifth of its value of 20 years ago. They argue that there is no guarantee that equities outperform, and even if they perform better on average, not everybody gets the average returns. If some people achieve outperformance then by definition other investors will underperform, they argue. Furthermore, the cost of active fund management will reduce actual returns. If you are not prepared to take the risk that equities might underperform then you should opt for more cautious investments.

Table 9.3: The power of equities: value of £100 invested at the end of 1899, income reinvested gross

Asset class	Nominal return	Adjusted for inflation
Equities	£1,152,944	£17,571
Gilts	£23,916	£365
Cash	£19,891	£303

Source: Barclays Capital, reprinted with permission

In its commentary attached to the 2009 study, Barclays adds that the drastic market correction that followed the banking crisis of 2008 means that company valuations are now more realistic than they have been for many years.

The issue of whether equities should be the main vehicle for long-term growth was examined in detail in the wake of the stock market crash that followed the dot.com bubble at the turn of the millennium. In 2003, when the FTSE stood down at around 3,300, the FSA asked PricewaterhouseCoopers (PwC) to consider whether its projection rates of 5, 7 and 9 per cent for long-term savings products such as pensions were correct. Under these projections the middle rate is given as an indication of the most likely outcome.

In that research PwC concluded that the best estimate for the likely outperformance of equities over fixed interest, known as the 'equity market risk premium', is between 3 and 4 per cent. PwC revisited the issue of whether 5, 7 and 9 per cent were the correct projection rates in December 2007 and confirmed that it believed they were.

Table 9.4: Equity performance since 1899

Number of consecutive years	2	3	4	5	10	18
Outperform cash	72	75	78	78	92	91
Underperform cash	36	32	28	27	8	1
Total number of years	108	107	106	105	100	92
Probability of equity outperformance	67%	70%	74%	74%	92%	99%
Outperform gilts	75	81	82	79	81	83
Underperform gilts	33	26	24	26	19	9
Total number of years	108	107	106	105	100	92
Probability of equity outperformance	69%	76%	77%	75%	81%	90%

Source: Barclays Capital, reprinted with permission

Building your portfolio

If you feel sufficiently confident in your understanding of financial matters to make decisions about your investment strategy then you can move on to selecting the funds you will hold in your pension. However, you should never invest in things you do not understand and if you are unsure, you should get professional financial advice.

If you are going to create your own portfolio there are a number of sources that will give you ideas to help you on your way. You can get suggestions for your portfolio from financial websites from IFAs, financial services providers and market data companies. It is important to understand that this information is guidance and not advice, which means you do not have any redress against the firm giving you the information if it proves to be wrong, which is not the case if you pay for face-to-face advice from an IFA. That said, if the investments that an IFA recommends through paid-for financial advice perform badly, you are still unlikely to have any redress.

There are thousands of different collective funds available to UK investors. No two are identical and many have different objectives, which mean performance can also vary considerably. Some will be trackers mirroring the performance of a stock market index such as the FTSE 100 or the FTSE All Share. Others will be actively managed, investing in a small concentration of stocks. Specialist funds, such as those investing in single stock market sectors such as healthcare, financials and commodities, can be prone to big swings in performance – shooting the lights out one year and on the floor the next. These funds are generally unsuitable as a core holding in a pension portfolio.

Hargreaves Lansdown offers portfolio ideas for SIPP investors on its website at www.h-l.co.uk/pensions/investment-ideas-for-your-sipp. Other stockbrokers, SIPP providers and online share dealing services also have information on favoured funds and portfolio construction ideas.

Multi-manager funds

The concept of multi-manager funds seems ideal for pension investors who do not want the hassle of having to review their portfolio every year. Get a specialist to pick and choose the best fund managers for you. But despite the simplicity of the idea, the extra costs inherent in multi-manager funds mean that many pension advisers are yet to be persuaded of their attractiveness. This is despite the fact that there are some multi-manager fund groups who have achieved consistent outperformance.

There are broadly two types of multi-manager funds, which are inherently different from each other: funds of funds and managers of managers.

■ *Fund of funds* A fund of funds is a single fund whose underlying portfolio is made up of a collection of OEICs and unit trusts. These can be further sub-divided into 'fettered' and 'unfettered' funds. If a fund of funds invests only in one investment group's unit trusts or OEICs, it is known as 'fettered'. Unfettered funds of funds, on the other hand, invest in funds from a variety of companies, from big fund groups to investment boutiques. Many IFAs question whether there is a case for the fettered option because of their obvious limitations.

■ *Manager of managers* A manager of managers (MoM) fund is more akin in management style to institutional pension funds. A MoM hires different fund management groups to run bespoke segments of portfolios according to a set mandate, rather than investing in off-the-shelf unit trusts or OEICs.

The major criticism with funds of funds is that they are expensive in comparison with conventional funds because of the double layer of charges – one levied by the underlying investments, the other for managing the fund. Some have total costs of nearly 3 per cent a year, more than double the charges on some actively managed funds, and while some have consistently delivered extra returns to justify these extra costs, many have not. However, many have delivered performance far surpassing that of default funds through the recent stock market volatility.

Is active fund management worth paying extra charges for?

The debate over whether active fund management delivers better returns than passive has been running for decades and is likely to continue for years to come.

Active fund managers are supposed to outperform the market by using their knowledge, research and investment process to buy stocks cheaply before they go up and sell them before the pack when they fall. The investor pays an increased annual management charge for this expertise, which in theory is more than made up for in the above-average returns that the fund manager generates. In some years the fund manager will beat the benchmark that the fund has been set, but in other years will fall short.

Passive funds, known as trackers, have much lower costs and simply buy and hold assets that replicate a portion of the market, such as the FTSE 100 for example. Year in, year out they will deliver on, or very close to, their benchmark, which is the average performance of the section of the market they reflect.

The average annual management charge for British managed unit trusts and OEICs is 163 basis points, or 1.63 per cent, according to data from Lipper, the fund information company. It is possible to get access to passively managed funds that track an index, such as the FTSE All Share, for an annual management charge of just 25 basis points, or 0.25 per cent. The question is therefore: are active fund managers capable of delivering an extra 1.3 per cent growth in your fund, year on year?

Critics of active fund management say they are not, and that, as a result, your fund performance will be held back by these charges. Numerous studies have shown that the average actively managed fund falls short of its benchmark more often than not, and active management critics say markets are so efficient these days that there is little scope to beat the market. Because there are so many people analysing every detail of every company's accounts and the markets they operate in, it is virtually impossible to steal a march on everybody else, they argue.

Figures from Standard & Poor's published in April 2009 back this view up, with an overwhelming majority of actively managed funds performing worse than their sector averages. Over the five-year market cycle from 2004 to 2008, the S&P 500 outperformed 71.9 per cent of actively managed large cap funds, S&P MidCap 400 outperformed 79.1 per cent of mid cap funds and S&P SmallCap 600 outperformed 85.5 per cent of small cap funds. These results are similar to that of the previous five-year cycle from 1999 to 2003.

Further evidence of the inability of most fund managers to deliver consistently higher returns was put forward in 2007 by John Bogle, chairman of passive fund giant Vanguard Investments. Bogle's book, *The Little Book of Common Sense Investing*, argues that out of 355 equity funds launched in the past 36 years, in America and till 2007, only 24 managed to outpace the S&P 500 by more than 1 per cent a year.

While both sets of data relate to the US market and not our own, critics of active management argue that it is barely conceivable that UK fund managers should be able to fare any better than their American counterparts. The reputation of active management is also dragged down, they argue, by the fact that not all 'active' funds are very active in their management strategies. Balanced managed funds in particular, which are common default options in pension plans and therefore hold huge amounts of the assets of uninformed investors, take a passive approach to investing to ensure that their performance will never fall too far below its benchmark.

Supporters of active management argue that just because the majority do not outperform the index, it does not mean that none do. They point to those star fund managers, like the now-retired Anthony Bolton, who have managed to beat their index consistently over a number of years. These men and women, they argue, have experience and expertise that makes them able to beat the index year on year.

They also point out that trackers do not always do what they say they will. Performance of trackers can be affected because of a combination of charges, and because they do not have absolutely identical holdings to the indices they are meant to be mirroring. Over 10 years some trackers can fall short of the index they are tracking by more than 10 per cent.

In 2002 the Investment Management Association commissioned research from Charles Rivers Associates to determine whether past performance was in any way indicative of how well a fund would perform in the future. That study found that there is strong evidence of consistency of returns among poorly performing funds but only mixed evidence of persistently good returns among the top performing funds.

The active versus passive debate is by no means over, and you will get different opinions depending on whom you talk to. But looking at the issue broadly, if you are the sort of person who will never revisit their investment portfolio once it has been fixed, passive funds are more likely to be suitable. If you are taking an active interest in your pension assets, active fund management may be more appealing.

Active or passive – which is best?

There is no definitive answer to whether active or passive management is best. But whichever path you follow, avoid the pitfalls.

Active

Even supporters of active management agree that the majority of actively managed funds are poor performers. There are a number of freely available recommendations of who to go for and who to avoid. Hargreaves Lansdown publishes its 'Wealth 150', which are the top funds it recommends out of a universe of 2,000 actively managed offerings (www.h-l.co.uk). Bestinvest, another IFA, publishes an annual 'Spot the Dog' list of names and shames the worst performing funds (www.bestinvest.co.uk). The Spot the Dog list helps investors to avoid poor fund managers by singling out those that have underperformed their benchmark for the previous three years and have delivered 10 per cent less than their benchmark over the last three years.

Passive

If you have a personal or stakeholder pension plan it is likely to offer you access to a tracker fund, usually with charges of around 0.3 per cent a year. But not all tracker funds are cheap. If you have a SIPP, there are likely to be several tracker options open to you.

The Virgin UK Index tracker has an annual management charge of 1 per cent a year, making it the most expensive fund of its sort available. The HSBC All Share tracker is available for a charge of 0.25 per cent a year, although its performance has fallen short of its peers over the last five years. The F&C All Share tracker has an annual charge of 0.3 per cent and has returned 3 per cent more than the HSBC offering in the five years to April 2009. You can get almost identical exposure to indices through exchange traded funds (ETFs) at very low prices. ETFs are growing in popularity in the UK as an alternative to tracker unit trusts. They track indices as shares, rather than units, which means their administration costs are lower. ETFs cover sectors or geographical areas and have less likelihood of tracking error than traditional passively managed funds.

Ethical investing

You may be unhappy with putting your money in funds that invest in companies whose products and practices do not match your ethical principles. You may object to companies engaged in animal testing, tobacco, weapons, pornography, genetic testing or nuclear energy, or those with a poor record on human rights or environmental issues.

If so, you are not alone. Billions of pounds a year are invested in UK ethical investment funds and around four-fifths of large pension fund assets are invested in companies that have adopted socially responsible investment (SRI) practices.

Virtually all personal pension and stakeholder providers offer investment funds with some form of ethical or SRI investment process. SIPPs offer access to lots of these funds. These funds screen out funds that do not meet certain set criteria, and aim to generate good returns from progressive companies.

Trustees of occupational pension funds are required to spell out the extent to which, if at all, they take ethical, social and environmental factors into account when instructing investment managers on behalf of pension members. This is included in the 'Statement of Investment Principles'. They are not obliged to include any ethical screening, although many do so.

Types of approach to ethical/SRI investment

- *Negative screening* The most common form of ethical or SRI funds operate negative screening. This means they exclude companies that engage in certain activities, for example, producing tobacco.
- *Positive screening* These funds invest in companies that are actively promoting responsible business practices, products or services. This could be through adopting sustainable environmental principles, local community involvement or ethically monitored supply chains. This process can include oil, airlines and mining companies, provided they adopt the practices set by the fund, so read the fund factsheets to make sure you are happy with what you are investing in. Certain oil companies could be excluded, on the other hand, if their activities take place in countries where human rights issues have been raised.

■ *Dialogue and engagement* Fund managers will invest in companies that will take steps to adopt more responsible business standards for example in relation to climate change and transparency of trading practices. As with positive screening, this can lead to companies that some people may not consider ethical or socially responsible being accepted within the fund.

The stronger the ethical or SRI principles, the more of the market is excluded. These funds can end up investing in small and medium-sized companies and, as a result, can have a higher level of volatility.

You can contact an IFA who is expert in ethical and SRI investment issues at www.ethicalinvestment.org.uk

State pension provision

10

State pension

What topics are covered in this chapter?

- State pension: what will I get?
- State second pension
- Delaying state pension
- Inheriting state pension

The UK has one of the lowest state pensions in the developed world. It may come as no great surprise to learn that an average earner in continental Europe can expect to retire on a state pension of almost double that of their UK counterpart. Lord Turner's 2004 Pension Commission report found that workers in France, Germany and Italy typically retire on 70 per cent of salary. In the UK the average is just 37 per cent. Perhaps even more surprising is the fact that the UK system is even less generous than the US system. Americans receive 45 per cent of average earnings from the state pension system.

UK state pension is made up of the basic state pension and the state second pension, formerly SERPS.

Basic state pension has dwindled since 1980 when the Thatcher Government stopped increasing it in line with average earnings, and instead giving annual increases in line with the lower Retail Price Index. This is due to be reversed during the next parliament, no later than 2016, but that will simply stop the disparity between pensioners' and workers' incomes growing, without redressing the gulf between the two groups. At £95.25 a week for a single person for 2009/2010, it represents a fraction of what most people expect to live off.

But a state pension that is inexpensive to the Treasury has been a policy goal of successive governments of both right and left, and since 1997 the Labour Party has done little to increase in real terms the amount of basic state pension that is paid. In 1979 the basic state pension stood at 26 per cent of average earnings. By 2007 it had fallen to 16 per cent.

In 2007 the UK government spent just 6.6 per cent of GDP on state pensions, including basic and secondary pensions and means-tested Pension Credit. This is considerably less than half the figure spent in France, Italy and Austria. This peculiarly Anglo-Saxon approach to state pensions means the emphasis is on the individual to provide for their own retirement. (See Table 10.1.)

But just because state pension in the UK is not very generous, it doesn't mean it is worth ignoring.

Table 10.1: State expenditure on pensions, as proportion of GDP, as at 2007

Austria	12.8%
Belgium	10.0%
France	13.0%
Germany	10.4%
Italy	14.0%
Spain	8.4%
UK	6.6%
EU-27	10.1%

Source: Working Group of the European Commission Expenditure Ageing Report, © European Communities 2009, http://ec.europa.eu/economy_finance/publications/publication14992_en.pdf

For women in particular, indeed anyone with a broken work record, building up full entitlement to state pension can be a very efficient use of retirement saving. Whether you have taken a career break to bring up children or have been abroad for significant periods of time, buying extra years' state pension credit can be extremely good value if you are in the position of being likely to fall short of full entitlement to state pension. This is more likely to be the case for those born in the 1960s and earlier, as the system has been made more generous in recent years.

For couples where one partner has traditionally been the one earning and the other not, topping up the non-earning partner's credits can also be great value where he or she does not have a full contribution record.

State pension is not, on its own, going to be enough to live off, but getting the maximum possible out of the system is one of the most affordable ways to build a solid foundation to your strategy for a decent retirement income.

History of state pension

The Old Age Pension was introduced in 1908 by then Chancellor of the Exchequer David Lloyd George. It was payable to those aged 70 and above, but drunkards, criminals and those who had refused work when able were barred from receiving it under a 'character test'. In 1908 the full pension was five shillings (25p) for a single person and seven shillings and sixpence (38p) for a married man. Adjusted for inflation, that adds up to £19.30 and £29 respectively. In 1908 only one in four people made it to age 70 and those who did lived for an average nine months longer.

Today, 84 per cent of people in the UK reach state pension age, and live on average for a further 24 years.

State pension: what will I get?

State pension comes in two parts – basic state pension and state second pension, which replaced SERPS (State Earnings Related Pension Scheme) in 2002. SERPS was introduced in 1978 and replaced an earlier second-tier state pension known as Graduated Retirement Benefit.

Nobody, not even the government, expects people to be able to live on the state pension in this country. The basic state pension, at £95.25 for a single person for the year 2009/2010, falls short of the minimum £130 a week the Government says a single person needs to live on.

State second pension will bring most people over that benefits threshold. But a significant minority who do not have full entitlement to state second pension will have their income topped up by the means-tested Pension Credit. Pension Credit is currently paid to around 2.7 million pensioner households, although around a third more people are eligible to receive it but do not claim.

State pension age

State pension is payable from your state pension age, which is currently 65 years for men. Women's state pension age is increasing from 60 to 65 between 2010 and 2020, rising by a year every two years. This graduated rise will affect women born between 6 April 1950 and 5 April 1955. Between 2024 and 2046 state pension age is increasing from 66 to 68 for both sexes. You can find out your state pension age online at www.pensionadvisoryservice.org.uk

Basic state pension: how it is calculated

Basic state pension is a flat-rate pension based on the number of years you have made National Insurance contributions or accrued credits because you have been looking after children or those with disabilities. Full basic state pension stands at £95.25 for a single person and £152.30 for a married couple or civil partnership for the year 2009/2010.

The more years you contribute, the more you get, but high earners and low earners working for the same number of years will get the same amount. The number of years' contributions needed for full basic state pension is being reduced from 6 April 2010. Men who reach state pension age before that date need 44 years' credits to qualify for full basic state pension. Women need 39 years' credits.

From 6 April 2010 onwards both men and women will only need 30 years' credits to get full basic state pension.

You need to have at least 10 years' credits by the time you reach state retirement age to get any basic state pension at all. You accrue entitlement to basic state pension if you pay Class 1 National Insurance contributions, which are paid by most people in work. The self-employed pay Class 2 and Class 4 National Insurance contributions but it is their Class 2 contributions that provide entitlement to basic state pension.

You can also be credited with contributions if you are incapable of work because of illness or disability, or if you are receiving Carer's Allowance, Working Tax Credit, Statutory Maternity Pay, Statutory Adoption or Child Benefit for a child under 12. You also get credits for basic state pension if you are unemployed and actively seeking work. These are credited to you automatically through the benefits system so there is no need to claim them.

Buying back extra years' basic state pension

As many as 70 per cent of women and 15 per cent of men do not qualify for full basic state pension. By topping up their entitlement to basic state pension they can effectively buy pensions worth thousands of pounds for a fraction of their market price.

> As many as 70 per cent of women and 15 per cent of men do not qualify for full basic state pension

Women who gave up work in the 1970s to look after children have most to gain from buying back extra years. This is because the system of giving credits for those in receipt of Child Benefit was not introduced until 1978. But people of both sexes with broken National Insurance contribution records, whether from periods out of the workforce for some reason or as a result of living abroad, can profit from buying back extra years. These credits are known as Class 3 National Insurance contributions.

Spouses or unmarried partners who have not had children and who have never worked because their partner is wealthy and has been able to provide for both of them can also buy back extra years. In these situations the spouse or partner who is earning the money will normally have considerable pension income of their own, and will be taxed on it in retirement. By buying added years of state pension for the other spouse or partner, the couple can not only get retirement income at bargain prices compared to what they would have to pay an insurance company for an annuity, but the state pension would be received tax-free provided the non-earning spouse or partner had no other income.

In the most extreme cases, buying extra years' pension credits can give you a return on investment of 5,700 per cent. This is because of the 'cliff edge' created by the fact that you need a minimum of 10 qualifying years of National Insurance contributions before you get any basic state pension at all. Once you hit the 10-year threshold, you are entitled to a pension of 26 per cent of the full basic state pension, but if you only have 9, you don't get any at all. For 2009/2010 someone with 10 qualifying years' credits would get a pension of £24.76 a week.

Buying one extra year would cost £626.60, but would be the difference between nothing and a pension of £24.74 a week, or £1,286 a year for life. To buy an annuity paying £1,286 a year would cost a woman aged 60 as much as £36,270 – which is not a bad return for an initial outlay of just £626.60.

Of course such a return on investment is not going to be possible for everybody. But buying extra years of state pension is still one of the best-value pension deals on the market, even if you are only increasing your contribution years on a one-for-one basis.

The cost of buying the same income provided by each extra year's state pension bought varies between £2,711.06 and £4,066.44, depending on the age you retire. At a cost of £626.60 per year, this still works out at a return of between 433 and 650 per cent.

Added years – what does it cost?

Cost of buying one added year of basic state pension (annual income of £128.65)	£626.60
Cost of buying equivalent income through an annuity	£2,711–£4,066 (depending on what your state retirement age is)

You can buy back up to a maximum of 6 years' missing National Insurance contributions from previous years, and you can make the contributions in the current year either as a one-off payment or by paying at the weekly rate of £12.05.

Paying the same sum into a personal pension would give you far less. A full 30 years' credits would give a full basic state pension of £95.25 a week, or £4,953 a year, which would cost more than £138,000 to buy with an annuity in 2009. Contributing £12.05 a week for 30 years into a personal pension would only build up a fund of £41,382 adjusted for inflation, a third the cost of buying the state pension income, assuming an annual return of 7 per cent and charges of 1 per cent.

Should I buy extra years?

Buy extra years' basic state pension if …

■ You will not have accrued 30 years' basic state pension contributions by the time you reach state pension age, provided you can build up at least 10 years' entitlement by then.

Don't buy extra years' basic state pension if …

■ You do not have time to buy 10 qualifying years by the time you reach state retirement age. You can only buy an additional 6 qualifying years at one time.

■ You are on course to accrue 30 qualifying years by the time you retire (including years of credit when looking after children or caring for sick and elderly relatives).

■ You will be entitled to State Pension Credit in retirement because your income is low.

■ You are married or widowed and pay reduced National Insurance, also known as the 'small stamp' or 'married women's stamp'.

How can I find out how much state pension I have already accrued?

Get a pension forecast by completing form BR19 at the Pension Service website (www.pensionservice.gov.uk) or by contacting the State Pension Forecasting Team inquiry line on 0845 3000 168.

State second pension

State second pension is an earnings-related income paid in addition to basic state pension. The amount you get depends on your earnings and National Insurance contributions paid during your working life. It was introduced by the Labour Government in 2002 with the aim of giving more additional pension to low and moderate earners and also to carers and people with long-term disabilities. It replaced SERPS (State Earnings Related Pension Scheme).

More than 21 million people are accruing state second pension, making up 59 per cent of the working age population. You will not be accruing state second pension if you are self-employed or if you contracted out through your employer's company pension scheme or into a personal pension. Employees who earn more than a certain amount, called the lower earnings limit (£95 for 2009/2010), are entitled to state second pension provided they pay standard-rate Class 1 National Insurance contributions.

A high earner retiring 25 years from now could expect to receive around £92 a week or £4,784 a year in today's money, from state second pension and SERPS, which are known together as additional pension.

To put that into perspective, when compared with some of the apparently sizeable funds people have built up by contracting out of state second pension and SERPS, you would need a fund of over £95,000 to buy an annuity offering a comparable income from an insurance company.

Unlike basic state pensions, there is no cap to the number of years you can accrue state second pension – you get a year of accrual to state second pension for each year worked or credited, which means you can accrue from age 16 to state pension age.

Changes to state second pension

Fundamental changes to state second pension are being introduced in 2012. State second pension will gradually cease to be earnings related, which means low and moderate earners will get more but higher earners' will get less. By 2030 everyone will accrue state second pension at the same rate, regardless of how much they earn. The decline in higher earners state second pension will start to be felt by those retiring around 2035. Someone on £40,000 a year or more would expect to get a pension of £75 a week if they reach state pension age in 2050, compared to £90 a week in 2035.

The government argues that this change is one part of a package of measures and that the reduction in state second pension suffered by higher earners will be more than made up for by the increase in basic state pension that higher earners will get as a result of the reintroduction of inflation increases that are linked to earnings rather than prices.

Abolition of contracting out

Another significant change in state pension provision is that contracting out into personal pensions is being abolished at some point in the future, although the government has yet to confirm exactly when this will be. However, this change will not affect occupational money purchase or final salary schemes. If your employer offers an occupational money purchase scheme that currently receives your National Insurance contributions, it will be able to continue to do so. Members of such schemes will continue to fail to accrue state second pension.

How much state second pension and other additional pension will I get?

People reaching state pension age in 2010, who have been employed most of their working life:

Low earner on £14,200	£2,392 a year
Medium earner on £25,800	£4,732 a year
High earner on £42,000 or more	£7,956 a year

People reaching state pension age in 2025, who have been employed most of their working life:

Low earner on £14,200	£2,444 a year
Medium earner on £25,800	£3,900 a year
High earner on £42,000 or more	£5,564 a year

People reaching state pension age in 2035, who have been employed most of their working life:

Low earner on £14,200	£2,860 a year
Medium earner on £25,800	£3,848 a year
High earner on £42,000 or more	£4,784 a year

People reaching state pension age in 2050, who have been employed most of their working life:

Low earner on £14,200	£3,380 a year
Medium earner on £25,800	£3,848 a year
High earner on £42,000 or more	£4,160 a year

Source: Data provided by the Department for Work and Pensions

Delaying state pension

You can increase the amount of pension you receive by deferring the date you receive it until after your state pension age.

For many, the idea of putting off receiving a pension they have paid into for perhaps 45 years may seem unappealing. But for the growing group of people with insufficient private pension savings who face having to work well past 65, deferring state pension, both basic and state second pension, can be a very good deal.

Department for Work and Pensions figures released in 2008 showed that 11 per cent of people over state retirement age are either having to or choosing to work after state retirement age. More than 1.2 million people are now working past their state retirement age. The effect on women is particularly severe, with 800,000 working after the age of 60, up more than 9 per cent between 2007 and 2008. And with the collapse in financial markets that has taken place since then, experts are predicting that figure to rise even higher.

If you have other income to live off, choosing to defer state pension is an efficient way to save for the future. You can choose whether you receive the additional money as increased pension income, or, if you defer for at least a year, you can take it as a lump sum. You can defer both basic state pension and state second pension.

Deferred state pension: increased income option

State pension is increased by 1 per cent for every five weeks you put off claiming. You can put off claiming for as many years as you want. For example, someone entitled to a weekly state pension of £100 who puts off claiming their pension for two years would get at least £120.80 for the rest of his or her life in today's terms. Delay it for five years and it grows to £152 a week. In reality the amount will be even more because the state pension will go up each year during the period to reflect inflation. This equates to an increase of around 10.4 per cent of pension, paid for the rest of your life, for every year you delay drawing it.

This is a better uplift than you would get by delaying the purchase of an annuity with a personal pension, which would increase your income by about 8 per cent if you waited from 65 to 66. Delaying annuity purchase is generally a good idea if you have got other income to live off and you do not expect to have an exceptionally short lifespan, because the extra you receive to reflect your shortened life expectancy soon overtakes the amount you have forgone.

However, this effect is even more pronounced when you defer state pension, where it takes just six and a half years before the amount you have forgone has been recouped. Given the fact that men aged 65 today are expected to live for a further 20.8 years, for most of those who can afford to do so, deferring state pension is a good deal. Women of 65 are expected to survive a further 23.3 years on average. And that life expectancy of 85.8 years for men today is an average for the entire population. Non-smokers and those leading healthy lifestyles can expect to live even longer, thereby recouping even more benefit by deferring their state pension in return for a higher starting income.

The same can also be said of those who have saved in pensions and buy annuities, as they are generally wealthier and have tended to lead healthier lifestyles than those who have not. The life expectancy among males buying annuities is four years longer than the average for the population as a whole. For this group of people, deferring state pension by a full five years could pay dividends in the order of an income more than 50 per cent higher over two decades.

> The life expectancy among males buying annuities is four years longer than the average for the population as a whole

To put into perspective just how valuable boosting your income by delaying state pension actually is, it is worth considering how much someone with combined basic and state second pension of £200 a week would have to put away to duplicate the same income. By deferring for five years, an extra £104 a week would be achieved, making an annual pension of £5,408. To buy an equivalent income through an annuity would cost a 70-year-old male £98,000 and a 65-year-old female £114,000. (The reason this costs more for women is because they are expected to live longer).

The downside is of course that you might drop dead the day before you start claiming, or within the six and a half years it takes to recoup the pension that you have forgone. If this happens, not only have you lost the enjoyment of the money, but you will also be unable to pass anything on to your family or friends through a will. This is not the case for somebody deferring buying an annuity with a personal pension, as this can be passed on to beneficiaries.

Deferred state pension: lump sum option

Instead of increasing your annual pension income, you can opt to defer your state pension and receive a cash lump sum. The lump sum you receive equals the pension you would have received plus a return of 2 per cent above the Bank of England base rate.

Waiting a year can make sense if you are planning to retire mid-way through a tax year, particularly if you are a higher rate taxpayer. By deferring your pension income you can pay tax on it at a lower rate and take advantage of the higher rate of return.

Extra income or lump sum: which is best?

If you can afford to defer taking your state pension then you need to choose whether a one-off lump sum or an increased pension income for life best suits your circumstances.

If you receive extra pension income it will be treated like any other income for the purposes of calculating Pension Credit. But if you choose a lump sum, it is ignored for the purposes of calculating Pension Credit, Council Tax Benefit or Housing Benefit.

Extra state pension incurs income tax in the same way as any other income. Lump sums also attract income tax at your marginal rate, but you only pay it at the rate of your other income. In other words, you will not be pushed into a higher tax bracket on account of receiving the lump sum.

Inheriting state pension

Surviving spouses and civil partners can inherit some of the state pension – whether basic state pension, state second pension or SERPS – that their deceased partner was entitled to. However, because the government has a long-term policy objective of moving away from a historic reliance of wives on their husbands' pensions, the proportion that you are entitled to claim can depend on a number of factors.

Basic state pension

A widow can claim the basic state pension her husband was entitled to at the time of death, based on his National Insurance record. If she is entitled to basic state pension of her own, the total cannot exceed the maximum for an individual (£95.25 in 2009/2010).

A widower or civil partner can claim a basic pension equal to their spouse or partner's entitlement only if the deceased is also over state pension age at the time of death. If the deceased dies before their state pension age, a widower or civil partner cannot claim a pension in respect of them unless they reach state pension age on or after 6 April 2010. They may, however, be able to substitute periods from the deceased's National Insurance record for theirs if this would increase their entitlement.

Additional state pension (SERPS and state second pension)

The maximum amount of additional state pension that any person may receive (through a combination of both their own additional pension and any inherited additional pension) is £154.70 a week in the 2009/2010 tax year. This applies to both SERPS and state second pension or a combination of both.

The amount of additional state pension you are entitled to inherit from a spouse or civil partner depends on whether it is SERPS or state second pension.

SERPS

It is possible to inherit the SERPS pension of your spouse or civil partner after they die. The government has a long-term policy objective of reducing from 100 per cent to 50 per cent the amount of SERPS that can be passed on. This means the proportion of SERPS that you are entitled to inherit depends on when you were born, the year you reached state pension age and your sex.

But the total amount of additional SERPS you can inherit is capped at a total combined personal and inherited SERPS level, which stood at £151.10 in 2008/2009. If your SERPS income would have been taken over this level because of extra SERPS inherited from a spouse or civil partner then it is reduced to this cap. The deceased had to have been old enough to be entitled to claim at the time of death for a spouse or civil partner to benefit. (See Table 10.2 and 10.3.)

Table 10.2: The maximum proportion of SERPS entitlement that a man's wife or civil partner can inherit

Man's date of birth	Maximum inheritable SERPS
5 October 1937 or before	100%
Between 6 October 1937 and 5 October 1939	90%

▶

Table 10.2: The maximum proportion of SERPS entitlement that a man's wife or civil partner can inherit *continued*

Man's date of birth	Maximum inheritable SERPS
Between 6 October 1939 and 5 October 1941	80%
Between 6 October 1941 and 5 October 1943	70%
Between 6 October 1943 and 5 October 1945	60%
6 October 1945 or after	50%

Table 10.3: The maximum proportion of SERPS entitlement that a woman's husband or civil partner can inherit

Woman's date of birth	Maximum inheritable SERPS
5 October 1942 or before	100%
Between 6 October 1942 and 5 October 1944	90%
Between 6 October 1944 and 5 October 1946	80%
Between 6 October 1946 and 5 October 1948	70%
Between 6 October 1948 And 5 July 1950	60%
6 July 1950 or after	50%

Inheriting state second pension

The rules for inheriting state second pension are straightforward. There is a flat 50 per cent entitlement to a spouse or civil partner's state second pension, and there is no cap on the combined amount of personal and inherited state second pension you can receive. As with SERPS, the deceased had to have been old enough to be entitled to claim at the time of death for a spouse or civil partner to benefit.

Under these provisions, the surviving member of a professional married couple who both received £4,680 in state second pension could expect to receive a further £2,340 on becoming widowed, bringing their individual state second pension up to £7,020. To buy a pension with an equivalent spouse's benefit at the age of 65 on the open market today would add around £20,000 to the cost of a pension.

In extreme cases it is possible that marriage or civil partnership could be the difference between as much as £7,000 a year extra. If one partner has less than 10 years' National Insurance contributions, perhaps through having brought up children in the 1970s and then spent many years working part time below the contribution threshold, marriage or civil partnership would entitle them to a full basic state pension of £95.25 a week, or £4,953 a year, based on their partner's contributions. If the deceased also received in excess of £4,000 in state second pension, a surviving spouse or civil partner would be entitled to 50 per cent of that on top, making a combined income approaching £7,000.

People living together who are not married or in civil partnerships cannot inherit their partner's state second or SERPS pension, even if they have been living together for decades and had children together. For people in this situation who have no principled objection to getting married, entitlement to extra secondary pension is a genuine financial incentive to doing so.

11

Pension Credit and means-testing

What topics are covered in this chapter?

- Extra money for lower income pensioners
- How Pension Credit works
- Pension Credit, means-testing and the disincentive to save
- Pension Credit, means-testing and Personal Accounts

Extra money for lower income pensioners

Pension Credit is a means-tested benefit paid to people over the age of 60 whose income falls below a certain minimum. Most of us hope not to have to rely on state benefits in retirement, but today more than 40 per cent of pensioners are eligible to receive Pension Credit. Pension Credit increases each year in line with wage inflation, while the state pension only increases in line with prices, which means that more people are entitled to claim the benefit every year.

If you have a decent pension then Pension Credit and other benefits will not be relevant to you personally, but you may have elderly relatives who are entitled to the extra income it offers but who are not receiving it. However, eligibility for Pension Credit and other state benefits in retirement is not limited to those on low earnings in retirement. Because of the collapse in workplace pension provision, there are many middle-class people in work today who could be on benefits in retirement.

While the prospect of living on benefits may not be an attractive one, for some people who have left it until their fifties to start saving for their retirement, it could be a reality. For this group it is important to consider whether pensions are the best vehicle for long-term saving. To find out whether it pays to save, or whether you or your relatives are entitled to extra income in retirement, you first of all need to understand Pension Credit.

How Pension Credit works

There are two elements to the benefit: the Guarantee Credit and the Savings Credit. The Guarantee Credit provides a minimum floor below which older people's income should not fall, whether they have saved during their working life or not. However, they only get this guaranteed minimum income if they actually claim. The Savings Credit is a mechanism that gives more Pension Credit to those who have saved during their working life, but have not built up enough pension to take them off means-tested benefits. Some pensioners may receive both.

1 *Guarantee Credit* tops up the income of the less well off to a guaranteed level of £130 a week for single people and £198.45 for couples.

2 *Savings Credit* rewards pensioners over the age of 65 who have saved for their retirement with up to £20.40 a week for single people and £27.03 for couples. You do not have to receive the Guarantee Credit to receive Savings Credit.

Guarantee Credit

The way the Guarantee Credit is calculated is straightforward. If your relevant income in retirement is less than the Guarantee Credit of £130 for a single person in 2009/2010 and £198.45 for couples, then your income is automatically topped up to match it.

Weekly income after tax is calculated by adding up:

■ state, work and personal pensions

■ some benefits

■ any earnings from work.

Not included in the calculation are:

■ Housing Benefit

■ Council Tax Benefit

■ Disability Living Allowance

■ Attendance Allowance.

Savings and investments above £10,000 count towards income, with £1 a week income being added on for each £500 of eligible savings you have. For example, somebody with £8,000 of savings, whether in bank accounts, ISAs, PEPs or premium bonds, would be considered as having a further £4 a week income.

There are certain circumstances, such as for people with disabilities or those with housing costs, where Pension Credit can be higher than the standard levels.

Savings Credit

Savings Credit is designed to give more Pension Credit to those pensioners who have at least put away some money for their retirement than to those who have saved nothing throughout their lives. It pays 60p in the pound on savings between the level of the full basic state pension and the Guarantee Credit threshold. So in 2009, when the basic state pension is £95.25, somebody who has a combination of state pension and private income totalling £105.25 will be £10 above the threshold and therefore entitled to £6 a week Savings Credit.

Savings Credit ceases to be paid if your income is more than £181 a week (over £9,000 a year) for a single person or £266 a week (around £13,800 a year) for a couple. If your income is below these levels you are likely to be entitled to Savings Credit. For people with certain housing costs such as high service charges or mortgage payments and those entitled to extra income because of disability, the figure can be higher. Unlike Guarantee Credit, which is paid from age 60, Savings Credit is only paid from age 65.

Example

Jean is 64 and lives alone. Her state pension is £90 a week and she has a further £20 from an occupational pension. Her total income is therefore £110, so she is entitled to Guarantee Credit of £20 a week to bring her up to the £130 threshold. She is not entitled to any Savings Credit because she is under 65.

When she turns 65 she will also be entitled to Savings Credit because her personal income is £14.75 higher than the rate of full basic state pension of £95.25. This means she is entitled to Savings Credit of £8.85 (60 per cent of £14.75) plus Guarantee Credit of £20, making a total Pension Credit entitlement of £28.85 a week.

Pension Credit: key facts

- You can get Pension Credit provided you are over 60. It does not matter if your partner is not over 60.
- The starting age for receiving Pension Credit is rising in line with the state retirement age for women, which is increasing from 60 in 2010 to 65 by 2020.
- Pension Credit is not paid automatically. You have to make a claim to receive it.
- The definition of a couple for the purposes of Pension Credit is a husband and wife, civil partnership or people who live together as though they are married or in a civil partnership.
- You can backdate a claim for Pension Credit by up to three months.
- If you get Pension Credit you may also be able to get Housing Benefit and Council Tax Benefit.

How to apply for pension credit

- By telephone on 0800 99 1234.
- By filling in a form you can download at www.thepensionservice.gov.uk.

The Pension Service website has a Pension Credit calculator that will quickly work out how much extra income you are entitled to. However, a formal application is required, either on the telephone or in writing, to actually claim.

Poor take-up of Pension Credit: are your relatives affected?

Take-up of Pension Credit among the elderly is low. The most recent Department for Work and Pensions research into the issue in 2007 found that somewhere between 33 and 41 per cent of pensioners are not claiming Pension Credit that they are entitled to. Pensioner groups say this is as a result of complexity and confusion over the process, lack of awareness of what is available, resistance to receiving 'handouts from the state' and a dislike of filling in forms.

Yet the benefit of claiming can be huge. Somebody with full entitlement to basic state pension of £95.25 in 2009/2010 but no other pension savings would see their income uplifted by £34.75 a week or £1,807 a year. The cost of buying such an income from age 60 through an annuity is at least £44,000. Given that 70 per cent of women and 15 per cent of men do not even qualify for full basic state pension, some pensioners will be forgoing even more than this.

Pensions charities urge friends and relatives of elderly people who may be entitled to Pension Credit to help them make a claim and persuade them that there is nothing wrong with taking money from the state.

Pension Credit, means-testing and the disincentive to save

Pension Credit was introduced by the Labour Government to tackle poverty among pensioners. Rather than take the costly option of increasing basic state pension for all pensions, it opted to increase the income of those on low incomes. But the policy has been criticised for extending the scope of means-testing, which in turn has increased the number of people for whom it may not pay to save in pensions. Lord Turner's Pension Commission report of 2005 calculated that 40 per cent of today's pensioners are entitled to means-tested benefits, principally Pension Credit.

The problem stems from the fact that the basic state pension, which is the only personal retirement income many people in the UK have, is simply so low that it is less than the amount the government says is sufficient to live on.

Pension Credit tops up the income of all pensioners to the level of the full basic state pension, and rewards those with modest savings above that level at a rate of 60 per cent. But this means that if somebody saves in a pension that pays out £1 of income above the basic state pension, they are only 60p better off than the person who did not save at all. Many people see this as a 40 per cent tax on pension saving. Financial advisers are loath to recommend saving in a pension if an individual's circumstances mean this will be the likely outcome.

But this disincentive to save already existed under the Minimum Income Guarantee, which was the policy that Pension Credit replaced. Supporters of the Pension Credit policy argue that the Minimum Income Guarantee in fact created an even more pernicious disincentive to save. Under the Minimum Income Guarantee, which stood at £102.20 a week in 2003 when Pension Credit replaced it, many pensioners who actually made the effort of saving lost 100p in the pound of their savings above the full basic state pension rate. Back then, basic state pension was £77.45 a week. Somebody with full basic state pension who had made the effort to put away £20,000 in a personal pension could have got an annuity income of around £20 a week, giving a total income of £97.45. But despite saving, this pensioner would have been no better off than the person who had never saved a penny. Both got their income topped up to the Minimum Income Guarantee of £102.20 a week (in 2003).

Pension Credit introduced at least some level of reward for those who made the effort to save, giving them 60 per cent of their saved income between the thresholds. In the above example, the person who saved would have got an extra £12 a week Savings Credit, giving them a total income of £114.20 a week. But the introduction of Pension Credit also extended the group of people caught in the means-testing net, reducing incentives for those on slightly higher incomes. Policy-makers call the proportion of pension lost through means-testing 'the withdrawal rate'.

> Pension Credit introduced at least some level of reward for those who made the effort to save

In the words of Lord Turner's 2005 Pension Commission report:

> *As a result of the introduction of Pension Credit ... a smaller proportion of pensioners face very high withdrawal rates, but 40 per cent of all pensioners face combined tax and benefit withdrawal rates of over 50 per cent ... . Compared with the Minimum Income Guarantee, the Pension Credit improves incentives for some people but worsens them for others.*

So what should I do?

This may sound like an academic argument on the subject of state benefits, but with 40 per cent of people retiring being eligible for state help, the question of whether it pays to save is a genuine one, particularly for those starting to save late in life. The issue will gain increased focus in 2012 with the introduction of Personal Accounts and auto-enrolment, the government's policy of forcing every employee in the land to join a pension scheme.

How much do I need to avoid the benefits system?

£43,789 – the pension pot the average person needs to avoid being below the threshold for state benefits

£91,191 – the pension pot the average self-employed person needs to avoid being below the threshold for state benefits

Source: Hargreaves Lansdown

The gulf between the basic state pension and the upper threshold for Pension Credit is so great that a substantial pension is needed before you rise above the benefits system. People relying on money purchase pensions alone may be surprised at how much they need to put away.

The average combined basic and state second pension in 2008 stood at around £140 a week for a single person. Because the upper limit for entitlement to the Savings Credit element of Pension Credit is £181 a week, an average saver needs to be able to buy an annuity paying more than £40 a week before they reach that level.

The average employee therefore needs to have built up a pension pot of over £43,000 by the age of 65 to avoid being below the threshold for state benefits in retirement, according to research carried out by Hargreaves Lansdown, in 2008.

For the self-employed, who do not accrue state second pension because they do not pay Class 3 National Insurance contributions, the figure is even higher. They need more than £91,000 to break through the means-testing barrier. To put this into context, the average pension pot in the UK is around £30,000, although some people have final salary pensions as well. Not many people are self-employed through their entire working life, but even one or two decades working on a self-employed basis will be enough to put a dent in your state second pension.

> Not many people are self-employed through their entire working life

The Pensions Policy Institute says these amounts are only enough to keep today's 65-year-olds off benefits. An even bigger sum is needed to remain off benefits throughout retirement. This is because state pension is currently indexed to prices, and most annuities do not have any inflation protection at all. The threshold for benefits, on the other hand, goes up in line with wage inflation.

So should I give up on pension saving altogether?

On seeing such big figures, this is not an unreasonable question. But to actively decide not to save in a pension is a huge step for any individual to take. Doing so on the basis that the incentive to do so is not great enough because of means-testing involves accepting that you will live out your retirement on state benefits.

There are all sorts of risks in taking this view. One of the most significant is the attitude of future governments to means-tested benefits for the elderly. There is no certainty that the means-tested benefits for the elderly that are here today will be here in 20 or 30 years' time. On the other hand, with older people far more likely to vote than the young, it would be a very brave government that made radical reductions to the proportion of national earnings that the poorest pensioners receive.

If you are one of the millions of people for whom the effect of means-testing amounts to a potential loss of 40p in the pound, what are your alternatives? When you are in your seventies and eighties, 60p in the pound is better than nothing.

People asking themselves whether saving is a good idea if they are losing 40p in the pound should also remember that in all cases they will have got at least 20 per cent tax relief on their contributions, and possibly 40 per cent, and may be paying no or lower income tax in retirement.

Furthermore, if an employer is contributing to the pension scheme then the disincentive may be completely cancelled out. In addition, it should be noted that tax-free cash falls outside the Pension Credit calculation, so a quarter of the individual's saving is not affected at all.

Another consideration is the fact that small pensions, of 1 per cent of the lifetime allowance for pension saving (see page 47), can be withdrawn as a cash lump sum, rather than as income. The maximum size allowed for a small pension to be withdrawn as cash for the 2009/2010 tax year is £17,500.

There are also risks in saving. Once the money is paid in, it is tied up until retirement and three-quarters of it must be taken as an income. Even if you have runaway debts you cannot access the cash until you take a pension from it. Furthermore, as you are likely to be saving in a money purchase arrangement, there is no certainty about the returns that you will get or the annuity rates that will be available when you retire.

Factor in the complexity of the benefits and pensions systems and individuals' personal circumstances and it is obvious that there are no one-size-fits-all answers. Deciding whether pensions are the best home for your money will depend on a number of factors – see the checklist box.

Checklist – factors affecting the incentive to save in pensions

Why it could pay to save in a pension:

■ *Tax relief on contributions* Everyone will receive 20 per cent tax relief on the contributions they make. Higher rate taxpayers will receive 40 per cent relief (unless earning more than £150,000 a year).

■ *Tax-free cash* A quarter of your fund is paid out to you as a tax-free lump sum, making a disincentive of 40p in the pound effectively one of 30p in the pound.

■ *Employer contributions* If the contributions you make are matched by your employer then this, combined with tax relief, can wipe out completely any disincentive to save.

■ *Small pensions* If your pension pot does not exceed the £17,500 (in 2009/2010) threshold for small pensions, you can receive the entire sum back, 25 per cent of it tax free.

■ *Ownership of your own pension* Nobody knows what future governments' pensions policy and attitude to means-tested benefits will be.

■ *What else can you do?* Even if you do not get back all you put in, you have got to save somewhere, and money saved in bank accounts, ISAs and other savings products is included within the calculation for your entitlement to Pension Credit.

And why it could not:

■ *You may be little or no better off* You may have so much to save before you will even start to get credit for your savings that it is not worth doing so. You may be better off enjoying spending it while you are working.

■ *Your money may be more efficiently spent elsewhere* If you have credit card and hire purchase debts, for example, you are often better off clearing them with the money you would have used to pay into a pension.

■ *Tax* Although you get tax relief on the contributions you make into your pension, you also get taxed on the income you receive from your pension.

■ *Other benefits* Your entitlement to other benefits such as Council Tax Benefit and Housing Benefit could be affected by saving. You also may have a higher Pension Credit threshold if you are paying a mortgage or service charge costs or if you are disabled.

■ *Investment risk* If you pay into a personal pension there is no guarantee that the investments within your plan will go up and not down. You may not achieve the growth that the people selling you the plan project.

■ *Annuity risk* By the time you come to retire, annuity rates may have gone down, meaning you will not get as much pension income for your pot as you could have done today.

Does it pay to save?

People who could lose out through means-testing generally fall into two groups: those with total income including private income above the level of the full basic state pension who could 'lose' 40p in the pound through the Savings Credit, and those whose total income is below it who could 'lose' 100p in the pound. For those in the former group, pension savings will be more likely to be worthwhile. For those in the latter group, there is a greater chance that money that could be paid into a pension could be used more effectively, such as for clearing debt.

However, it is worth re-emphasising that the concept of 'losing' 40p or 100p in the pound is an oversimplification of the situation. As the check-list box demonstrates, there are numerous factors that can make the disincentive more or less than 40p or 100p in the pound.

Examples

Example 1: Loses 40p in the pound?

David is 55 and earns £30,000. He is on course to receive combined basic and state second pension of £125 when he retires at 65. He has final salary pension entitlement that will boost his income by a further £30 a week, but he still needs another £26 a week to take him above the upper limit for Pension Credit. This means that, provided the benefit rules are the same in 10 years' time as they are today, he will need to build a pension of around £30,000 to reach the benefits threshold.

By saving 6 per cent of earnings, or £150 a month into a personal pension, he could expect to reach three-quarters of this target, a fund of £22,500 by the time he is 65. This will be enough to buy him an income through an annuity £14.62 a week, but the effect of the Savings Credit means he only gets £11.70 a week income for that extra saving. However, he will also be entitled to a tax-free lump sum of £5,625.

Example 2: Loses 100p in the pound

Frances is 55 and will reach state pension age in January 2018 in eight years time when she is nearly 64 (because the pension age for women is gradually rising to 65 between 2010 and 2020). She is currently earning £35,000 a year.

▶

Example *continued*

She brought up children through the 1970s and has been self-employed for much of her career when she finally returned to work. Both of these factors have contributed to a low projected combined basic and state second pension income of just £60 a week. She has no other pension income.

She needs to build a private pension income of £35.25 a week before she will receive any reward for saving at all. To buy an annuity that will get her income up to this level will cost her £46,290 and it will not increase her income by a penny. And if she wants to retire at her state retirement age of 64 she has only got six years to build it up.

Even if she puts away 12 per cent of earnings, totalling £350 a week, she can only expect to build up a fund of £43,330, and still will be no better off. If she puts in 12 per cent and her employer puts in 6 per cent, her fund could be expected to grow to £64,995. This would allow her to take a tax-free cash lump sum of £16,248 but then give her an additional private income of just £2 a week. The effect of the Savings Credit on this level of store would mean she ended up with £1.20 more income than if she hadn't bothered saving. Her £16,248 tax-free cash lump sum is dwarfed by the £33,600 pre-tax contributions she has made, without even taking into account the contributions made by her employer.

Example 3: More than recoups outlay

Philip is 55 and has spent much of his working life either working abroad or self-employed. He is now working for a company and earns £20,000 a year. Because of his broken National Insurance contribution record his basic state pension is projected to be just £70 a week when he retires in 10 years' time. He has no other pension.

He has only just started accruing state second pension and that is projected to boost his income by a further £10 a week. He therefore needs a fund that will boost his income by £15.25 a week just to get him to the £95.25 a week of the basic state pension, the threshold for the Savings Credit. Unless he can get over this figure, there is no point whatsoever in him saving for income in retirement. To get to the Savings Credit threshold he will need a fund of £23,469.

Philip has access to a stakeholder pension scheme through his employer. Under the terms of the scheme the employer offers to match employees' contributions up to a maximum of 4 per cent. Philip decides he can afford to pay 3 per cent of earnings into the scheme, a figure of £50 a month from gross earnings, which his employer matches. After 10 years his fund has grown to £15,000, well short of the £23,469 he needs to break past the Savings Credit and get at least some increased pension for the saving he has made. Buying an annuity with his fund will be a total waste of time. He will have lost 100p in the pound on the money he has saved and would have been better off enjoying the extra income while he was earning.

But because his pension pot is below the £17,500 small pensions threshold, he is allowed to take the entire sum in cash, without having to buy an annuity. He can take 25 per cent of the fund tax-free, while the remaining three-quarters will be treated as income and taxed at his marginal rate in the year of receipt. To get this £17,500 lump sum his contribution from gross salary is £3,000, being £2,400 from net pay. Even if his employer contributed nothing and he made the full 6 per cent contribution himself, his net outlay would only have been £4,800. However, he needs to bear in mind that if the £17,500 takes his savings above the £10,000 disregard, his Pension Credit will be reduced accordingly.

Pension Credit, means-testing and Personal Accounts

The effect of means-testing on pensions saving is likely to become a political hot potato in 2012 when around 10 million people are enrolled into company pension schemes for the very first time.

From 2012 employers will be required to enrol all staff, both existing and new joiners, into a company pension scheme that meets certain legal requirements. This process is called 'auto-enrolment', and is the centrepiece of a key government policy to increase the level of pension saving among UK workers. The policy is one of the proposals made by the Pension Commission, headed by Lord Turner, which delivered its final recommendations in 2006.

Employers must automatically enrol in a scheme that contributes at least 8 per cent of salary between a band of £5,035 and £33,540 a year at 2006/2007 earnings levels. Employees are expected to contribute 4 per cent, employers 3 per cent and the government adds an extra 1 per cent in tax relief.

Employers who do not currently offer a contributory company pension scheme have the option of arranging one with a life insurance company by the time the requirement becomes law. Those employers that choose not to will join Personal Accounts, a new form of low-cost government-backed pension scheme that is being established.

The reason this policy is so controversial is that employees will see 4 per cent of earnings deducted from payroll without their ever having agreed to it. Employees are allowed to opt out of the scheme, but they have to make an active decision to do so, and the government is hoping that at least 7 million will not opt out of Personal Accounts.

> Employees are allowed to opt out of the scheme, but they have to make an active decision to do so

If saving 4 per cent of income were mandatory then the policy would be perceived as a tax. Furthermore, some people with very low state pension entitlement have no chance of ever rising above the benefits threshold through private saving. By allowing people the option to leave the scheme if they want to, the government is able to claim that those who stay put are saving on a voluntary basis.

The policy is a classic example of 'nudge theory', the concept developed by two American academics, economist Richard Thaler and legal scholar Cass Sunstein. The idea is that government decides the best option for people, i.e. saving in a pension, and leaves the other options open to them.

Apathy plays a large part in the government's calculation of the numbers that will choose to stay put. Critics argue that some low earners who save in Personal Accounts or their company pension schemes after being automatically enrolled will never build up enough pension to actually get more out than they have put in. They will simply end up paying for benefits they would have received anyway, they argue. The government accepts this is the case for a fraction of those who sign up, but puts the figure at less than 5 per cent. Those affected are likely to be those closer to retirement.

Critics of the government's research, however, point out that these figures are based on a consistent 7 per cent a year return on the investment funds within these pensions. They say that the government's figures fail to reflect the possibility that investment markets may perform badly, as they have done in recent years.

The government, and supporters of automatic enrolment, argue that the vast majority of people will be better off as a result of the policy, receiving more than twice as much out of the system as they put in. Automatic enrolment, in conjunction with reforms to basic and state second pension, is also designed to reduce the level of means-testing in the future.

A 2009 report from the Department for Work and Pensions on the effects of the policies says that by 2050 the proportion of Gross Domestic Product to be spent on contributory benefits (basic state pension and additional pension – which includes state second pension and SERPS) is projected to rise from 5.3 per cent to 5.9 per cent, while the spend on pensioner income-related benefits is projected to fall from 1.1 per cent to 0.5 per cent as more people are lifted off income-related benefits by the more generous state pension and increased private pensions.

The pension reforms that are being introduced are designed to reduce the amount of means-testing over the long haul. They include increasing basic state pension in line with earnings, raising state second pension for low and middle earners and reducing the number of years needed to qualify for full basic pension. This will mean that in future virtually everyone will have full state benefits – around 95 per cent will receive basic state pension by 2025, according to the government.

Against a backdrop of higher average basic and state second pension, people who save in Personal Accounts or other company schemes should be less affected by means-testing in future, and likely to get out more than they put in. But it will take several decades to get to this position. As a very rough guide, people who are under 45 today are generally likely to be better off in retirement by saving in Personal Accounts or other pensions and get back considerably more than they paid in. For people over 45 today, the situation is less clear – almost everybody will be better off in retirement, but there will be some people, with very poor state pension contribution records and low incomes, for whom it is not certain they will get back as much as they put in.

12

Contracting out of the state pension system

What topics are covered in this chapter?

- How contracting out works
- Contracted-out occupational schemes
- Claiming compensation for incorrect advice to contract out

Contracting out of the state second pension, formerly SERPS, into a personal or occupational pension is a way of building up an independent pension of your own. For more than two decades opinion has swung back and forth as to whether it is better to be in or out of the second tier of state pension. The prevailing current view is that, in purely financial terms, staying in is in most cases the best bet. But you may want to continue being contracted out, or contract out for the first time, if for you the increased flexibility that doing so offers is more important to you than having a bigger pension in retirement.

How contracting out works

You are allowed to divert some of your and your employer's National Insurance contributions away from your state second pension into a pension of your own. One of the key potential benefits of doing so is that if the investments you select perform well you could get a pension that exceeds what you would have got from the state. But by contracting out you also take on board the risk that your investments will perform poorly, and that annuity rates will decline, both of which could leave you worse off. A report carried out for the FSA has found that the majority of people have ended up worse off as a result of contracting out.

Even if you end up worse off in purely monetary terms, there are still extra flexibilities to contracting out that can make it attractive to some people. Since April 2006 you have been allowed to take a quarter of your contracted out pot as a tax-free lump sum from age 55 (50 until April 2010).

You are also able to draw income from your contracted out pension from this age, and single people can bequeath a contracted-out pension pot to their heirs if they die before they start drawing benefits. None of these features are available with state second pension.

The ups and downs of contracting out

Contracting out was first introduced in 1978 for employees enrolled in occupational schemes. The National Insurance contributions paid over into these schemes are used to support the cost of offering more generous benefits.

In the following decade the Conservative Government wanted to encourage more people to take responsibility for their own retirement. To encourage this it extended contracting out to all employees, whether their employer offered a pension or not. From 1988 all employees were allowed to divert National Insurance contributions into plans called appropriate personal pensions. These are very like today's personal pension and stakeholder plans, but have certain restrictions on the way pension benefits can be taken.

Around 8 million people have contracted out at some point in the career, although less than 3 million remain outside the state scheme today.

To kick-start the policy the government offered employees who contracted out of the state system a rebate of 5.8 per cent of National Insurance contributions plus a sweetener of an extra 2 per cent on top. The theory was, that by investing this money in the stock market and then buying an annuity with the proceeds you could build a bigger pension than you would have got through the state.

In the early years this was what happened, and in the first five years after contracting out was rolled out to all employees, most people did well out of it. But the rebate was reviewed every five years and in 1993 was reduced to 4.8 per cent plus 1 per cent extra for those over 30. In April 2007 it fell so low that financial advisers and pension companies say most people should contract back in again.

The situation was made worse for those who contracted out by poorer investment returns on their money purchase pensions, and on increases in life expectancy that made pension annuities more expensive to buy. These factors created a situation where it became increasingly difficult to justify contracting out of the state system.

In 2005 the consumer group Which? published a scathing report into contracting out, claiming that 71 per cent of those who opted out of state second pension would be worse off as a result of having done so. That report argued that the average contracted-out pension will be 20 per cent less than state second pension.

Which? says that part of the reason for the shortfall was the charges taken out of the pension products that people transferred into. Its 2005, report calculated that, of the £35bn paid over by the government in National Insurance rebates, around £3bn had been paid to pension providers and financial advisers in charges.

The FSA was so concerned about contracting out that it commissioned an independent report into the matter from Oxford Actuaries and Consultants (OAC). That report, published in 2005, found an average reduction of £200 a year in the pensions of those who contracted out from 1988 to 2005. But some were much worse off. A 45-year-old man who was contracted out between 1988 and 2005 had a £33,600 shortfall on the fund he would need to buy the same income as offered through state second pension, leaving him £27.30 a week worse off – a fall in pension of 31 per cent.

In 2007 OAC published an update to its report, showing that a year later a market rebound had caused his shortfall to shrink to £14,300, or £12.63, amounting to a reduction of 14.5 per cent of his pension. These newer figures reflected a 21 per cent increase in pension fund returns in the time since the first report. But since then markets have fallen far below their 2005 level and the actual size of the shortfall will continue to go up and down with the stock market until individuals actually buy an annuity. This demonstrates the volatility to which anyone in a money purchase pension is exposed, particularly if they are invested in equities.

Contracting out became even less attractive from April 2007 when National Insurance rebates were restricted even more. For several years now pension providers have been writing to some or all of their contracted out clients, advising them to contract back into the state system. Because many of these letters will never be opened, let alone read or acted upon by apathetic customers, some providers have taken matters into their own hands. Pension companies such as Aviva, HSBC, Equitable Life, Pearl and NPI are so concerned at the reputational and regulatory risk of having thousands of customers lose out through remaining contracted out that they have taken the drastic step of automatically contracting all of their clients back in to the state system, unless they expressly state otherwise.

Can I get compensation if I have lost out?

In the wake of the OAC report into returns on contracted-out pension funds, the FSA conducted its own investigation to see whether advisers and pension providers who had recommended that consumers switch out of state second pension were guilty of misselling. That investigation, which was concluded later in 2007, found that there had been some instances of misselling but that they were not widespread. Of the 8 million approved personal pension plans sold, around 120,000, or 1.5 per cent, went ahead where the individual involved was above the age recommended for contracting out. The FSA concluded that many of these people must have been misadvised, but that some may have gone ahead on the basis that they valued the flexibility offered by contracting out.

Who is most likely to have lost out through contracting out?

Those most likely to suffer the greatest financial shortfalls are:

■ males aged over 45 and females aged over 40 at the time they contracted out
■ those who first contracted out in the period 1988/1989 to 1996/1997
■ those who have remained contracted out for periods in excess of five years.

Contracted-out occupational schemes

If your employer offers a contracted-out occupational scheme, whether a final salary arrangement or an occupational money purchase plan, you are usually better off by being a member of it. This is because almost all contracted-out occupational schemes include extra contributions from your employer, which means that your income in retirement will be greater.

The Pensions Advisory Service advises that employees in contracted-out money purchase schemes will be worse off in terms of their own contributions if they are aged 49 or older. But your employer's contributions will normally tip the balance in favour of joining or staying in the scheme.

If you have the chance to join a final salary scheme, the benefits on offer are normally so valuable that you should jump at the chance. But there is a caveat. If your employer goes bust before you retire and leaves the pension scheme with a substantial deficit, you may not get the pension you are entitled to. If the scheme is wound up and cannot pay all the benefits it has promised then you may have to claim compensation from the Pension Protection Fund (PPF). This generally gives you protection of 90 per cent of your pension entitlement up to a cap of £28,742.69 for the year 2009/2010. But this is only payable from age 65, even if your scheme has an earlier retirement date, and the inflation protection it gives is often less generous than the scheme you are leaving. Combining both these factors means that the benefits you get from the PPF work out at roughly 70 per cent of your original entitlement up to the cap, with no protection thereafter. See page 75 for a more detailed explanation of the PPF.

In reality only a tiny proportion of schemes have fallen on the PPF to date, and most scheme members who have done will get more out of the PPF than they will lose by not accruing state second pension. No financial adviser will tell you to turn down the chance of joining a final salary scheme.

You can take tax-free cash from contracted-out occupational schemes, subject to the scheme's rules, both money purchase and final salary, from age 55 (50 until April 2010), although most do not allow it. You could get round this by transferring to a personal pension, although if you did so while still employed by the sponsoring company you would be likely to miss out on future contributions.

'Protected rights'

The funds built up by contracting out are called protected rights

The funds built up by contracting out are called protected rights. There are certain restrictions on the way protected rights can be used because the government requires that they replicate many of the features that state second pension offers.

Protected rights can be held in personal pensions, stakeholder pensions and SIPPs but have to be ringfenced from other non-protected rights assets. If the pension plan holder is married or in a civil partnership then a 50 per cent survivor's benefit must be purchased when protected rights are used to buy an annuity. Furthermore, for occupational money purchase schemes that are contracted out, protected rights relating to contributions prior to 5 April 1997 must buy pension income that increases in line with RPI up to a maximum of 3 per cent. After that date protected-rights payments must increase in line with RPI up to a maximum of 5 per cent (known as Limited Price Indexation).

Contracting out via a personal pension

Q *How often should I review my decision whether to contract out?*

A Every year. The decision you make this year will not change the decisions you made in previous years as each year is treated on its own.

Q *Can I make extra contributions into an appropriate personal pension or stakeholder pension plan?*

A Yes. And you will get tax relief on your contributions.

Q *When do I have to make my election to opt out or back in again?*

A Make an election by the end of the tax year and that will affect your benefits for that tax year.

Q *I have heard that contracting out is to be abolished for defined contribution pension schemes. When is this happening?*

A The government has yet to decide this, but it will not be before 2012.

Q *How do I contract out?*

A Contact a pension provider that offers appropriate personal or stakeholder pensions. If you already have a pension, ask your existing provider as they may offer one.

Q *How do I contract back in to the state second pension?*

A Contact your pension provider or HM Revenue & Customs. They will send you form CA 1543, which you must complete and return.

Should I be in or out?

Whether you are currently in or out of the state scheme at present, the factors that determine what you should do this year and in future years are identical. (See Table 12.1.)

Deciding whether to contract out of state second pension or opt in will depend on the way you want to receive your benefits and your attitude to risk. In purely financial terms, contracting out today is finely balanced, but if you are over the age of 43 then most experts agree you are likely to be worse off by being contracted out. This is the case even taking into account the fact that you are allowed to take a quarter of your contracted-out pension pot as a tax-free lump sum, an option that is not available if you remain contracted in.

For people under 43, there is some chance you may be better off, but there is also a chance that you will be worse off. By contracting out you need to accept that you may end up with a lower income when you retire. If you are not prepared to take this risk you should contract back in again.

Table 12.1: The ins and outs of contracting out

	Contracted in	*Contracted out*
How much will I get?	The amount of state second pension you get depends on the level of contributions you have made and the level of pension that the government of the time says is payable. By remaining contracted in you bear the risk that a future government will change the way state second pension is paid, which could leave you with more or less than you are currently projected to receive.	Your contracting-out rebate, which is made up of part of your National Insurance contributions and some tax relief, is paid into an approved personal or stakeholder pension plan. You can invest your plan in a range of assets, including the stock market. The amount of pension you will get will depend on the rebates paid in, the performance of your investments, the charges taken out of your pension by the pension provider, and the annuity rates available at retirement. Your investments can go down as well as up. Similarly, annuity rates can go down as well as up. Both these factors could mean you end up with a smaller pension than the state second pension you would have got. If you are married or in a civil partner ship, you must buy an annuity that pays out 50 per cent of income to them if they are still alive after you die.

Table 12.1: The ins and outs of contracting out *continued*

	Contracted in	*Contracted out*
How can I take my pension?	You receive your state second pension at the same time as your basic state pension. This is payable at your state retirement age, which is 65 for men and 60 for women (rising to 65 by 2020). State retirement age for both sexes is rising to 68 by 2046. You can defer receipt of your state second pension, together with your basic state pension, to build up an enhanced income or lump sum (see page 159)	You must use at least 75 per cent of your fund to pay a pension income. You can start receiving this at age 50, rising to 55 from April 2010, but you cannot start later than your 75th birthday. Most people take income in the form of an annuity bought from a life insurance company. The level of income you get will depend on your age when you buy the annuity, your health and lifestyle factors such as whether you smoke. See Chapter 14 for how to get the most out of an annuity. You can also draw your tax-free cash and leave the rest of your pot invested in the stock market until age 75 through unsecured pension, also known as income drawdown.
What about tax-free lump sums?	There is no tax-free lump sum option if you remain contracted into state second pension. But if you defer state second pension and basic state pension you can take your additional benefit as a taxable lump sum.	You can take 25 per cent of your contracted-out fund as a tax-free lump sum from age 50, rising to 55 from April 2010.

▶

Table 12.1: The ins and outs of contracting out *continued*

	Contracted in	*Contracted out*
What happens to my contributions when I die?	If you are married or in a civil partnership, your spouse or civil partner may be entitled to half of the state second pension you have accrued whether you die before or after starting to receive benefits. If you are not married or in a civil partnership, your estate will not receive anything.	If you die before taking benefits and you are married or in a civil partnership, your contracted-out pot must go towards paying a pension to your spouse or civil partner. If you are not, your pot goes into your estate. If you die after taking benefits and your spouse or civil partner is still alive, he or she will continue to receive the 50 per cent survivor's benefit from your annuity.

Claiming compensation for incorrect advice to contract out

You may be able to claim compensation from the pension provider or financial adviser that advised you to contract out of state second pension. The FSA estimates that 120,000 people may have been wrongly advised to contract out. This amounts to less than 2 per cent of the 8 million people who opted out of the state scheme.

What do I need to prove?

■ *Attitude to risk* Poor investment performance on your contracted-out pension pot is not grounds for compensation. You can only get compensation if the advice you received was incorrect or inadequate. The adviser should have ascertained your attitude to investment risk. The adviser should have explained to you that you might get less through contracting out, and that you were happy to accept that risk.

■ *Age* Your age at the time you received the advice is also a significant factor. When contracting out was rolled out in 1988, actuarial estimates showed that people in their late 40s or older were unlikely to be better off by contracting out. The FSA says you are most likely to have a claim for incorrect advice on contracting out if you were advised to contract out between 1 July 1988 and 5 April 1997 and you were over 45 if you are male or were over 40 if you are female, at the time you contracted out. This is known as the 'pivotal age'.

■ *Charges* The adviser should also have explained the charges in the approved personal or stakeholder pension plan you were moving to, and the effect these would have on your fund's performance.

Two steps to claiming compensation

1 Make a complaint to the pension provider or financial adviser that advised you to contract out. They are required to have an internal dispute resolution process. You are entitled to free copies of the sales paperwork that the adviser used at the time, although they may no longer have this as they are only required to keep documents for six years.

2 If your claim is rejected but you still think you are entitled to compensation, make a claim to the Financial Ombudsman Service (for address, see Useful Contacts). You must do this within six months of receiving a final refusal from your pension provider or financial adviser in response to your complaint. There is no charge for making an application to the Ombudsman. If the Ombudsman finds in your favour, its decision is binding on the provider or adviser that advised you. The Ombudsman can order that you be paid compensation. If you are not satisfied with the Ombudsman's determination you are still allowed to take the matter through the civil courts, but you will have to pay court fees and possibly legal costs.

What if the firm that advised me has gone out of business?

If the company that advised you to contract out is no longer in existence you may be able to claim compensation from the Financial Services Compensation Scheme.

What compensation could I get?

If the Ombudsman finds in your favour it can order the pension company or financial adviser that gave you the faulty advice to pay a cash lump sum into your approved personal or stakeholder pension, to bring it up to a level where it would be on course to deliver an equivalent income to what you would have got had you remained contracted in.

Should I use a claims management company?

Claims management companies have proliferated in the wake of the endowment review, where many hundreds of thousands of people were paid billions in compensation. Claims management companies will charge you a fee, running into hundreds and possibly thousands of pounds, for making a claim. Some require an up-front fee, others operate on a no-win, no-fee basis, taking a percentage of any money you win.

The Pensions Advisory Service has warned consumers about paying anything up front to a claims management company as there is always a chance you may not get any compensation at all. It also points out that claiming to the Ombudsman does not cost anything and is straightforward. However, if you would like the assistance of a professional organisation when making a claim it pays to shop around on the internet for a claims management firm that offers the best terms. Claims management companies operating in England and Wales must be registered with the Ministry of Justice and are required to follow a code of conduct.

part

4

Wealth management
in retirement

13

Managing your retirement

What topics are covered in this chapter?

- Choosing when to retire
- Non-pension assets
- How will your income needs vary through retirement?
- How to convert your pension into income
- Early retirement
- Working later than you had planned
- Raising cash on your home: equity release

Retirement is a time when you make key decisions about all aspects of your life. The choices you make at retirement will have as much bearing on the amount of pension income you receive as those you made through your working life, in some cases possibly more so. For this reason you need to plan carefully how to use what you have got to finance the retirement you want.

Some of the choices you will face may require the assistance of a financial adviser. Others you can do on your own with the help of this book, or with the assistance of agencies whose contact details are set out in the following chapters.

The astonishing advances in life expectancy in recent years mean that retirement can easily extend into three and even four decades. Making your money last for 30 years or more is not easy, and you need to ensure that it works hard for you. This chapter looks at the issues you face prior to and at the time of retirement, and some of the ways you can manage your money in the most efficient way possible.

Choosing when to retire

For some people, inadequate pensions mean that they will have no choice but to work longer than they had hoped. Others may be in the position to choose when they want to stop working, and even retire early. There will also be those who can afford to retire but don't want to and those who will start winding work down by going part time.

The private pension system has been made as flexible as possible to ensure that whichever of these categories you fall into, the rules will not stop you from making the choice you want. As to the state system, aside from raising the retirement age for women, measures have been put in place to encourage people to work longer, either full or part time.

The closer you get to retirement, the better your picture of when you can afford to retire will be. In the years before you retire it is worth carrying out the retirement savings plan exercise in Chapter 2 to see whether you are on course to retire on the income you want. If you are not, you may need to consider working later, saving more, downsizing or releasing some equity from your home. And whether your pension saving is on target or not, it is still crucial to convert it into income in the most efficient way. You can easily increase your income in retirement quite considerably by making clever choices with your pension pot, giving you spare cash to play with or put away for a rainy day.

Non-pension assets

You may have built up considerable savings that are not contained in pensions, such as cash on deposit, ISAs, investment funds, shares and property. Managing these assets efficiently through retirement can be as important a part of your financial planning as converting your pension pot into an income in the most effective way.

For pensioners, generating income from your assets is normally the top priority, while at the same time attempting to keep pace with inflation. Managing non-pension assets through retirement is dealt with in more detail in Chapter 16.

How will your income needs vary through retirement?

It is highly unlikely that you will spend money at the same rate throughout a retirement that could easily span three decades. Experts talk of three phases of retirement: active, passive and care. The active phase is just after stopping work where retirees are mobile, enjoying hobbies and going on holiday. Spending can be high during this phase. Most people then move into a phase where they are frailer, less keen to travel or go out, and happy to spend the majority of their time at or near their home. As a result, spending is generally lower. The third phase is the period where their physical condition has deteriorated and they either need care at home or have to move into sheltered accommodation. This phase, while normally shorter than the other two, can be very expensive indeed.

> Experts talk of three phases of retirement: active, passive and care

You should bear these stages in mind when planning how to draw your pension income and savings through your retirement.

How to convert your pension into income

If you have a final salary pension then the amount you receive will be fixed by the scheme and paid to you from your normal retirement date. But for people with money purchase arrangements, retirement means converting their pension pot into an income. This is known technically as moving from the accumulation phase of pension saving to the decumulation phase.

A quarter of your fund can be taken as a tax-free cash lump sum and the remaining 75 per cent must be used to take an income in one of two ways: by buying an annuity or by going into unsecured pension, also known as income drawdown.

You do not have to convert all of your pension into income the day you finish work. You can leave some or all of it invested in the stock market if you have other sources of income to live on.

Annuities

An annuity is a contract between an individual and a life insurance company whereby part or all of the pension fund is handed over in exchange for an income for life. Income is normally paid monthly, quarterly or annually. The annuity can pay a reduced income to a spouse or partner after death, and can also be guaranteed to pay out for up to 10 years, whether the person buying it lives that long or not. But after death or the end of the guarantee period, whichever is later, no more payments are made and the insurance company keeps the pension fund.

There are many sorts of annuity on the market and the shorter your life expectancy, the higher income you can get. Smokers, the obese and those with pre-existing medical conditions can get significant income uplifts by shopping around. Even healthy people can get 15 per cent more by shopping around for the best annuity deal. There are also annuities that give you some exposure to the stock market. Finding the best annuity deal is dealt with in more detail in Chapter 14.

Unsecured pension/income drawdown

You do not have to draw anything from your pension at all until the age of 75

Rather than buy an annuity, you can keep your pension invested and draw an income from it each year. This facility is called unsecured pension or income drawdown. You do not have to draw anything from your pension at all until the age of 75. At 75 you must either buy an annuity or go into alternatively secured pension (ASP), a more restrictive form of income drawdown. How to make the most of income drawdown is looked at more closely in Chapter 15.

Variable annuities

Variable annuities attempt to give investors the potential to benefit from increases in the stock market while at the same time guaranteeing that their capital is not eroded. In terms of risk they sit between traditional annuities and drawdown, which is why they have been dubbed 'third way' annuities.

Variable annuities are a relatively new concept in the UK, having arrived from the USA in the last few years. However, one of the three American insurance giants to launch a product in the UK, Hartford Life, has since pulled out of the market. They are discussed in more detail in Chapter 14.

Annuity or drawdown: which is right for me?

The great majority of people take out an annuity when they retire rather than opt for drawdown. Annuities are far more secure, offering a guaranteed income for the rest of your life. In drawdown you remain invested in a mixture of the stock market and more secure investments such as bonds and gilts, drawing an income from your fund. If your investments go down in value and you carry on drawing income, it is possible to erode your pension pot quite quickly. You also carry the risk that by the time you come to buy an annuity, the rates on offer will have become even more unattractive than they are today.

On the other hand, if you are in a position to be able to take on this level of risk, you may be able to benefit from growth in the stock market and increase your income. Exposure to the stock market can play a crucial role in the battle against inflation, which erodes the spending power of most annuities over the long term.

How inflation erodes pensioners' spending power

Value in real terms of £10,000 a year pension income not protected against inflation

Number of years	Inflation at 2.5%	Inflation at 3.5%
10	£7,760	£7,000
20	£6,020	£4,900
30	£4,670	£3,430

One of the biggest threats to pensioners is inflation. The rampant inflation of the 1970s reduced pension incomes drastically, and many experts believe the effect of the government's attempts to reignite the economy by increasing the money supply will lead to a similar bout of inflation in years to come. But even a modest level of inflation reduces the spending power of most annuities, which are not indexed to prices.

Four-fifths of people buying annuities opt for level annuities that pay a fixed income for life, offering no protection against inflation whatsoever. The reason so many people opt for level annuities is the fact that you get a higher starting income than you do with an inflation-protected annuity. But as the years go by, their real value declines. To illustrate the point, a pensioner in their nineties today who bought a level annuity when they retired could easily be living on an income fixed when James Callaghan was prime minister, and will probably be having it topped up by state benefits today.

There are a number of strategies you can follow to attempt to deal with inflation. Maintaining some exposure to the stock market is one solution. If inflation takes off, the value of shares tends to rise too. You can maintain exposure to the stock market either through unit-linked annuities, variable annuities or unsecured pension. There are also annuities that rise in line with inflation.

Because they have to be able to be sure they can pay out on them, life insurers back annuities with gilts and long-term bonds. The very low returns that are paid on gilts and long-term bonds are one of the reasons that annuity payments are so seemingly low. Opt for an inflation-linked annuity and you will have to accept a starting income around 35 per cent lower than you get from a level annuity that never goes up in price.

Supporters of drawdown argue that, given the lengthy retirements stretching well into 30 years that are becoming prevalent today, having some exposure to equities is the only way pensioners can keep pace with rising prices.

Death benefits are also better in drawdown before the age of 75 than through an annuity, where the fund is lost to the life insurer on death. One factor in favour of annuities over drawdown, which should not be overlooked, is the fact that the investor does not have to worry about underestimating or overestimating how long they will live. You may plan to run your drawdown pot with the aim of spending it all by the time you are 85. But if you live to 95 you will have nothing to live on for the last 10 years. Alternatively, you might decide to be frugal in the early years in the expectation of making it to 95, but die after a short, austere retirement at the age of 75.

By taking your retirement income from your own pot through drawdown you have to deal with what is called 'mortality drag'. Because annuities pool thousands of people together, they are able to pay out an amount broadly equal to your fund plus its investment growth over the number of years you are expected to live, less a profit margin for the insurer. In this way, those who die younger than predicted by their life expectancy subsidise those who die older. However, it does not have to be an 'either/or' decision – you can go into drawdown for several years and then buy an annuity later on. By doing so you will not have to worry about trying to guess how long you are going to live. Or you can buy an annuity with part of your pension pot and go into drawdown with the rest.

How much risk can I afford?

One key factor when considering whether to go for an annuity or drawdown is how much risk you can afford to take. As a basic principle, the more money you have, the more risk you can afford. Put the other way round, if you barely have enough to live on in retirement, can you afford to risk losing it? (See Table 13.1.)

For this reason, most income drawdown providers require a minimum fund of £50,000 before they will accept business. However, a pension fund of £50,000 might only generate an income of £3,500, and this limit is only this low to accommodate people with retirement income from other sources, such as savings, other pensions and property. As a general rule you should not be contemplating risking your money on the stock market through income drawdown if your total retirement income assets are worth less than £100,000.

Table 13.1: Annuity versus drawdown

	Annuity	*Drawdown*
Secure income?	Yes	No
Potential for stock market growth?	No, apart from unit-linked or with-profits annuities	Yes
Benefits from cross-subsidy through pooling?	Yes	No
Able to pass on fund at death?	No	Yes, subject to tax to surviving spouse or dependant
Able to vary income?	No, for most products	Yes, can increase or decrease to suit cir cumstances
Simple to administer?	Yes – payments made monthly, quarterly or annually	No – needs regular assistance of a financial adviser, which increases cost

Early retirement

Not surprisingly, retiring early usually involves getting a reduced income, unless your employer makes you a generous offer to leave.

Not only are you receiving income for longer, but also you are contributing less. If you start paying in at age 35 and expect to live until 85, retiring at 65 means you will build up a fund over 30 years and spend it over 20 years. Retire at 55 and the fund you build up over 20 years will have to last you 30 years.

Early retirement

■ *Money purchase* Early retirement means you have a smaller pension pot and you get a lower annuity rate because your expected lifespan is longer.

■ *Final salary* Early retirement means you accrue less years into the scheme, so your pension is reduced proportionately. If, in a 1/60th scheme you join at age 35 and retire at 65, you will get 30/60ths or half of your final salary. Retire at 55 and you will get 20/60ths, or one-third, payable from your normal retirement date. Furthermore, you may have missed out on salary enhancements that would increase your final salary.

Ask to receive your pension early and the scheme's trustees will reduce the amount you get even further.

Working later than you had planned

You may decide you have to work later than you had planned. Unfortunately the law does not protect you from age discrimination in the workplace after the age of 65, although political pressure for this rule to change is growing. This may mean you will not be as secure in your current job as you had been. On the other hand, employers are taking an increasingly positive view of older workers, and it may be possible to get a full- or part-time post.

It is also important to remember that different pensions will start paying out at different ages. Some company pensions pay out from age 60 or 65, while state pension pays out at any point between 60 and 68, depending on your age and sex.

If you work part time but do not earn enough to live on, you can draw part of your pension and leave the rest of it to continue growing until it suits you to start drawing it (unless it is a final salary scheme, where it is likely to be difficult to draw it before the scheme's retirement date). You can draw your personal pension in as many tranches as you like.

Deferring state pension

By deferring your state pension you can build up a lump sum of up to £30,000 or increase your income by 1 per cent for every five weeks after your normal retirement date that you put off taking it. This works out at an increase of 10.4 per cent for every year of delay. For more on deferring state pension, see Chapter 10.

Spread income between couples

People over 65 pay no tax at all on the first £9,490 of income (2009/2010), and even higher for the over 75s (see Chapter 2). Couples should therefore ensure that income is held in both parties' names up to this level, allowing a tax-free household income of £18,980.

Gifts between spouses and civil partners are free of Capital Gains Tax, so it is possible to pass assets such as shares, savings, ISAs and property into the name of the partner with the lowest income. Even non-working partners can get 20 per cent tax relief on pension contributions up to £2,880, so it can also be worthwhile for the partner who is earning paying into a pension for the one who is not.

Use tax-free cash lump sums efficiently

People in final salary schemes should make sure they draw tax-free cash from AVC arrangements where possible. This will mean they will not have to forgo valuable final salary benefits to get their cash lump sum. It can even be worth borrowing over the short term to fund pension contributions just before retiring to avoid having to surrender final salary income to get tax-free cash (see Chapter 6).

Recycle your tax-free cash lump sum into your pension

It is possible to pay your tax-free cash lump sum back into your pension and not only get tax relief on it, but also get another tax-free cash lump sum in relation to the amount paid in.

This sounds like a good deal, and for higher rate taxpayers it is. For this reason the government has restricted how much of this tax-free lump sum 'recycling' is allowed. Experts point out that if an individual makes a contribution into a pension shortly after drawing some tax-free cash, the government has no way of knowing whether the contribution is from the tax-free cash or from the individual's other funds. The real effect of the rule is that it stops advisers and providers from marketing the solution for amounts above the permitted limits.

Recycling is allowed for tax-free cash withdrawals of less than 1 per cent of the lifetime limit, meaning £17,500 for 2009/2010 in any 12-month period, rising to £18,000 from 2010/2011 to 2016/2017.

Example

How tax-free cash can boost your pension pot

In the 2010/2011 tax year Angela is 57 years old, earns £90,000 a year and has a pension pot of £200,000. She draws benefits from £72,000 of her pension, giving her a tax-free cash lump sum of £18,000. She leaves the remaining £54,000 invested through unsecured pension.

She then pays the £18,000 into her pension fund, which is grossed up by basic rate tax relief of £4,500 immediately, and receives a further £4,500 back in her hand through her tax return.

The following year she draws an identical sum of tax-free cash. She pays the £18,000 plus the £4,500 higher rate tax relief back into the pension. This £22,500 contribution is automatically grossed up by basic rate tax relief of £5,625. She receives a further £5,625 cash in hand through her tax return.

Before recycling:

■ fund to buy an annuity: £150,000

■ potential tax-free cash: £50,000

After recycling:

■ fund to buy an annuity: £214,625

■ potential tax-free cash: £26,656

■ tax-free cash in hand: £5,625

(not allowing for any investment growth)

By recycling, she has reduced her available tax-free cash by £17,719 but increased her pension fund by £64,625. This will give her a pension for life that is 43 per cent higher than she would have got. If she is a basic rate taxpayer in retirement, the extra pension income she receives is likely to exceed the amount of the tax-free cash lump sum after around seven or eight years.

She can continue to recycle tax-free cash for as long as she is working and paying tax at 40 per cent, right up to the age of 75 if she wishes.

Retirement – getting your affairs in order

If you are just about to retire you need to get your finances straight before you do so.

Checklist

■ Claim state pension. Decide whether you want to draw it from your state retirement age or defer it to get a higher income or cash lump sum. Work out whether you should buy back missing years (see page 000).

■ Claim other benefits you may be entitled to. These include means-tested benefits such as Pension Credit, Housing Benefit and Council Tax Benefit, which you may even be entitled to if you have a modest private pension. Non-means-tested benefits include Disability Living Allowance for the under 65s and Attendance Allowance for the over 65s. Most people over 60 are entitled to a winter fuel payment. Check the online benefits calculator at the Age Concern website (www.ageconcern.org.uk).

■ Notify the tax office that you have retired. State pension is paid without tax being deducted, but private pensions and income from cash on deposit and other financial products are normally paid with basic rate tax already deducted. You may be entitled to a tax rebate if your income is below your personal allowance. Alternatively, you may be able to receive private pension income gross – check with your pension provider or pension scheme trustees to see if this is possible. Check that the tax office correctly changes your tax code at age 65 and 75. Mistakes are not uncommon.

■ Get your debts under control. It makes sense to sort out debts at any time in your life, but if your income is about to drop considerably, it makes sense to clear as much of your debt as possible before it does. You may wish to use some of your tax-free cash lump sum to clear your debts. If your debts are a problem contact the National Debtline on 0800 808 4000, or at www.nationaldebtline.co.uk

■ Trace lost pension. Track down lost pension through the Pension Advisory Service's pension tracing service. See page 236 for more detail.

Raising cash on your home: equity release

If you own your own home you may wish to use it to raise extra cash to fund your retirement. You may choose to sell up and downsize to a smaller property or alternatively opt for equity release, whereby you transfer entitlement to all or a part of your home to a financial services company in return for a cash lump sum or income, while retaining a right to remain in the premises until you die.

Releasing cash from your home may seem like easy money, but the FSA warns consumers against taking out equity release without considering all other options beforehand. By going into equity release you may find your options are less flexible in the future (you may not be able to downsize and release cash) and the cash you receive could affect your entitlement to means-tested benefits from the state.

These are the factors to consider before going into equity release:

■ Can you raise money from other sources?

■ Can you release cash by moving to a smaller property?

■ Will the cash you receive reduce your entitlement to means-tested benefits?

■ Can you get home improvement grants from your local authority?

■ Have you discussed inheritance issues with your family?

Equity release plans allow you to release a percentage of the value of your home depending on your age. This percentage is based on the equity release provider's estimate of how long you are likely to carry on living in the property before you die.

All equity release plans carry some set-up costs such as arrangement fees and legal expenses. You will also have to pay buildings insurance.

There are two different sorts of equity release which are quite different in the way they operate: lifetime mortgages and home reversion plans.

Lifetime mortgages

Under a lifetime mortgage you receive a loan secured on your home and retain the right to live in the property for the rest of your life. Because the loan is secured on your home, the property still belongs to you. When you die or move out the loan must be repaid. If the debt is bigger than the value of your home then the difference may have to be paid from the remainder of your estate. To protect against this scenario most providers offer a no-negative-equity guarantee that you will never have to pay back more than the value of your home. Providers that are members of Safe Home Income Plans (SHIP), an industry standards body, all offer a no-negative-equity guarantee.

Lifetime mortgages come in different types:

■ *Roll-up lifetime mortgage* Interest is charged on the money you borrow, and rolls up year after year until you die or move out. You can either take a lump sum or draw income down in tranches from the property.

■ *Home income plan* The money you borrow buys a regular annuity paying you an income. Anyone under the age of 80 is unlikely to get a large amount of income because for younger pensioners the interest payments will eat up much of the annuity being paid.

■ *Interest-only mortgage* Interest is paid monthly and you repay the principal loan when you move out. You should watch out for variable rate plans as repayments may rise higher than you can afford.

■ Fixed repayment lifetime mortgage. The repayment rate is set at the outset, depending on how long the insurer thinks you will live. These plans work out better value if you end up living longer than the life insurer expects you to.

The speed at which interest rolls up on lifetime mortgages

Getting hands on easy cash for purchases such as a new car or home improvements may seem tempting, but you will probably still be racking up interest long after the things you bought have been scrapped or thrown away. Interest rolls up on a compounded basis, meaning that the amount you owe increases exponentially. Generally speaking costs will roughly double every 12 years. This means that for every £10,000 you release from your home, you will owe around £20,000 after 12 years, £40,000 after 24 years and £80,000 after 36 years.

Home reversion plans

With home reversion plans you sell all or a proportion of your home for a cash lump sum or regular income, but you retain the right to remain in the property until you die under a lease paying a nominal sum. You can normally get between 20 and 60 per cent of the value of your property, depending on how old you are, with older home reversion plan investors getting more to reflect their reduced life expectancy. The FSA says home reversion plans are more suitable for people over age 70.

14

Annuities

What topics are covered in this chapter?

- ▓ Shopping around for the best deal
- ▓ Inflation protection
- ▓ Providing for a spouse or partner after your death
- ▓ Guaranteed annuity payments
- ▓ How do I want to be paid?
- ▓ Annuities for smokers
- ▓ Annuities for people in poor health
- ▓ Fixed-term annuities
- ▓ Investment-linked annuities: with-profits annuities
- ▓ Investment-linked annuities: variable annuities

Shopping around for the best deal

If there is only one piece of advice that you take from this book, it should be this – if you are buying an annuity, shop around for the best deal you can find. Choosing the right annuity is arguably the most important decision relating to your pension that you will ever make. There is probably no other situation where you can increase your income for life by up to a third just by making a minimal amount of effort.

It is up to you when you start drawing an income from your pension, provided it is between the ages of 55 (50 until April 2010) and 75. You are allowed to take 25 per cent of your fund as a tax-free lump sum. The remaining 75 per cent must be used to give you a pension income. People in final salary schemes do not have to buy an annuity because the scheme pays them income for life.

The 'open market option'

Your pension provider will send you an offer of an annuity in the months before your stated retirement date. You should not accept this offer without seeing if you can get a better deal. You have the right to buy an annuity from any provider you wish. This is called the 'open market option'.

Smokers and people with certain medical conditions can get their income increased by up to 35 per cent by taking a specialist annuity. You can even get a better deal if you live in an area where people tend to die younger. Surveys have shown that around 40 per cent of people could get an enhanced annuity of some sort or another, yet only a fraction of them actually do.

You can get an idea of the difference between the conventional annuity rates available on the market by looking at the pension annuities section on the FSA's website (www.fsa.gov.uk/tables). These tables will give you the best rates based on age, sex and whether you smoke, both for level and indexed annuities, with or without guarantees and spouse survivor benefits. But they will not show you how much you could get if you have a medical condition or based on your postcode.

Lower annuities for healthy people

The number of factors that insurers will take into account is increasing, meaning that annuities are becoming increasingly closely matched to an individual's actual life expectancy. This trend is actually bad news for people who are healthy and who are expected to live a long time.

The bad news for healthy people is that as more people with shorter life expectancy are pulled out of the annuity pool by products designed for them, conventional annuity rates go down. But the good news is that even healthy people can get up to 20 per cent more income than their pension provider is offering them just by shopping around.

Making the right annuity purchase is absolutely crucial because it is a once-in-a-lifetime purchase. Once you have bought your annuity there is no turning back if it is not suitable or if you realise you could have got a better deal.

> Making the right annuity purchase is absolutely crucial because it is a once-in-a-lifetime purchase

Pension companies make a considerable amount of their profits from uninformed customers who take the easy option of accepting the poor value annuity that they are offered. Some even pay commission to the IFA that sold you the pension years ago if you do not switch, even though you may not have spoken to the adviser for 10 years or more.

Your pension provider is supposed to inform you that you have the right to look for better deals elsewhere, but many companies have dragged their heels, making their marketing literature confusing so that the message fails to get across.

A report by the FSA in 2008 found that 38 per cent of providers failed to give adequately clear information that would allow consumers to make an informed decision. The FSA also found a gulf of up to 20 per cent between the best and worst rates available on the market, underlining the benefits that even those in good health can draw from shopping around. Yet getting the right annuity is not hard, and you can often get professional advice and assistance without it costing you a penny more.

The one area where it is unlikely to be in your interests to switch provider is if your existing provider has promised you a guaranteed annuity rate. Some pensions taken out in the 1980s and earlier offered valuable guaranteed annuity rates that are far higher than those available today.

Beware trustee recommendations

Just because an annuity has been recommended by the trustees of your scheme does not mean it is the best deal you can get or suitable for your circumstances. There are many instances where pension companies give poor quality deals to trustees. Some companies that offer increased annuities for people who live in postcodes where life expectancy is shorter only do so where customers are approaching them for the first time – these deals are not necessarily available to their existing pension customers.

Furthermore, trustees will not necessarily ensure that any medical conditions you suffer from have been taken into account when sending you an annuity offer. And trustees will not make sure that all the possible options available when buying an annuity have been looked at. It is worth getting independent financial advice even if your annuity has been recommended by the trustees of your scheme.

Six questions on buying an annuity

There are many different sorts of annuity, and you may want to buy more than one to spread your risk.

There are six key questions you need to ask yourself to find the best annuity:

1 Do I want inflation protection?

2 Do I want to provide a survivor benefit to a partner?

3 Do I want to guarantee payments after I die?

4 How do I want to be paid?

5 Do I qualify for any enhancements because of my medical condition or for smoking?

6 Do I want to risk part of my income in the hope of getting stock market growth?

Professional advice

It makes sense to get professional advice on which annuity is suitable for your circumstances. An IFA will take you through these questions and help you understand what will work best for you.

People with pension pots worth £30,000 or more can get professional advice on annuity purchase from an IFA effectively for free. This is because annuity providers will pay advisers a commission of between 1 and 1.5 per cent of the value of the product. Annuity providers give consumers the same deal whether they pay this commission or not, so you may as well take professional financial advice on which product is most suitable for you.

Even if your fund is smaller than this, it is still advisable to pay a few hundred pounds to get professional advice on your annuity options. The money you will save is likely to outweigh the cost of the advice. You can contact a financial adviser in your area through IFA Promotion at www.unbiased.co.uk

Spread your risk: buy more than one annuity

As in all areas of financial planning, spreading risk is always a good idea. You can spread your pension pot into as many different annuities as you want, provided you meet the minimum purchase price, typically £10,000 per provider. By buying two, three

You can spread your pension pot into as many different annuities as you want or even four different types of annuity you can give yourself some of the benefits that each class of product offer while reducing the risk of making a single big mistake. But you should bear in mind that there is an administrative loading of around £250 contained within the cost of each annuity, which means you get slightly lower rates for having three or four small annuities than you would for one large one.

Annuity supermarkets

You can search for real-time live annuity quotes on the internet through online annuity supermarkets. They will give you an indication of how much more you can get by shopping around, and will in a great many cases be able to point to an annuity that is better than the one being offered by your pension provider. However, many do not offer access to every single annuity provider on the market, and by completing the application online, you may end up selecting a product you do not fully understand. Furthermore, you will not benefit from a qualified adviser finding out your circumstances and then recommending a solution that is suitable for you.

Most have telephone staff to help you through the online application process, but it is important to understand that these are not qualified financial advisers. When you buy from an annuity supermarket you do so on an execution-only basis, which means you alone are responsible for the choice of annuity and you have no comeback if it turns out to be the wrong choice.

Converting your pension to income is an extremely important decision, and if your fund is £30,000 or more you can usually get professional advice at no extra cost to yourself.

Rebating commission

If you have a large pension pot then you should seek out an IFA that charges a fee that is taken out of the commission paid by the provider. Good advisers will charge you an hourly rate and then rebate any commission left back to you in the form of an increase in your annuity income.

For example, if you have a £100,000 pension pot, the annuity provider may pay up to £1,500 commission. A fee-based adviser may charge you £600 for the advice, and then rebate the remaining £900 into the product, which would give you an increased income, albeit a slight one of less than 1 per cent.

There are a few online annuity discount brokers that will rebate upwards of 50 per cent of the commission on the product back to you provided you buy the annuity on an execution-only basis online or over the telephone. For example www.annuitydiscount.co.uk will give you 51 per cent of commission on annuities up to £100,000, which would increase your monthly payment by between 0.5 and 0.75 per cent. But buying on an execution-only basis means you have no comeback against the company if you end up with the wrong product. Given the once-in-a-lifetime nature of buying an annuity, it should only be an option for people who are absolutely certain they know which sort of product they want.

Inflation protection

Inflation erodes the value of annuities over time unless they have inflation protection. This is set to create a serious problem for tomorrow's pensioners as life expectancy continues to grow. A quarter of today's 50-year-old males can expect to live to the age of 93. Today 30 years of retirement is a possibility for anyone in reasonable health at the time they stop working. Yet after just 20 years of inflation averaging 3.5 per cent, an annuity without protection against rising prices will lose half its spending power. Unfortunately, buying an annuity with inflation protection means you have to accept a starting income nearly 40 per cent lower than you get from a level annuity. This means that at current levels of inflation you have to live well into your eighties before the amount you receive from an inflation-linked annuity exceeds that of the level annuity, which is one of the reasons that less than one in five people choose inflation-linked annuities. Some people opt for the higher income available from a level annuity because they want to be able to spend more in their sixties and seventies while they are still active. (See Table 14.1.)

Table 14.1: The cost of inflation protection: annual income for a 65-year-old male non-smoker, with 50% income to a surviving partner, £50,000 fund

Type of annuity	Annual income	Difference
Level annuity	£3,132	–
Rising 3% a year	£2,172	30% less
Rising with RPI	£1,896	39% less

Providing for a spouse or partner after your death

If you are married, in a civil partnership or long-term stable relationship you may wish to provide for your life partner after you die. You can choose whether to have an annuity that stops when you die, known as a 'single life' annuity, or one that pays an income to your spouse or partner for the rest of their life too, known as a 'joint life annuity'. Joint life annuities can pay a survivor's benefit of 100 per cent, 66 per cent or 50 per cent.

The bigger the survivor's benefit, the less the starting income. Figures from Standard Life show that around three-quarters of married annuitants have bought products that do not protect their spouse. It is not known in what proportion of cases the unprotected spouse actually knows that a single life annuity has been bought. If you are financially dependent on a spouse or partner you should discuss with them whether or not they will be opting for a single or joint life annuity, because if they opt for a single life annuity, your income will drop severely if they die first. This issue is more commonly faced by women, who typically have less pension income of their own than men, tend to be younger than their spouses and partners and have a longer life expectancy. (See Table 14.2.)

Table 14.2: The cost of providing an income for a surviving spouse or partner: annual income for a 65-year-old male non-smoker, level annuity, £50,000 fund

Type of annuity	Annual income	Difference
Single life	£3,516	–
Joint life – 50% survivor's benefit	£3,132	11% less
Joint life – 67% survivor's benefit	£3,024	14% less
Joint life – 100% survivor's benefit	£2,844	19% less

Guaranteed annuity payments

You may resent the thought of the life insurance company scooping virtually your entire pot if you die the day after you buy an annuity. You can buy a guarantee that the income will continue to be paid to a named beneficiary after you die. Guarantees normally last for five or ten years. The beneficiary will pay income tax on the money received. The cost of a five-year guarantee for a 65-year-old male is negligible, and even a ten-year guarantee only reduces income by 2 per cent.

You can also buy an annuity that protects the value of your fund in the event that you die before age 75. This option, called 'value protection', will pay named beneficiaries a sum equal to the difference between the cost of the annuity and the amounts paid out on it before you died, subject to 35 per cent tax. (See Table 14.3.)

Table 14.3: Cost of guaranteeing annuity payments: annual income for a 65-year-old male non-smoker, single, level annuity, £50,000 fund

Type of annuity	Annual income	Difference
No guarantee	£3,516	–
Five-year guarantee	£3,504	0.34% less
Ten-year guarantee	£3,444	2% less

How do I want to be paid?

You can ask to be paid monthly, quarterly or annually, either in arrears or in advance.

Annuities for smokers

Smokers can improve their income by around 18 per cent by seeking out an annuity provider that offers special rates for those who smoke. For a pension provider whose conventional annuity is poor value, the combination of getting the best rate on the market and getting the smoker's enhancement can easily boost the annuity purchaser's income by as much as 35 per cent. You typically need to have been smoking ten cigarettes a day for the ten years prior to buying the annuity.

Annuities for people in poor health

You do not have to be seriously ill to get an increased annuity rate. Obese people and those with high cholesterol, high blood pressure, hypertension and diabetes mellitus can also get enhanced annuities because of their shorter life expectancy. Annuities for smokers and for people with these milder conditions are called lifestyle annuities.

You can often get between 10 and 20 per cent more than the best conventional annuity for chronic illnesses that are not life threatening.

Annuities for people with more serious illnesses

The more serious a threat your condition poses to your life, the higher the annuity you can get. Impaired life annuities can pay considerably higher incomes than lifestyle annuities to people with more serious illnesses, such as cancer, chronic asthma, diabetes, heart disease, high blood pressure, kidney failure, multiple sclerosis or stroke. You will be asked to provide the insurance company with a report from your doctor to back up your claim, but you will not normally have to undergo a medical examination.

Annuities based on postcode

Lifespans vary hugely around the country and, to reflect this, insurance companies have in recent years started offering annuities based on where people live. Aviva (formerly Norwich Union), Legal & General and Prudential now offer annuities that offer enhancements for people who live in postcodes where lifespans are shorter. This also means that those living in places where longevity is greater, usually more affluent areas, get less.

For example, when Aviva introduced postcode annuities in 2008, a 65-year-old male with a £100,000 pension pot could get an annuity of £7,668 a year wherever they lived. Since adopting postcode underwriting, those in the best postcodes saw their income cut to £7,590 – £228 a year less than those in the postcodes with the worst mortality statistics, who see their income increased to £7,818. Insurers underwrite down to street level, covering 1.5 million areas across the country.

Fixed-term annuities

Fixed-term annuities can be beneficial for people who are healthy and do not qualify for an impaired life annuity when they retire at, say, 60 or 65, but who later in life develop some form of medical condition that would entitle them to an enhanced annuity. Rather than lock into a basic conventional annuity when you are healthy, fixed-term annuities allow you to receive an income, while allowing you to renegotiate terms for another annuity, potentially with ill-health enhancements, years later.

Fixed-term annuities are riskier than conventional annuities because there is the possibility that annuity rates across the board will have gone down by the time you come to buy a new annuity. However, they do not carry any of the stock market risks that investment-linked annuities carry.

Living Time is one provider that offers these fixed-term annuities. It pays an income equal to the best level annuity available on the market, for a fixed period. Then at the end of the fixed period it pays a lump sum equal to the amount needed to buy an annuity that would carry on paying out at the same rate. That amount is fixed as at the date the fixed-term annuity is purchased, so there is a risk that annuity rates will have got worse by the time the pensioner comes to buy a new annuity. On the other hand, ten or so years later, that pensioner may have developed a medical condition that entitles them to an impaired life annuity, giving them the opportunity of an enhancement of between 10 and 35 per cent more income.

Figures from the Office for National Statistics show that the number of years of healthy life that can be expected at 65 is 10.1 for men and 10.6 for women, indicating that a considerable minority of people are expected to develop some form of medical condition by the time they are 75.

You can get fixed-term annuities for periods as short as three years. These can be beneficial if you think you face having to buy an annuity at a time when annuity rates are unusually low, for example when long-term interest rates have dipped. However, you carry the risk that annuity rates will get even worse during the period you hold the fixed-term annuity.

Example

Alex is just turning 65 and is in good health. In January 2009 his £100,000 pension pot will buy him a conventional level annuity of £7,416 a year for life. Alternatively he opts for a fixed-term annuity, which pays him an identical figure for ten years and then ceases the day before he turns 75. At this point he has to either buy a lifetime annuity or move into alternatively secured pension (ASP).

The day before his 75th birthday, in January 2019, the fixed-term annuity repays him a guaranteed maturity amount of £74,202, for him to buy a new pension income. This is the amount it would have cost a 75-year-old to buy an income of £7,416 in January 2009.

Scenario 1

Since January 2009 Alex has had a heart attack and developed diabetes. He uses the guaranteed maturity amount to buy an impaired life annuity and is able to secure a 20 per cent income enhancement.

Example *continued*

> **Scenario 2**
>
> At age 75 Alex is as fit as ever. He has to use the guaranteed maturity amount to buy a conventional annuity. Annuity rates may have gone down since January 2009 and he is worse off. Alternatively, they may have improved and he is better off. This annuity rate risk is the risk that comes with a fixed-rate annuity.

Investment-linked annuities: with-profits annuities

With-profits annuities allow you to retain some exposure to the stock market, while receiving an income. As the name suggests, your income is linked to the performance of a life insurance company's with-profits fund. Unlike with conventional annuities, which provide a guaranteed income, there is a chance that your income from a with-profits annuity could go down. On the other hand, over time a with-profits annuity could give you some degree of protection against inflation, as share prices tend to rise when inflation is high.

With-profits annuities: how they work

People taking out a with-profits annuity have to select an anticipated bonus rate (ABR). This is the rate the with-profits fund needs to grow by to give you a steady return, and also sets your starting income. Your future income is then increased or decreased by the difference between the ABR and the actual return on the with-profits fund, known as the with-profits bonus. If the with-profits fund declares a return higher than the ABR you selected, your income goes up. If the with-profits bonus is lower than the ABR you selected, your income goes down.

The level of income, and therefore ABR you go for, will determine whether your income goes up or down. If you choose a cautious ABR and take less income, you will have a greater chance of the fund outperforming, giving you more returns in the future. Take a bullish view and you will get a higher starting income, but you will also run a higher risk of your income falling in the future if the with-profits fund does not generate an annual return higher than your ABR figure. To compare with-profits annuities with conventional annuities, it is helpful to choose an ABR that gives an identical starting income. Pick an ABR at whatever the returns on gilts are at the time, and you will get a starting income close to what you would have got from a level annuity. In 2009 you needed an ABR of between 3.5 and 4 per cent to give a starting income matching a level annuity.

While with-profits funds are designed to smooth out the peaks and troughs of the market, their performance is still linked to the stock market.

With-profits annuity: how it works

A with-profits annuity with an ABR of 4 per cent pays £1,000 in year 1.

- If the with-profits fund declares a bonus of 5 per cent in year 2, the year 2 income is: 1,000 × 1.05 1.04 = £1,009.62
- If the with-profits fund declares a bonus of 3 per cent in year 2, the year 2 income is: 1,000 × 1.03 1.04 = £990.38

Source: William Burrows Annuities, reprinted with permission

How well your with-profits annuity performs is generally linked to what stage the stock market is at in the economic cycle when you join, and the starting income and ABR you choose. People who have bought with-profits annuities at or near the top of a bear market have usually seen their income fall over time. People going into a with-profits annuity near the bottom of the market are more likely to see it rise.

Investment-linked annuities: variable annuities

Variable annuities offer a guaranteed income and some exposure to investment markets. They are also known as 'third way annuities' because they aim to offer investors some of the benefits of drawdown with reduced risk while also offering some of the security of annuities with potential for stock market growth.

Technically speaking, variable annuities are not annuities but a form of guaranteed income plan offered through income drawdown. The theory behind variable annuities is straightforward. The investor's money is invested in a life insurance fund linked to the stock market. An annual charge is made to pay for a guarantee that the fund value will not fall below a certain level. The cost of this guarantee goes up or down depending on how much exposure to risky assets the investor wants to take. The investor selects a rate of income they want to withdraw.

How they work

■ *In rising markets* If the return on the life insurance fund exceeds the combined cost of the income withdrawal, the guarantee charge and the other management charges of the plan, the investor's fund grows and they can take more income in future years. Gains can be locked in, thus guaranteeing an increased secure income for life, every three or five years.

■ *In falling markets* If the return on the life insurance fund is lower than the combined cost of the income withdrawal, the guarantee charge and the other management charges of the plan, the investor's fund shrinks below 100 per cent of its starting value. Income is still guaranteed but the investor's fund has to rise above 100 per cent of its starting value before any increases in income will be added.

For example, if the guarantee and plan charges total 3.5 per cent, and the income withdrawal rate is 5 per cent a year, the fund needs to return more than 8.5 per cent for income to rise. If the fund posts a negative return of 10 per cent in the first year, the investor's pot is reduced by 18.5 per cent to 81.5 per cent of starting value. With a further 8.5 per cent set to come out of the pot in year 2, the fund needs to grow by 33 per cent in that year for the investor's fund to be restored to 100 per cent of its starting value.

How risky are variable annuities?

Variable annuities have lower starting incomes than conventional level annuities and there is no guarantee that the income they generate will ever overtake them. On the other hand, if you go into a variable annuity when markets are rising, you may get more.

For those that guarantee to provide you with a fixed income for life, the risk you are taking is effectively limited to the difference between what you would have got from a level annuity and what you are guaranteed to get from the variable annuity. With both level annuities and variable annuities there is the risk that inflation will erode the value of the guaranteed payments. However, variable annuities do offer some potential for protection from inflation because asset values tend to rise when inflation surges.

Other variable annuities guarantee to return capital in full at age 75. People taking out these plans carry the risk that annuity rates may have gone down by the time they come to buy one, years down the line.

Variable annuities vs. conventional annuities vs. income drawdown

The different variable annuities on the market all have different features, charges, guarantees and withdrawal rates, so it is hard to compare performance. Furthermore, because these products are still relatively new, statistics comparing their performance to conventional annuities is thin on the ground.

That said, in general terms you are likely to do well through going into a variable annuity if the date you take one out is at or near the bottom of the equity cycle. Conversely, if you take one out when equity markets are at the top of the cycle you are less likely to see your income beat that of a conventional annuity over the long term (but on the plus side, you are likely to be going into the product with a bigger pot if you do so at the top of the market).

The reverse effect is true when comparing variable annuities to income drawdown with no guarantees. The cost of the guarantees in variable annuities holds back gains when markets are rising. However, when markets fall, these guarantees protect investors. People who took out variable annuities in 2007 and early 2008 may be unlikely to ever get income higher than they could have got by buying a conventional level annuity. But they are considerably better off than those who invested in income drawdown and carried on drawing income from their fund.

Types of variable annuity

The variable annuities on the market today all approach the problem of offering security of return and exposure to fluctuating asset values in different ways. You will have to go through an IFA to get access to a variable annuity, and they will discuss with you the options available.

There are three providers offering guaranteed income through drawdown in the UK: Lincoln Life, MetLife and Aegon. (See Table 14.4).

Table 14.4: Variable annuities and their features

Company	Lincoln	MetLife	Aegon
Product	i2Live	Retirement Portfolio	Income for Life
Overview	Drawdown and variable annuity with option of an income guarantee and death benefits	Personal pension with capital guarantee for accumulation phase and income guarantee for drawdown phase	An unsecured pension with a guaranteed level of income for life
Income	Investors can take up to 100% of the Maximum Supportable Income without affecting the guarantee	Depends on age, but varies from 3.8% to 6.2% guaranteed for life	Dependent on amount invested and age when regular income taken
Guarantees	Guaranteed income is based on 75% of Maximum Supportable Income; gains are locked in every five years	Every three years investors lock into any gains; this can increase capital value or income value depending on type of guarantee selected	Can lock in up to 100% of investment gains
At age 75	Option to convert to flexible annuity	Capital guarantee will mature or income guarantee can continue beyond age 75	

Source: William Burrows Annuities, reprinted with permission

Variable annuities are popular in the USA but have only been widely available in the UK since 2006, when three of America's largest insurers and a handful of other providers started to market the products. These products offer guarantees underwritten by investment banks, and since the near-collapse of the banking system in 2008 the cost of securing these guarantees has risen considerably. As a result, Hartford Life, one of the USA's biggest variable annuity providers, pulled out of the UK in 2009. Those providers who are still in the UK say their commitment to the market is unshaken. Some have had to increase the cost to consumers of offering guarantees, however.

Some IFAs question whether other providers will follow suit, and argue that the more expensive the guarantees get, the less chance there is of plan-holders benefiting from rises in the stock market. Variable annuity providers argue that the higher cost of the guarantee simply reflects the greater risk of asset values falling in the current economic uncertainty. This increased uncertainty, they say, makes the guarantee even more valuable to investors.

People taking out these products should also ask their advisers about the security of the banks offering the guarantees to the variable annuity providers.

15

Income drawdown

What topics are covered in this chapter?

- How income drawdown works
- Benefits on death
- Alternatively secured pension (ASP)

Income drawdown is the ability to leave your pension invested in the stock market, while having the option of drawing an income from it. This facility, which is also known as unsecured pension, is available from retirement age up to 75, after which you must either buy an annuity or go into alternatively secured pension (ASP).

ASP is similar to unsecured pension but is far more restrictive in the amount of income that can be withdrawn. Tax on any remaining fund in your ASP pot after your death is punitively high.

With increased life expectancy meaning that retirement can stretch well into three decades, many experts now argue that remaining in the stock market is the best way to manage your money. Annuities are backed by gilts, yet with an investment horizon of 20 or even 30 years or more it can be argued that at least some exposure to assets such as equities is more appropriate. While it exposes you to considerably more risk, drawdown can also give you a hedge against inflation. If you can afford to lose some of your pension, drawdown can also potentially increase it.

Choosing income drawdown is not a once-in-a-lifetime decision – you can buy an annuity with your fund at any time. So you could use drawdown to keep your fund invested and take an income from it if annuity rates are particularly low at the time you come to retire. Annuity rates are linked to long-term interest rates and life expectancy data. Life expectancy is not cyclical, and so far has only grown, creating a long-term downward trend in annuity rates. But over the medium term, annuity rates can go up and down. This is because long-term interest rates fluctuate with the economic cycle. Buying an annuity when long-term interest rates are at historic lows may not be your best option.

Timing annuity rates carries its own risks, however, and there are no guarantees that rates will come back up again.

The pros and cons of income drawdown

Advantages of income drawdown:

- Allows you to put off buying an annuity if rates are low.
- Improved death benefits.
- Potential for growth and protection from inflation by remaining invested in the stock market.
- Freedom to increase and decrease withdrawals at will to suit your income needs or reduce your tax bill.
- Access to a wide range of investments.

Disadvantages of income drawdown:

- Income is not guaranteed.
- Principal sum invested is not guaranteed.
- Annuity rates could fall by the time you come to buy one.
- No benefit from cross-subsidy of other people buying annuities.
- Requires regular input from a financial adviser which can push up cost.

How income drawdown works

Income drawdown is an option that becomes available when you take benefits from your pension, such as drawing your tax-free cash lump sum. Most personal pension, SIPP and SSAS providers offer a facility allowing you to move into income drawdown. If not, you will have to move to one that does.

You can draw an income from your fund, which must vary between zero (i.e. you do not have to take any income at all) and 120 per cent of a fixed notional pension determined by the Government Actuary's Department (GAD). GAD publishes tables setting these limits for men and women of different ages in terms of the percentage of fund that can be withdrawn.

For example, in 2009, GAD rates allowed a 65-year-old male to withdraw 7.56 per cent of their fund, while a 55-year-old could withdraw 6 per cent of fund. These maximum limits are recalculated every five years, and fluctuate with annuity rates. However, you should review your investments with your financial adviser every year to see that they are on course to meet the growth and income requirements you want.

The investor, usually with their adviser, decides on the investment portfolio for the assets and on how much income will be withdrawn. Provided the withdrawals and charges combined add up to less than the return on the fund, the portfolio will grow. If income from other sources permits, it is advisable to try to reduce or stop withdrawals altogether in years when the fund posts flat or negative returns. This will slow the erosion of the fund.

You can draw income monthly, quarterly or annually, either in arrears or in advance. Drawing income at the end of the year rather than at the beginning will give you greater returns, because you will have a greater principal sum invested, but you will have no income for that year.

You are free to stop your income drawdown plan at any time and buy an annuity. At age 75 you have to use your drawdown pot to either buy an annuity or buy an alternatively secured pension (ASP).

What are the risks?

Income drawdown is generally considerably more risky than buying an annuity and should only really be considered by people who have got enough assets to be able to afford to take that risk. As a general rule, you need combined pension and other retirement savings worth £100,000 or more before you should be considering income drawdown.

Precisely how risky it is depends on the investments that you hold within your drawdown plan. You could invest cash on deposit and have no risk to your capital at all. Alternatively, invest in emerging markets, commodities or technology funds and your fund could potentially rise considerably, but could also suffer significant losses.

Structuring your portfolio to make sure it meets your risk/reward profile is more important for people in income drawdown than for investors at any other time of their life. The same basic rules of portfolio construction apply to income drawdown as to other pension investments, and are explained in greater detail in Chapter 9. Most providers only access income drawdown with the assistance of an IFA, although some will let you operate without advice, on an execution-only basis. This is only recommended for people who have a high understanding of pension and investment issues.

Example

Income drawdown in rising and falling markets

Market rising 10 per cent a year for two years in a row:

■ Lukas has £100,000 in his income drawdown fund. After set-up charges he has £97,000, which rises 10 per cent to £106,700. He draws income of 5 per cent at the end of year one (£5,335). His fund value at the end of year 1 is £101,365.

■ By the end of year 2 his fund has risen to £109,981 net of charges. His second-year income is £5,499 and his fund value at the end of year 2 after income is deducted is £104,481. (If he had opted to maintain his income at £5,000 his fund value would be even bigger.)

■ His fund has grown by 4.48 per cent.

Market falling 10 per cent a year for two years in a row:

■ Henrik has £100,000 in his income drawdown fund. After set-up charges he has £97,000, which falls 10 per cent to £87,300. He draws income of 5 per cent at the end of year 1 (£4,365). His fund value at the end of year 1 is £82,935.

■ By the end of year 2 his fund has fallen to £73,397 net of charges. His second-year income is £3,700 and his fund value at the end of year 2 after income is deduced is £69,697. (If he had opted to maintain his income at £4,365 his fund value would be even smaller – so much so that, depending on his age at the time, GAD limits might not have permitted him to withdraw such a sum.)

■ His fund has fallen by over 30 per cent. But because his principal investment is now so small, it will need to grow in year 3 by 45 per cent before charges before he gets back to his starting value. (Assumes charges of 3 per cent in year 1 and 1.5 per cent a year thereafter.)

The risks and rewards of deferring annuity purchase

One of the big risks with income drawdown is that annuity rates are worse when you come out of income drawdown than when you went in. Even if your fund grows over the period you are in drawdown, you may still get a smaller pension pot when you finally come to buy an annuity if rates have fallen.

Improvements in life expectancy have had a drastic impact on annuity rates over the last 20 years. In 1989 a 65-year-old male could have expected a rate of around 11 per cent for an annuity rising at 3 per cent a year, with a 50 per cent surviving spouse's pension and a five-year guarantee. This would give somebody with a £100,000 pension fund an income of around £11,000 a year. By 2009 that figure had fallen by more than half to around 4.8 per cent, giving less than £5,000 a year.

Compounding this annuity rate risk with investment market risk can mean that unlucky income drawdown investors can lose out badly. For some income drawdown investors, a combination of falling equity markets and falling annuity rates have combined over a decade to give pension incomes of half what they would have got from an annuity. (See Figure 15.1.)

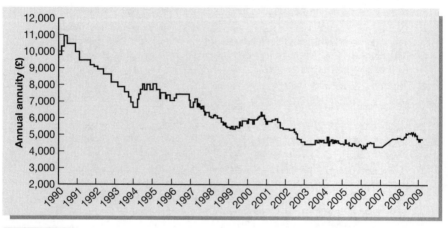

Figure 15.1   Annual income for a male buying an annuity with 3 per cent escalation, 50 per cent spouse's pension and five-year guarantee, 1990–2009

Source: The Annuity Bureau, www.annuity-bureau.co.uk, reprinted with permission

However, there are instances where delaying annuity purchase can be beneficial. Even if your fund value stands still, you will usually be able to get a bigger annuity years down the line because you will be older when you purchase it, meaning your life expectancy will be lower. Today a healthy 70-year-old will receive an income around 28 per cent higher than that paid to a healthy 60-year-old buying an annuity with the same value pot.

Furthermore, most people are healthy when they retire, and do not qualify for enhanced rates for impaired life annuities. Some people will develop medical conditions during the period they are in income drawdown that will entitle them to better rates when they finally come to purchase their annuity. This subject is treated in greater detail in Chapter 14 on annuities.

Investment options

Most pension providers will let you invest in the full range of funds they offer to their other pension investors. You are not allowed to make new commercial property investments with funds that have moved into income drawdown. Commercial property already held within a SIPP or SSAS, however, does not have to be sold on going into drawdown.

Benefits on death

If an income drawdown investor dies before the age of 75, there are three options open to surviving spouses, civil partners or financially dependent partners of either sex:

1   Withdraw the fund as a lump sum subject to 35 per cent tax, but with no liability for Inheritance Tax.
2   Remain in drawdown and continue to draw an income.
3   Use the fund to buy an annuity.

Alternatively secured pension (ASP)

When they reach age 75, people in income drawdown have to either buy an annuity or move into ASP. ASP is more restrictive than the unsecured pension form of income drawdown permitted to those under 75.

When the government brought in the reforms that introduced ASP in 2006, had not wanted to permit savers to avoid buying an annuity at 75. But during the legislative consultation, the Plymouth Brethren successfully managed to argue that an alternative to annuities should be offered. They have a religious objection to annuities because of the way they involve potentially profiting from the death of others. However, when framing the rules the government was keen to ensure that ASP should not be seen as an attractive alternative to annuities, so it made withdrawal rates restrictive and the tax on funds left after death punitively high.

In ASP you must withdraw a minimum of 55 per cent and a maximum of 90 per cent of the GAD rates. For anyone drawing the maximum 120 per cent of GAD allowed pre-75, moving into ASP will involve a considerable reduction in income.

The amount you can withdraw must be calculated every 12 months, taking into account performance of the investment fund and GAD rates.

You are free to use all or some of your fund to buy an annuity while you are in ASP, and you are also allowed to transfer from one ASP provider to another one.

Death benefits

■ *Spouses and dependants* On death any remaining fund can be used to provide a pension to any dependants, which include spouses and anyone financially dependent on you. The fund can be used to buy an annuity or, if the dependant is under 75, it can go into an unsecured pension. If over 75, the dependant can take the fund into ASP.

■ *Where there are no dependents*

– *Charity* If there are no dependants, the plan-holder can nominate a charity to receive any residual fund left after death.

– *Paid out to non-dependant* The residual sum can be paid out to non-dependants nominated by the plan-holder, but this will be treated as an unauthorised payment by HM Revenue & Customs and subject to tax charges totalling up to 82 per cent.

16

Retirement savings not held in pensions

What topic is covered in this chapter?

■ Investment approach

Most people have some savings that are not held within pensions by the time they retire. ISAS, unit trusts, shares, cash on deposit, premium bonds and fixed-term bonds can all contribute to your retirement income.

With retirement stretching beyond 25 years for increasing numbers of people, inflation is a threat to your retirement wealth. Maintaining some exposure to the stock market through your non-pension savings is one way to make sure you keep pace with inflation.

When you come to retire it is crucial to get your money to work harder for you. Shopping around for the best value income-generating products is one way to boost your income. But the way you structure your portfolio is equally important as it can also have a significant effect on the amount of tax you pay, giving you more cash in your hand in retirement.

Investment approach

The same basic principles of portfolio construction apply for those in their sixties, seventies and eighties as much as they do for younger investors. Spreading your investments across a range of asset classes is key, as is creating an investment strategy that matches your objectives.

It is even more crucial for older people to understand the relationship between risk and reward because they are far less likely to be in a position to earn some more money if they lose what they have. For older investors, the adage that you should not invest what you cannot afford to lose is even more appropriate than it is for everybody else. This means that as a general rule the older you are, the more cautious you need to be. The principles of investment portfolio construction are covered in greater detail in Chapter 9.

Retired people are generally looking for income from their assets rather than long-term growth

Retired people are generally looking for income from their assets rather than long-term growth. This is because they need the money to actually spend rather than put away for the future. But in some situations it is more tax efficient to invest for growth rather than income, as is explained below.

Keeping tax to a minimum is a priority for pensioners, so it is important to make use of all available tax breaks. These include ISAs, annual Capital Gains Tax allowances, and for married couples and those in civil partnerships, maximising both partners' personal allowances.

ISAs

Individual Savings Accounts (ISAs) offer an efficient shelter from Capital Gains and Income Tax. Over 50s can save up to £10,200 in an ISA (under 50s can too from April 2010), up to £5,100 of which can be held in a cash ISA. The balance, or the entire £10,200 if you decide not to opt for a cash ISA at all, can be held in a separate stocks and shares ISA.

It is worth using up your annual ISA allowance to put as much of your savings into an ISA as possible, year after year. By doing so, you will be able to avoid Income and Capital Gains Tax on an increasing proportion of your non-pension assets. But you should watch out for up-front charges when switching into ISAs.

You can avoid initial set-up charges on ISA investments by going through a discount fund broker such as Chartwell Direct, Cavendish Online or Hargreaves Lansdown. These brokers will generally rebate the up-front commission, typically 5 per cent of your investment. However, dealing through discount brokers is done on an 'execution-only' basis, which means you have nobody to complain to if the investments selected turn out to be unsuitable. If you have a large amount to invest and are not confident about choosing investments yourself, you should consult an IFA.

Efficient use of tax allowances: Capital Gains Tax

Each individual has a Capital Gains Tax allowance of £10,100 (for 2009/2010) for each tax year, and capital gains above that level are charged at 18 per cent. This makes investing for growth more attractive than investing for income, up to the limit of the allowance, which can be very efficient for people with large portfolios of investments outside pensions, particularly if they are higher rate taxpayers.

Unlike income investments, which usually pay dividends or interest, growth investments are made in companies that are focused on increasing their value. You can access a range of growth funds that aim to do this in various sectors and geographical areas of the world.

Married couples and civil partners can make use of both Capital Gains Tax allowances by giving half of their assets to their partner. This is because no Capital Gains Tax liability arises on gifts between spouses or civil partners.

Example

Where it pays to invest for growth rather than income

Emily and Alison are both retired and pay tax at 40 per cent because of their generous final salary pensions. They have both used up their ISA allowances and have £100,000 portfolios of non-ISA investments.

Emily invests in growth stocks, and the value of the companies and funds she invests in go up in value by 10 per cent, increasing her portfolio to £110,000. She can draw £10,000 from her portfolio without incurring tax.

Alison invests in income-generating stocks and her £100,000 investment generates £10,000 of income. She is taxed £4,000 on her income, leaving her with just £6,000.

Why it pays to maximise personal allowances

Karl and Eva are married. Karl is retired and pays tax at 40 per cent. He also has a £200,000 portfolio of non-ISA investments, which is invested in growth stocks. He is expecting the fund to return 10 per cent a year. Eva has no investments. If he retains the £200,000 in his own name, and it rises to £220,000, he will pay Capital Gains Tax of £1,800 when he cashes in his investment.

If he gives half of his money to Eva, then by using both partners' Capital Gains Tax annual allowances they will not incur a tax charge.

Cash on deposit

Depending on the ability of banks and building societies to pay interest, placing cash on deposit is an attractive place for at least some of your money. It makes sense to have access to some money in case of emergencies, and for those seeking absolute security, cash on deposit is a good solution up to the level covered by the Financial Services Compensation Scheme (FSCS). Since October 2008 deposits in banks and building societies of up to £50,000 are guaranteed. You should not put more than £50,000 in any one banking institution, but note these caveats:

■ Couples with joint accounts are covered up to £100,000.

■ Cover is per bank or building society, and not per account.

■ Some offshore banks may not be covered by a protection scheme, or it may not be as generous as the UK's FSCS.

■ Some merged banks count as a single bank. For example, you only get £50,000 of cover for accounts with Halifax, Bank of Scotland, Birmingham Midshires and Intelligent Finance because they all come under HBOS for the purposes of the FSCS. But RBS and NatWest count as separate institutions for compensation purposes. Ask the bank before depositing the money.

Over 50s can save up to £5,100 a year in a mini cash ISA without attracting income tax on interest. You can search for the best cash deposit rates either through tables in the weekend papers or through online comparison websites.

National Savings & Investments

Backed by the government, National Savings & Investments (NS&I) products have proved attractive to investors wanting financial certainty. NS&I offers premium bonds and index-linked savings, amongst other products. All NS&I investments are exempt from income tax and do not have to be declared on a tax return.

Immediate vesting pension: a way to generate higher income

In times when interest rates are very close to zero, investors seeking security can find it very difficult to generate income from their cash. Income-seeking pensioners saw deposit account rates falling to 1 per cent and below in 2008 and 2009 as banks grappled with the fallout of the crisis in the financial system.

But it is possible to generate returns of up to 12 per cent a year, provided you are prepared to tie up your cash for life. You can get such high rates of return by paying into a pension that lets you draw money out straight away, called an immediate vesting pension. Anybody, even those who have retired or are not working are allowed to pay £2,880 into an immediate vesting pension, provided they are between the ages of 55 (50 until April 2010) and 75. People still working can pay in an amount equal to their annual taxable earnings, up to £245,0000 a year.

Rates of return on immediate vesting pensions vary between 8 and 12 per cent. The older you are, the higher rate you get, reflecting your reduced life expectancy. The older you are when you take out an immediately vesting pension, the less likely you are to profit from it. The average 75-year-old man will recoup £2,410 on a net £1,980 investment before dying, compared to £3,471 for a 60-year-old woman.

Even the latter case may sound like a poor deal when compared with spending down the principal sum and interest. But by taking out an immediate vesting pension you insure against the risk of living longer than average.

Immediate vesting annuity: how it works

A 75-year-old male pays £2,880 into an immediate vesting pension, and gets £720 added through tax relief, making a total pension pot of £3,600. The pension is then drawn immediately, giving him a tax-free cash lump sum of £900. An annuity is then bought with the remaining £2,700, paying £218.30 a year.

Pros:

■ High income guaranteed for life.

■ Benefits from tax relief.

Cons:

■ If you die soon after taking out the plan your money is lost.

■ Nothing to pass on through your will.

■ You lose access to the cash.

17

Disputes and unclaimed pensions

What topics are covered in this chapter?

- Disputes over pensions
- Unclaimed pensions

Disputes over pensions

You may find yourself in dispute with your pension scheme. Disputes can arise in situations where members of occupational schemes believe they are entitled to ill health early retirement but the trustees of the scheme or employer refuse an ill health pension. Disputes can also arise where mistakes have been made on the calculation of entitlement and over- or underpayments have been made.

Ill health early retirement disputes

Some occupational pension schemes will offer an early pension in the event of the permanent incapacity of the scheme member due to physical or mental illness. Depending on the scheme's rules, it may be necessary to be incapable of doing the member's current job, or alternatively any job at all to qualify.

How to complain

1   Write a letter of complaint to the trustees of the scheme explaining why you think their decision is wrong. Under the statutory internal dispute resolution procedure the trustees can decide whether they go for a one-stage process or a two-stage process. The two-stage process effectively allows for an extra exchange of complaints and responses.

2   The trustees are required to give you a written response within four months, whichever process is followed.

3   If the matter is not resolved, you can refer the case to The Pensions Advisory Service (TPAS) (telephone 0845 601 2923). TPAS is an independent non-profit organisation that provides free advice and guidance on pensions matters. It will endeavour to resolve your complaint for you. You can contact TPAS at any stage of the process, and it makes sense to do so as soon as you think you have a problem.

4   You can also complain to the Pensions Ombudsman once the internal dispute resolution procedure has been exhausted. Applications to the Pensions Ombudsman are free. Applications need to be made within three years of becoming aware of the event being complained about. Determinations of the Pensions Ombudsman are binding unless either party goes to the High Court on a point of law. Complaints about state pension cannot be taken through the Pensions Ombudsman. If you have a dispute over state pension you should contact TPAS for assistance.

Bad advice on pensions

If you think the person or body that recommended a pension product to you gave you bad advice you may have a claim against them. Claims in relation to non-occupational schemes are dealt with by the Financial Ombudsman Service (FOS).

Your claim could relate to the type of pension or annuity product you have been offered, or to whether the investments you have been placed in accurately reflect your stated risk profile. You could also have grounds for complaint if you have been mis-advised on transferring out of a final salary scheme into a personal pension or on contracting out of state second pension (for more on advice relating to contracting out, see page 180). Your claim could be against a bank, insurance company, stockbroker or financial advisory firm.

Your claim could be against a bank, insurance company, stockbroker or financial advisory firm

However, just because your investments perform badly does not mean you have a case against the person who recommended the product.

How to claim to the FOS

1 Put in a formal complaint to the financial services company you wish to complain about. It is best to put in a written complaint and keep a copy. Companies governed by the FOS are required to deal with complaints promptly. You should make your complaint as soon as you become aware that you think you have a claim.

2 If you are not satisfied with the way the company deals with your complaint, put in a complaint to the FOS. You should do this on the FOS's complaint form, which you can find on their website. Call them on 0845 080 1800 if you need help filling in the form.

3 The FOS will then contact the company you have complained about, asking them for their version of events. Around 50 per cent of cases are resolved without a full investigation taking place. But if agreement between the parties cannot be reached, lengthier investigations can be necessary.

4 A determination is made which is binding on companies. However, consumers do not have to accept the decision and may take the matter to court instead.

Unclaimed pensions

Tens of thousands of pensions go unclaimed each year because the people entitled to them cannot track them down. Tracing these lost pensions is, in most situations, relatively straightforward provided it is the person whose pension it is that is carrying out the search. But if something happens to you that means your spouse or dependants are left trying to bring together all your assets, old pensions and other investment and savings products can easily get lost. For this reason it is always a good idea to make sure that pension schemes, insurance companies and other financial service companies are always kept notified of your correct address.

Around £3bn worth of occupational pensions are sitting in schemes' accounts waiting to be reunited with their rightful owners, according to the National Association of Pension Funds (NAPF). The NAPF reports that in most cases where pensions are lost the address held by the scheme is incorrect because the person entitled to the pension has put off notifying the scheme of the change of address, with the intention of doing so nearer retirement. However, by the time retirement comes along, that intention is forgotten. A surviving spouse may be unaware of the names of their deceased partner's former employers, let alone know how to trace them.

Other unclaimed investments

The £3bn of unclaimed pensions is just a fraction of the estimated £15bn of unclaimed assets across all types of financial services products, including bank accounts, investments, ISAs, insurance policies and share dividends. A further £300m worth of personal pensions is lying unclaimed in the vaults of the insurance companies that administer them.

Tracing lost pensions and other investments

There are several ways you can go about tracing lost pensions. Your first port of call should be the Pension Service's pension tracing service. This free service is part of the Department for Work and Pensions. Around 20,000 people a year ask it to trace pensions and it is successful in tracking down schemes in more than 90 per cent of cases, although not all of these find that they are entitled to any pension benefits.

You can either fill in a form online at www.thepensionservice.gov.uk/atoz/atozdetailed/pensiontracing.asp or call 0845 6002 537. It will then run the details you give it through its record of around 200,000 UK occupational schemes and personal pension arrangements. Many employers may no longer exist under the name they had when you worked for them. Some will have been bought by other companies or changed their trading name, while others will have gone out of business altogether. If it does have information about the scheme, the Pension Service will not be able to do any more than give you its contact details. You will have to contact the scheme administrator to determine what benefits you have.

For bank or building society savings contact the British Bankers Association or the Building Societies Association, both of which will send you an unclaimed assets claim form to complete. National Savings & Investments, the body that runs premium bonds, has a similar service.

If these avenues prove unsuccessful you can try the Unclaimed Assets Register, which is a subsidiary of credit reference agency Experian. It holds more than 400 million records on its databases, and for a £25 fee it will run a search of hundreds of thousands of commercial organisations looking for all of your lost financial services products.

Maintain good records

Rather than have to go through the unpredictable process of finding schemes years down the line, it will make life easier for yourself and your loved ones if you make sure that all the pension schemes and financial services providers you have ever dealt with have got your up-to-date personal details. You will need to contact your pension scheme or provider whenever your marital status changes or you start or finish a relationship with a long-term partner. Both occupational and personal pensions will pay valuable death benefits to spouses, civil partners and qualifying long-term unmarried partners, so if these change you should notify your pension administrator or provider accordingly. Incorrect recipients can be rectified after your death. But finding that death benefits are about to be paid to somebody you separated from years ago can prove to be very distressing to your surviving beneficiaries. And an unmarried partner may find it harder to prove their right to receive death benefits if you have not specified them as your nominated beneficiary.

It makes sense to keep all your pension documents in a safe place

As with all estate planning, it makes sense to keep all your pension documents in a safe place, together with all your other financial papers and your will, and make sure those close to you know where they are.

18

Retiring abroad

What topics are covered in this chapter?

- Residency requirements
- Currency risk

Literally millions of people are planning to retire abroad. Arranging your pension affairs for such a move is a complex business, involving more than one tax jurisdiction, and needs specialist advice. It is even possible to transfer your pension abroad and it can be tax efficient to do so, although there are situations where it is not.

Residency requirements

As a general rule you will be taxed wherever you are resident. HM Revenue & Customs will consider you resident in the UK for tax purposes if you spend 183 or more days in the UK in a year, or if your visits to the UK average 91 days or more over four years.

Popular retirement destinations such as France, Spain, Portugal and Italy have double taxation agreements with the UK, which means that you will not be taxed twice on the same income. You can also ask for UK-derived income that is normally paid net of basic rate tax to be paid gross. This applies to interest on bank accounts and income from annuities and bonds.

While their tax regimes differ from the UK's, there are few EU retirement destinations that offer markedly lower tax than the UK. Cyprus is one exception, though, with 5 per cent tax on pensions and no tax at all on bank interest and share dividends once you are resident. If you have satisfied HM Revenue & Customs that you are no longer domiciled in the UK (a stricter test than residency), and have become domiciled in Cyprus, your estate will not be eligible for Inheritance Tax.

Currency risk

> Currency fluctuations will also have a significant influence on your real income in retirement

Currency fluctuations will also have a significant influence on your real income in retirement. If your pension is paid in sterling then its spending power will go up and down with the exchange rate. Some people who retired to the eurozone when a pound bought 1.3 or 1.4 euros were forced to move back to the UK in 2008 when sterling approached parity with the Euro.

You can reduce the risk of currency fluctuation by gradually moving your investments into Euro-based assets in the years before you move. Specialist currency exchange providers such as HIFX allow you to fix currency rates for up to 24 months at a time to give you some security against these fluctuations.

Tax and financial planning pitfalls of retiring abroad

■ You will become liable for tax in your new country of residence. Tax ranges from 15 to 45 per cent in Spain, from 0 to 40 per cent in France and from 10 to 42 per cent in Portugal. For UK emigrants on median earnings there is likely to be little difference in tax overall to these countries. Some countries, such as Cyprus, have considerably lower tax rates for pensioners than the UK.

■ Watch out for wealth taxes. France charges residents a wealth tax of between 0.55 and 1.8 per cent of their total assets above a certain threshold every year. Spain's wealth tax starts at 0.2 per cent.

■ UK tax wrappers will not protect you in your new country of residence. For example, ISAs do not protect you against Capital Gains or Income Tax in France. It may be worth crystallising gains before you go, although you should watch out for up-front charges when you reinvest the money. This is a complex area and you should take specialist advice.

■ Be careful about moving abroad before taking your pension. Some countries will tax your tax-free lump sum.

■ Retire outside the UK and you may lose the inflation protection on your state pension. People retiring to the USA, Canada, Australia, New Zealand or South

Africa receive no annual inflation increases once they have moved abroad. Over time this will seriously erode the spending power of your pension. Those in the EU get the same annual RPI increase in their basic and state second pension that UK citizens get.

■ Inheritance laws are different all over the world. In some countries your will may be overridden to provide for children. The level of Inheritance Tax and the way it is levied varies from country to country.

■ You may need to take out a private medical insurance policy. People over UK state retirement age will be able to access local state health provision across the EU under a reciprocal agreement, but for those who retire younger than that, cover is not guaranteed. For example, France has recently stopped covering all UK citizens under retirement age. Some states require a contribution towards state healthcare. Non-EU states are unlikely to offer you any healthcare at all.

■ As a condition of long-term admission to Australia, UK citizens with no family connection with the country are required to demonstrate that they have sufficient wealth to support themselves through the remainder of their lives.

Offshore pensions

It is possible to move your UK pension to an offshore arrangement as you prepare to emigrate. To do so you have to transfer to a Qualifying Registered Overseas Pension Scheme (QROPS). QROPS schemes are available in a number of jurisdictions around the world including the Channel Isles, the Isle of Man and the Republic of Ireland.

By transferring to a QROPS plan overseas it may be possible to avoid having to buy an annuity at age 75. Until recently QROPS schemes had been used as tax loopholes for getting cash out of pensions. But since HM Revenue & Customs cracked down on the arrangements they are now required to have broadly similar tax and withdrawal arrangements to UK pensions, or be an approved scheme used by locals. Some QROPS schemes do allow a broader range of investment options than UK pensions, such as direct investment in residential property.

QROPS schemes may be attractive to internationally mobile people who have no intention of settling in the UK, or to those who wish to retire abroad and want to protect their money from potential future changes to UK tax laws. Their charges are generally higher than UK pensions, however, and you should seek specialist advice before taking one out. If you decide to do so, you should ask your adviser about the level of investor protection offered in the jurisdiction where the QROPS arrangement is in place in the event that the provider goes bust.

19

Inheritance Tax planning in retirement

What topics are covered in this chapter?

- Unmarried couples
- Gifts made when you are still alive

Death duties have become a concern for an increasing number of people in recent decades as personal wealth has grown faster than Inheritance Tax (IHT) thresholds.

The threshold is also known as the 'nil rate band'

IHT is payable at a rate of 40 per cent on all assets on death, including those held in trust and gifts made within the preceding seven years, above the threshold (£325,000 in 2009/2010). The threshold is also known as the 'nil rate band'.

Married couples and registered civil partners can increase their IHT threshold by double that amount if the executors or personal representatives of the deceased transfer his or her nil rate band to the other partner when they die.

Transfers that are exempt from IHT

■ Spouses or civil partners can inherit unlimited sums without attracting IHT.

■ Gifts to UK registered charities, whether while you are alive or through your will.

■ Potentially exempt transfers. Gifts made more than seven years before you die.

■ You can make gifts totalling £3,000 a year without attracting an IHT liability.

■ You can make as many small gifts, of up to £250 per individual, as you want each year.

■ Gifts on marriage are exempt. Parents can give £5,000, grandparents £2,500 and anyone else can give £1,000.

■ Regular gifts out of normal expenditure are exempt. This generous yet little understood exemption allows you to make unlimited gifts to any individual without raising an IHT liability, provided they are made regularly out of excess income that you do not need to live off. Capital cannot be passed on in this way, however.

Unmarried couples

Unmarried couples do not benefit from the spouse exemption. This can create unforeseen tax charges when one partner dies, even if they have been living together in the same home for years and have had children together.

Unmarried couples with a home worth more than two times the nil rate band (£650,000 in 2009/2010) will face an IHT bill when one of them dies if it is held as tenants in common, which is widespread. Property held as joint tenants is not affected in the same way, however. You should get specialist advice if this applies to you.

Gifts made when you are still alive

Unless they are exempt payments set out in the list above, gifts made in your lifetime will attract IHT if you die within seven years of making them. This is to stop people simply giving their money away as soon as they know they are going to die. Tax is levied on a sliding scale depending on the length of time between making the gift and death. (See Table 19.1.)

Table 19.1: How taper relief reduces IHT liability

Time between transfer and death (years)	Taper relief (%)	Proportion of IHT payable (%)
3 to 4	20	80
4 to 5	40	60
5 to 6	60	40
6 to 7	80	20

Note: No taper relief exists in the first three years after death.

Discounted gift trusts

Discounted gift trust plans allow you to remove assets from your estate immediately, while at the same time allowing you to receive income. The money is paid into an investment bond, which is held on trust by you for your beneficiaries. The income is yours to spend, although you will never be able to get your hands on the principal sum again, so you should only take this option if you can afford to do so.

IHT on trusts

There are many different sorts of trusts available for family succession planning arrangements

In recent years rules have been changed to levy tax on assets held in trust. This has made some trusts less attractive than they used to be, although they do retain advantages. There are many different sorts of trusts available for family succession planning arrangements. If you have complex succession planning issues you should take specialist advice from an expert legal or financial planning firm.

Non-quoted shares

You can get IHT relief by investing in AIM-listed shares and in unlisted companies. These assets become exempt from IHT altogether if they are held for two years. A downside of this exemption is that these sorts of companies tend to be more volatile than blue-chip companies, making them less suitable for those approaching retirement. This form of relief can be useful for people with assets over the nil-rate band.

Example

Using AIM-listed shares to reduce the IHT burden

Andrew is married and has a house worth £500,000 and assets of £525,000. He leaves £325,000 plus £100,000 of AIM-listed shares to his children, and the house and remaining cash to his wife, Jean. Provided he has survived for two years after buying the AIM-listed shares, his estate will incur no IHT. Jean can then buy the AIM-listed shares off the children with the £100,000 cash, meaning that £425,000 has been passed down, rather than £325,000, without suffering Inheritance Tax.

Inheritance Tax and pensions

If you buy an annuity you will not have anything to pass on after your death. However, guarantee payments made after your death to your named beneficiary will fall outside your estate, but may raise a liability to Income Tax for the recipient.

Money held in pensions that has not been converted into an annuity can be passed on to relatives. The Inheritance Tax consequences of different types of pension are covered in the relevant chapters.

Useful contacts

Financial Ombudsman Service
South Quay Plaza
183 Marsh Wall
London E14 9SR
020 7964 1000
www.financial-ombudsman.org.uk

Financial Services Authority
25 The North Colonnade
Canary Wharf
London E14 5HS
020 7066 1000
www.fsa.gov.uk

Financial Services Compensation
Scheme
7th Floor, Lloyds Chambers
Portsoken Street
London E1 8BN
020 7892 7300
www.fscs.org.uk

HM Revenue & Customs (HMRC)
www.hmrc.gov.uk

IFA Promotion
www.unbiased.co.uk

The Institute of Financial Planning
www.financialplanning.org.uk

The Personal Finance Society
www.thepfs.org

The Pension Service
0845 6060265
www.theoensionservice.gov.uk

The Pensions Advisory Service
0845 601 2923
www.pensionsadvisoryservice.org.uk

The Pensions Regulator
0870 6063636
www.thepensionsregulator.gov.uk

Index